Educated at Melbourne University and the Royal Melbourne Institute of Technology, Kevin Morgan has worked variously as a photographer, author, teacher, librarian, historian and researcher. His previous works include XIX, a thesis on mortality and the problem of evil, particularly as it affects children, and *The Particulars of Executions 1894–1967: The Hidden Truth about Capital Punishment*. His photo-essay 'Holocaustic', exploring the fate of a Jewish child in the Third Reich, was exhibited to much acclaim at the Jewish Museum of Australia. Kevin lives in Melbourne with his wife, Linda.

Gun Alley
Murder, lies and failure of justice

KEVIN MORGAN

SIMON & SCHUSTER
AUSTRALIA

First published in Australia in 2005 by
Simon & Schuster (Australia) Pty Limited
Suite 2, Lower Ground Floor
14–16 Suakin Street, Pymble NSW 2073

A CBS Company
Sydney New York London Toronto Singapore
Visit our website at www.simonsaysaustralia.com

This edition published in 2006

© Kevin J Morgan 2005

All rights reserved. No part of this publication may be reproduced, stored in a retrieval system, or transmitted, in any form or by any means, electronic, mechanical, photocopying, recording or otherwise, without the prior permission of the publisher in writing.

Cataloguing-in-Publication data:

Morgan, Kevin John, 1956– .
  Gun alley : murder, lies and failure of justice.

  Bibliography.
  Includes index.
  ISBN 0 7318 1293 X.

  1. Tirtschke, Alma. 2. Ross, Colin Campbell. 3. Trials (Murder) – Victoria – Melbourne. I. Title.

345.94502523

Internal design by Darian Causby, Highway 51
Cover design by Melissa Keogh
Cover painting by Charles Blackman, *Schoolgirl in the Lane*
Internal diagrams by Ian Faulkner
Excerpts from *Crime Chemist: The Life Story of Charles Anthony Taylor, Scientist for the Crown*, published by John Long, reprinted by permission of The Random House Group Ltd
Typeset in 11 on 15pt Sabon by KirbyJones
Printed in Australia by Griffin Press

10 9 8 7 6 5 4 3 2 1

For Linda

Acknowledgments

This book would not have eventuated without the commitment and giftedness of two remarkable women: my wife, Linda Tarraran, who contributed research assistance, encouragement and advice at every level; and Lucy Sussex, who unstintingly applied her wealth of editing expertise.

I am also grateful to Simon & Schuster Australia for its commitment to the Gun Alley story and in particular I acknowledge Jacquie Brown for her valuable editorial support.

For the courage and generosity of the families most affected by the Gun Alley tragedy—the relatives of Alma Tirtschke, Colin Ross, Frederick Piggott, TC Brennan and NH Sonenberg—in granting me interviews and providing assistance without reservation, I extend my sincere thanks.

My thanks to many others who gave their time for interviews, especially Alma's former schoolfriends Aggie Reid and Reg Allen, and the former colleagues and associates of superintendents Piggott and Brophy: Fred Hobley; HR (Bill) Donelly; George A Newton and Jim Rosengren.

I thank Dr James Robertson, Director Forensic Services, Australian Federal Police, for kind permission to reproduce his illustrated report on the Ross case exhibits. At the Victorian Institute of Forensic Medicine, I am grateful for the support of the Director, Professor Stephen M Cordner; the Deputy Director, Professor David Ranson; the Head of

Scientific Services, Professor Olaf Drummer; the Manager of Molecular Biology, Dr Bentley Atchison; and Senior Scientist April Smith. For helpful advice and support my sincere thanks also to Dr Rosetta Marotta of the Department of Clinical Neurosciences, St Vincent's Hospital, Melbourne. At the Victoria Police Forensic Science Centre I am grateful to Dr Roland van Oorschot, Maxwell Jones and Jane Taupin for advice and guidance. For his helpful comments, I thank Dr Vernon D Plueckhahn.

I gratefully acknowledge the assistance provided by the Victorian Office of Public Prosecutions, and thank particularly former directors Bernard Bongiorno and Geoffrey Flatman, and current director Paul Coghlan. Many thanks also to Peter Wood, Bruce Gardner, Michael Carter, Ken Dickson and Adrian Bendeler.

I thank former Director and Keeper of Public Records Ross Gibbs for the support of Public Record Office Victoria in this project and I particularly acknowledge the considerable assistance of Mike Tinsley, Ian MacFarlane, Charlie Farrugia and James McKinnon.

At the Victoria Police Historical Unit, I thank manager Peter Free and his colleagues Martin Powell and Brian Hodge for making the Unit's many valuable resources available for my study.

I gratefully acknowledge the assistance of James Butler, Supreme Court Librarian, and David Hassett, Librarian, Melbourne City Council. In addition I acknowledge the courteous assistance of both the State Library of Victoria and Australian Archives.

At the National Trust of Australia (Victoria) I owe a debt of thanks to Amanda Baker, Diane Gardiner and Richard Berman-Hardman for their boundless encouragement over many years and access to important resources, including especially the Old Melbourne Gaol itself.

For their support in drawing community attention to the

injustices of the Gun Alley story, I thank Deborah Fleming and Brigid Donovan of ABC TV's 'Australian Story'; at the *Sunday Age* I thank Steve Foley, Andrew Rule, John Silvester and Martin Daly.

During the 12 years it took to research and write this book, I received practical assistance from many generous people. I especially thank Gary Presland, Helen Harris, Colleen Woolley, Don Treble, Ken Allan, Alan Elliott, David Holland, Brian Quirk, Trevor McCandless and Joe Ragnanese.

Contents

Acknowledgments	vii
1. Errington	1
2. A schoolgirl	3
3. Until the day break	9
4. A popular sensation	16
5. Earning the reward	21
6. The search begins	27
7. Raising the stakes	38
8. 'A great country'	43
9. Crime chemist	62
10. Coroner's Court	66
11. 'Miss Matthews'	85
12. The only remaining witness	98
13. Colin Ross	110
14. Queen of Fortune-Tellers	123
15. Susso	125
16. The trial begins	133
17. Unsettled weather	147
18. A tangible memento	160
19. All in the same sugar bag	170
20. Judgment	197
21. Alma	210
22. In the midst of life …	226
23. Brennan appeals	234
24. 'Don't let them get you down-hearted'	259
25. Piggott	265

26. Seeking reprieve	268
27. The mysterious woman	282
28. The myth of instant death	286
29. A dandy 'D'	289
30. Farewell	292
31. Execution	294
32. Brophy	302
33. Ghurka's fortune	305
AN ANALYSIS OF THE EVIDENCE	307
34. Brennan's book	308
35. Piggott recalls	314
36. The evidence of the hair	323
WHO KILLED ALMA TIRTSCHKE?	327
37. Following the trail	328
38. At the edges of identity	334
39. Who killed Alma Tirtschke?	340
POSTSCRIPT: Subsequent Histories	345
APPENDIX 1 Totals of Reward and Sustenance Payments	349
APPENDIX 2 Dr James Robertson: Report of Examination of Hair Samples in the Case of *R v Ross* (1922)	350
APPENDIX 3 Letters Written to Colin Ross During his Imprisonment	355
APPENDIX 4 Letter to the People of Australia from Mrs Elizabeth Campbell Ross	359
Select Bibliography	361
Index	367

1. Errington

It is New Year's Eve, 1921, the city of Melbourne, early morning. Errington stands at the corner of Coromandel Place holding two sacks of bottles. He has sent his 11-year-old daughter Eva to have a look in a nearby easement. She comes back with a brown lager bottle.

Errington leaves his daughter's sack leaning against the wall for her, then moves across Little Collins Street. Here the footpaths are flagged and the gutters are broad drains of bluestone. Dollops of horse dung spatter the dusty road.

The chinking of hollow bottles: Eva catches him up. Errington squints down Alfred Place, towards the Paris end of Collins Street, although it's not squalid enough for a big find of bottles. He and Eva do better in the dead-end lanes, where offshoots or easements provide the privacy for a drunken binge. Up the hill, heading east, the next two lanes are strong chances.

''Ere Eva, you do the first 'un, Pink Alley; then meet me up. I'll be in the next 'un down.'

Behind them, 700 metres to the west, the gears click in the GPO clock tower; cogs are beginning to whirr and clatter. From the ledges of the tower's masonry, clusters of startled sparrows and pigeons take sudden flight. The pair pass a tailor's shop and a billiard-table maker. Then Pink Alley. Eva goes in—there are bottles here.

The GPO clock begins its hourly chime. Eva is getting tired and Errington knows it; she'll be whingeing soon. 'Da-aad, um 'ungry. Da-aad, can we go 'ome now?'

The clock begins to strike the hour. Not much further now. He can coax her the rest of the way with the promise of a lolly.

The second stroke and now the third ... Or the stick.

Fourth stroke ... For just an instant, above his head, a flock of pigeons clutters thickly.

Five ... He is now at the corner of Gun Alley, where Lane's Motors have their shop, 'Tyres All Makes—Pumps—Jacks—Generators—Valve Parts'. The clock strikes six.

On the other corner is Henry Stanley's barbershop, where a haircut costs ninepence. But Errington's eyes are for bottles alone. He walks into the alley, a 21-metre cul-de-sac. He hears his daughter coming down from Pink Alley to meet him.

Two-thirds of the way down Gun Alley, Errington looks to his left into the easement running behind Stanley's barbershop. He is confronted with the body of a female child. She lies on her back, naked, wantonly posed. Her left leg is bent up with the heel under the buttock; her right leg is also partly drawn up, and crossed under her left.

A stenographer will later smooth his enunciation. On oath Henry David Errington says: '... At 6am on 31 December 1921 I was in Gun Alley and I saw the body of a dead child ... I had my daughter with me and she was just coming into the lane at the time ... I put up my hand to stop her coming any further. I brought her back to Little Collins Street and went to Watkins' butcher shop and got them to phone the police ...'

2. A schoolgirl

Twelve-year-old Alma Tirtschke lived in the nearby suburb of Jolimont with her 74-year-old grandmother. Alma's aunt Maie Murdoch was paying the household a visit on the morning of Friday 30 December 1921, when old Mrs Tirtschke called Alma into the room—she was to collect a parcel from the butchers in Swanston Street, where Maie's husband John worked as secretary. Every Friday afternoon the Murdochs collected a parcel of smallgoods from the butchers, but that day neither Maie nor her son Gordon could do the errand.

Maie gave the young girl instructions: 'Ask Miss McAdam at the desk and give her this letter to be handed to Uncle John ... take [the parcel] back to our flat at Masonic Chambers [31 Collins Street] ... then come straight back to Grandma's here—don't wait for me.' Then she gave Alma the tram fare for the errand. The schoolgirl had taken messages into the city on previous occasions and knew where the butcher's shop was located, but because she attended school she hadn't previously been sent on this errand. Now, however, it was school holidays.

Since Alma was going into the city, she would need to look presentable. Her school uniform, that of the Hawthorn West Central School, was the neatest and handiest set of clothes: a white cambric blouse with blue polka dots; a navy-blue serge box-pleated overall dress; long black knitted socks; black lace-up shoes; and her white straw school hat with a ribbon around its crown.

Alma left at 12.30pm, choosing to save her tram fare by walking the 1.5 kilometres into the city. She headed west through the Fitzroy and Treasury Gardens.

'She came into the shop at about a quarter past one,' remembered Alice McAdam, cashier at the butchers, Bennet and Woolcock's. 'She went upstairs to see if her uncle was in; but he was out. She ... handed me a letter from her auntie ... then asked me if the auntie's parcel was ready.' Alice McAdam told her that it would be a 20-minute wait. 'The little girl waited for the parcel and after the lapse of about a quarter of an hour I gave it to her. That would be about half-past one ...'

Smallgoods butcher Cyril Castles had prepared the brown paper parcel: '... 3½ pounds of cooked corned beef, 2 pounds of Epping sausages, half a pound pork lunch and two bundles of frankfurts ... The total weight ... would be 8 to 9 pounds ...'

'[A]fter that we lost all trace of [Alma] ...' her uncle John Murdoch told the *Herald*. When she didn't arrive as expected at the Murdochs' flat in Collins Street, they thought she had gone home to her grandmother. When they discovered she was not there either, they searched for her and '... not being successful, we informed the police shortly after tea'.

The first policeman to whom Murdoch had spoken, on duty near the Treasury buildings in the city, suggested the girl might have gone down to one of the beaches on the tram, as it was a fine day. Murdoch knew that Alma didn't have enough money for the tram ride all the way to the beach. He headed to the nearest police station—at the intersection of Little Bourke and Liverpool streets—where the official in charge phoned several hospitals inquiring about the missing child, but without success. The policeman advised the distraught relatives to go back to the flat, in case their niece had returned during their absence.

But there was no further news at Collins Street. Murdoch then went to the Russell Street police headquarters with Mrs Alice Scott, another of Alma's aunts. They arrived between 7 and 8pm and were interviewed by an officer who, according to the family, treated the matter in 'a casual and desultory way, as if he were on a frivolous inquiry'. He advised the anxious pair to return home and not to worry.

Murdoch told the officer that Alma was such a reliable young girl—that her disappearance indicated something serious had happened. Constable Ramsay, in charge of the Russell Street switchboard that evening, began another round of phone inquiries to the hospitals. He also promised that a description of the missing girl would be sent to all police stations immediately.

Returning home to Collins Street, the family, including Mrs Tirtschke, maintained an all-night vigil. Soon after midnight, while Mrs Tirtschke was sitting in the parlour with the light burning and the door open, two constables entered. 'Have you found my girl?' she inquired. They looked puzzled and said they had come in because it was their duty to investigate where doors were open late at night and premises lighted. These constables were on beat duty in the section through which the girl should have passed on her way to Masonic Chambers, yet in four and a half hours the report of Alma's disappearance had not reached them.

Alma lies on a draining slab in a room of whitewashed walls. So extreme is the trauma of her death that blood vessels in her eyes have burst, staining them with blood. She is cold and rigor mortis has set in. The autopsy is performed by Crawford Henry Mollison, Coroner's Surgeon since 1893, Lecturer in Forensic Medicine at the University of Melbourne and Pathologist to the Melbourne and Women's hospitals. He notes for his report that the skin over the girl's right eye is very black, probably from a blow. Her face is swollen, her eyelids congested. Her height is '4 feet, 10 inches'. Her weight will subsequently be given as 'about 5 stone'. The hair of her head is loose and red in colour. Though her breasts are undeveloped, the child is approaching the age of puberty and there is fine down on her pubes.

'In cases of asphyxiation, the lividity [congestion of blood vessels after death] is usually well-marked,' Mollison wrote in his *Lectures on Forensic Medicine* (1921). 'Lividity occurs in whichever portion of the body is dependent after death ... As a general rule, if a body is found on its back and lividity is present on the front, the body has been interfered with after death.'

There is lividity on the right side of Alma's face and the front of her chest, which additionally shows small haemorrhages on the skin. Because her body was found on its back but with post-mortem lividity on the front, Mollison knows she has been turned from lying on her front, probably during the time her body was lying in the lane.

Her fingernails are also livid, and he makes an examination of the gaps between the nails and flesh. He discovers nothing: she did not apparently scratch anything that might give a clue. With a magnifying lens Mollison also examines the external injuries to the girl's throat. 'In cases of throttling, you sometimes find fingermarks on the neck, scratches or abrasions, and sometimes little pieces of skin are found to have been taken out of the victim's throat by the nails of the perpetrator.' He notes the abrasions on the front and left side of the neck, the largest measuring 6.4 centimetres in length by 1.1 centimetres in width at its widest part. It extends across the midline from the left side. Below this mark is another 3.5 millimetres in width while above it, along the lower jaw, there is an abrasion 25.4 millimetres in length by 7 millimetres in width. He notes too, that there are some small bruises on the right side of the neck.

'In cases of strangulation where a ligature has been used, the mark on the neck will be evident completely round the neck and there will commonly be ecchymoses, or signs of extravasation of blood into the tissues in the immediate neighbourhood of the mark, that is to say: bruising.' Mollison notes that lower down on the girl's throat there is a narrow pale mark which extends completely round her neck and measures 4.5 millimetres in width. 'Sometimes suspicious looking marks on the neck may lead to an erroneous opinion that strangulation has occurred by means of a ligature.' In his *Lectures*, Mollison warned specifically against misinterpreting marks caused after death by the pressure of a fold of skin or a tight collar. The test is to determine whether there is any bruising. With his blade, Mollison nicks the mark but finds only a watery secretion, no blood. He notes: 'There is no bruising beneath this mark.'

Mollison inspects the thoracic organs and finds the lungs distended with dark fluid blood, consistent with asphyxiation. 'In cases where death has been rapid and violent, you will probably find haemorrhage in the lungs and patches of air bubbles under the pleura from rupture of some of the air cells ...' He sees the spots of haemorrhage on the surfaces of her lungs, the bubbles of effused air.

He also notes that the girl's hymen shows a recent tear in its lower margin, penetrating the wall of her vagina. He finds blood and mucus there and takes a sample for analysis. He notes the girl's uterus is undeveloped. The wall of her bladder, he finds, is much thickened, suggesting that in life it would be a very irritable bladder.

In 1921 testing for alcohol was not an automatic procedure in post-mortems. Mollison had been given no directive that he should test for it, but when he opened the girl's stomach, he noted there was 'no abnormal or alcoholic odour about [its contents]'.

Mollison later tells detectives that the child had been dead for 12–16 hours, placing the time of death somewhere close to—or between—the hours of 6–10pm on the Friday night. When, as part of his report, Mollison states that he has found no evidence of semen, it is postulated by the detectives that some care has been taken to wash the girl: they had noticed a watery stain running down the girl's thigh. Mollison agreed that some washing of the private parts seems likely: he is of the belief there should have been much greater evidence of blood loss from the genital injuries.

3. Until the day break

Before 1938 detectives with the Criminal Investigation Branch in Melbourne had only on-the-job training. Chosen to work in the CIB on the basis of their experience and record of police work, they were appointed after an interview with senior officers. They had little, if any, background in science, let alone any significant appreciation of science as a tool for detection of crime. Brevet Sub-Inspector Frederick Hobley, who established a police scientific section and Australia's first detective training school in 1938, said: 'the idea that science could aid [police in solving] ... crimes ... was slow to develop'. The most significant and most common problem he encountered in his observations of police work prior to the advent of detective training was: 'the preservation of the [crime] scene ...' Police officers of the time often did not appreciate that a crime scene should be preserved absolutely until those qualified to examine it had done so.

In 1921 the responsibility for the examination and interpretation of a crime scene was exclusively that of the investigating detectives. There was no guarantee a photographer could be obtained at short notice from the Government Printing Office. Until a detective arrived at the crime scene, it was in the charge of the most senior policeman in attendance, who might, or might not, preserve the scene, depending—in the absence of formal training—on such diverse factors as his interpretation of his call to duty, experience, personality and psychological response to the crime.

Errington's news was received by the police at Russell Street at 6.13am. Senior Constable Salts and Constable Mason were despatched to the scene immediately, arriving by motor car a few minutes afterward. Mason was a police driver whose responsibility was the vehicle, 'the rattletrap' as it was called, a temperamental old Model-T Ford. Since Salts held the senior rank, he was the first police officer to view and take charge of the scene.

A soldier before joining the force in 1897, John Patrick Salts had 25 years' experience as a policeman. Now, he was carving a niche for himself as a quiet achiever behind a desk. Called out on this early shift five days after Christmas for what should have been, odds on, a prank, he was shocked by what lay in wait for him in Gun Alley. He ordered Mason back to Russell Street to fetch detectives urgently. At 6.30am, Senior Detective John O'Connell Brophy arrived and responsibility for the crime scene passed to the CIB. Shortly afterward, the body was removed to the morgue.

'A thorough search of the locality was made,' Brophy later told the coroner, 'and no signs of a struggle or blood or clothing were found that would lead us to suspect that the tragedy had been committed there.' Having inspected the scene, he departed without appointing anyone to guard it against subsequent public access. Inquisitive individuals were now free to stroll into the alley to look at the place where the body had lain.

Reporting to Superintendent Lionel Potter at Russell Street, Brophy urged that further men be assigned to assist him in the investigation, more particularly as the unprecedented seriousness of the crime would soon thrust it into the public eye.

In later years, Senior Detective Frederick John Piggott would recall how he became involved in the case: 'On the morning of New Year's Eve, 1921 ... Superintendent Potter came to our old muster room at Russell Street ... and told me to go down with Brophy to the city morgue ... He said a girl's body had been taken there and that he felt it would be a complicated case.' When Piggott demurred, reminding Potter that '... if this girl's body was found in the city, that's Brophy's division ... I'm on the south of the city ...' Potter replied: 'I know ... but you also happen to be the senior man. I'll need you both on this case ...'

Although Piggott was 47 and Brophy 43, Piggott was 'the senior man' because he had joined the Victoria Police two years prior to Brophy and was appointed senior detective 15 months ahead of him.

At the morgue Piggott viewed the body, listening intently as Brophy recounted how it was found. A detective of the first rank, Piggott's reputation for keen observation had already won him comparisons with Conan Doyle's famous sleuth. Since he was now heading the investigation, Piggott knew he had to see the scene of the body's discovery for himself. But it was now 9am, two hours after the body had been removed to the morgue and three since the discovery by Errington.

From Exhibition Street, the rattletrap burst into Little Collins and headed west, the rear of the Eastern Market looming along the northern side of the street. At number 95, Stanley's barbershop, the vehicle banged and clattered to a halt.

As Piggott alighted, he found a big crowd of Saturday morning shoppers making their own inspections of the area. Fortunately, however, the detectives were at this time joined by detectives Harper and Portingale, who had been deputed to assist them. The crowd was ordered out of the alley to allow Piggott and Brophy access.

In that night's paper a journalist commented on the accessibility of the scene to newsmen and the public, giving a snapshot of the changes which were rapidly affecting the alley's terrain:

> ... [E]arly this morning this writer visited the place where the body was found, and noted two new, long, indented scratches on the brick surface of the lane close where the victim's head had lain. They were obviously the marks of a heavily nailed boot which had skidded into the dry gutter near the fence under the pressure of some weight or physical exertion ... [T]his afternoon the writer again visited the spot. This time the shallow gutter was running, but across the slightly slime-filmed course of its bed were two obviously newly seared scars ...
>
> Possibly this boot trail was made by the constable who lifted the body to carry it to the morgue. On the other hand, it may not have been. In which case there remains a suggestion that the person who left that trail was the one who carried and placed the body in the place where it was found.

That Saturday night the *Herald* carried the first reports of the crime on its front page: 'Brutal Murder in City—Girl of 12 Strangled and Left in Lane'. At this point, none of the detectives had been prepared to speak to the press. Over the next 24 hours, however, the press found Senior Constable Salts a willing source of information. The *Age* reported that Salts found the body cold and that rigor mortis had set in. It further reported that he 'carefully searched the ground in the vicinity for signs of a struggle without finding any'. Salts gave a description of the body to all the newspapers: the deceased was naked, lying face upward with her head to the east. Her auburn hair was flowing straight out from her head 'giving the impression', reported the *Age*, 'that the body had been emptied out of a bag'. The body lay partly on the stones of the lane and partly on a rectangular cast-iron drain cover. The lewd position led to speculation in the *Herald* that the killer had laid the body out.

Salts *was* an experienced policeman but he was lacking in even rudimentary forensic instruction. When he examined the dead child's injuries he made the layperson's common error of confusing areas of lividity and post-mortem staining with bruises, the result being that injuries described by Salts and subsequently reported in the newspapers were not in fact perpetrated on the victim.

The most serious error in each of the four newspaper reports pertains to the narrow band of discolouration extending completely around the girl's throat. The *Midnight Sun*, Melbourne's Saturday night weekly, said of the dead child that: '*when found this morning*[†] there was the mark of a cord around the neck . . .' and went on to say that death was due to strangulation.

The *Midnight Sun* does not name Dr Mollison but the other reports do. In each of these cases, the cord is mentioned after reference to his post-mortem, as if he had confirmed the information. Mollison did not grant press interviews: he adhered scrupulously to the regulations, including the confidentiality of the autopsy report. Moreover, Mollison knew that the mark around the girl's throat was caused by post-mortem staining. The error almost certainly originated with Salts, and after news of the murder had broken, no more was heard from him; as if he had suddenly learned—or had been made to learn—discretion.

---

†Author's italics

Since the cord furphy was contrary to Mollison's autopsy report it was probably on his urging that a correction was eventually issued. The *Herald* of 6 January declared the child was not strangled by a cord, and added on 10 January:

> Alma Tirtschke was wearing a cotton blouse ... which reached up to her neck, encircling it in a tight fit. The top opening was fastened by a press-stud ... if it was firmly secured the mark seen on the neck after death was probably caused by the tight-fitting top of the blouse ...
>
> Consistent with death by strangulation, the flesh of the neck would become swollen, and if the blouse was tight at the top, the mark on the neck of the child, seen after death, would be made.

Notwithstanding these explanations, the myth of the cord was never fully laid to rest.

Tuesday 3 January 1922 was a bright summer's day. Alma's body was removed from the morgue that morning in a white coffin and taken to the home of her aunt and uncle Ivy and Bill Park, in Hawthorn. In front of the house a large crowd of young people, mostly girls and women, had gathered to pay their respects and were waiting to see the funeral cortege leave for the cemetery.

Detective George Portingale had a specific errand that morning:

> On Tuesday the 3rd January I went to the house of Mrs Park at 164 Burwood Road, Hawthorn, and I there saw the dead body of the girl, Alma Tirtschke. With a pair of scissors I cut a lock of hair from the left side of the head.

I placed that hair in an envelope and subsequently handed it to Detective Piggott.

A short, private service was conducted in the Parks' home by the Reverend Stanley Hollow, Anglican vicar of Hawthorn's Christ Church parish. Girls from the Hawthorn West Central School then paid a tribute to Alma, placing white flowers on her coffin. Six girls, among them Alma's schoolmates Doris Sharp and Melly Pooley, acted as pall-bearers. The *Herald* of that evening stated it 'moved many of the onlookers to tears. Most of them had known Alma Tirtschke as a quiet, well-behaved girl, and, as they thought of the fiendish treatment to which she had been subjected, and which had killed her, as well as of the added brutality in the method of disposing of the body in Gun Alley, they could not control their feelings.'

The motor-hearse and a coach carrying the relatives moved along Burwood Road, and the crowd watched until they were out of sight. At Brighton Cemetery the Reverend Hollow read the service at the grave. Alma was laid to rest alongside her grandfather, who had died the previous August.

The *Christ Church Chronicle*, newsletter to Hawthorn's Anglican parish, printed the following notice:

In Memoriam—Alma Tirtschke
Until the day break and the shadows flee away.

4. A popular sensation

'After the funeral,' said John Murdoch, Alma's uncle, 'with several friends, I went with Alma's father for a walk about the city with the object, if possible, of taking his mind off the dreadful happening. But he insisted on visiting the spot where Alma's body was found, and other places in the neighbourhood, and was much affected by the unrestrained display of horror and sympathy shown by the crowd of people that had gathered in the neighbourhood.'

Gun Alley had been overrun with people since the discovery of Alma's body. The *Argus* described the scene on the day of the funeral:

> ... crowds of people of all ages—from toddlers of three or four years to grey-headed men and women of advanced age—stood at the entrance to the lane where the body was found, exchanging views concerning the murder. Someone had marked a cross in chalk to indicate the spot where the body lay, and at intervals newcomers pushed their way through the crowd to gaze upon this spot.

A *Herald* journalist was also present that day, and reported:

> ... it was extraordinary how strangers discussed with strangers the revolting tragedy, how vehemently they condemned the murderer, and how fervently they hoped for his speedy capture by the police.
>
> 'The country would not be put to the expense of this trial if I saw him,' declared one man, 'for I would shoot him on sight, whether he be a sex maniac or not, as in any case such a being is not fit to live.'

Some people laid bundles of flowers and wreaths on the spot where Alma was found. Mothers brought their daughters to teach them lessons in wariness. Others came out of horror and disbelief, or morbid curiosity. Ed Reilly, then an eleven-year-old paperboy, was one of thousands who visited Gun Alley in the first weeks of January 1922. He and a few of his mates went there out of 'inquisitiveness, just to have a look; to see. It was ... talked about everywhere because it was such a sensation in the papers, especially being such a young girl too.'

A week after the murder, no arrests had been made. The *Age* asked on 6 January: 'Is crime to walk abroad, contemptuous of the law, working its wickedness upon the defenceless with impunity?' Sydney's *Smith's Weekly* also commented:

> What malignity of Fate ordains that, on an afternoon when the streets of Melbourne in the neighbourhood of a theatre were thronged with children trooping to the pantomimes, it should have been Alma Tirtschke, twelve years old ... whose vision inspired with the impulse of lust and murder a beholder who saw her pass?... How long does this creature in human shape with the instincts of a wild beast dwell in our midst in the heart of a big city ...?

Some of the speculation was bigoted. On 31 December, the first day of investigations, the *Midnight Sun* had declared:

... the perpetrator of the deed was of a more specialised type than the ordinary run of violent criminal as we know him in Australia. And in sexual offences in particular, cold-blooded carefully-considered preparations for the perpetration and 'covering-up' of the crime are most unusual. At least they are in Anglo-Saxon communities ...

Three days after the murder, the *Argus* reported:

A persistent rumour was current that a Chinese had been arrested in connection with the offence, and during the day the police at Russell Street received many telephone inquiries asking if this was so ... There was no foundation for the rumour.

By 6 January, it was clear those archrivals of the Empire, the Huns, had become the popular suspects. The *Herald* wrote:

Judging by the number of letters received by the police and the callers at the police office anxious to help in the capture of the murderer, persons of German appearance have been looked for by them principally. Several of that nationality have been referred to as men who would be capable of such an atrocity as that which was perpetrated on Friday.

The populace felt compelled to lay the blame somewhere. Alma's grandmother, Mrs Tirtschke, told the press on 5 January: '... if all the lanes and alleys in the city had to be lighted, by law, the murderer might have had some difficulty ...' These comments ignited further newspaper reports, which, consciously or unconsciously, alluded to the city's heart and to the darkness that had taken up residence there.

Perhaps the locality of the crime itself was to blame: the eastern end of Little Collins Street between Russell and Exhibition streets, bounded along the northern side by the Eastern Arcade and the Eastern Market. The *Age* referred to it as 'an unsavoury quarter' inhabited by 'undesirables', and pointed out that 'From the early days of Melbourne this section of the city has been the haunt of thieves and gamblers and other people of low type, and the low narrow arcade, with its dirty shops and saloons, has been many years a haven for evil characters.'

The *Herald* agreed: 'The atmosphere is squalid and depressing. In the arcade and market a pungent mustiness hangs in the air. The drab and dusty walls of the arcade where [its tenants] stand at the doors of their small dark shops gives a painful impression of meanness. In the market squalor again is the prevailing note. A poverty-stricken air hangs over everything.'

The Eastern Market building was built in the 1870s, to house produce merchants. In the early part of the 20th century these gave way to shooting galleries and hoop-la stands. With the arrival of picture shows, dance halls and similar rival attractions, these stalls too were being swept away. By 1922 the lower portion of the market presented an increasingly desolate appearance. A few businesses—pet shops, secondhand dealers, tobacconists, a Chinese herbalist—remained.

The Eastern Arcade was a long narrow building, a thoroughfare from Bourke Street to Little Collins Street. It housed more than fifty shopkeepers over two levels. Inside was a long, enclosed court paved with rough stone flags and covered by a convex roof glazed along the centre. Wooden stairways at either end led up to the second storey, the rooms of which abutted on a long encircling balcony overlooking the court below. There were 37 rooms on the ground floor and at least another 29 in the gallery.

Here were fortune-tellers, spiritualists, phrenologists, woodcarvers, sculptors, masseurs, booksellers, bookmakers, street strollers, actors, music teachers and Italian patriots. A prominent figure was the Russian seer, Madame Ghurka, who rented three shops on the western side of the arcade. She advertised each evening in the *Herald*:

> MADAME GHURKA—Famous Character Analyst, is not a crystal gazer, clairvoyant, etc. Better to be told the hard and honest truth by experts than to be fooled and flattered by humbugs ... Fee 2/6.

Close to the Little Collins Street entrance, occupying rooms 32 and 34, was the Australian Wine Saloon. On 6 January 1922 the *Age* reported:

> The licence of this saloon expired at the end of the year—on the day following the disappearance of the little girl. For a long time, the police say, the saloon has been the meeting place of men and women of evil repute, and only within the past few weeks a number of its frequenters were concerned in the shooting and robbing of a drunken man in the arcade. Patrons of the saloon and other undesirable persons could be seen at all times of day and night lurking about the Little Collins Street end of the arcade.

5. Earning the reward

To the Editor
   Sir,—The Government should lose no time in offering a substantial reward for information leading to the conviction of the murderer ... So far as public feeling is concerned, I am sure there would be little trouble in raising £500, apart from any reward the Government may think fit to offer. No time should be lost and no reward too great to bring this monster to the end he so richly deserves.
                    'FATHER OF ONE' (Port Melbourne)

Late on the afternoon of 4 January, WM McPherson, the Victorian State Treasurer, announced a reward of £250, small in comparison with former State Government rewards. The *Herald* was scathing: 'This miserly sum in no way represents what the public think of this horrible crime, or the fears that today stir many mothers' breasts. It would be well for the State to quadruple the amount.' *Herald* readers suggested sums between £3000 and £5000, raised by public subscription if necessary, and many offered donations. Each day, the paper published letters calling for an increase, and encouraged its growing readership of amateur sleuths:

EARNING THE REWARD
POINTS TO REMEMBER
Help for Amateur Investigators

A student of criminology, who has spent many years on the subject, both in Europe and in Australia, submits the following points to the consideration of those anxious to discover the murderer of little Alma Tirtschke.

1. The majority of criminals age from the years of 20 to 40 but in certain crimes there is no limit to the age of the offenders.
2. Criminals generally belong to the category of lodgers and are seldom householders or family men.
3. Proprietors of lodging houses and householders who let furnished rooms should, therefore, bear in mind the following points:–
   a. Has any lodger failed to return to his lodging since Friday night?
   b. It is a fallacy to suppose that murderers are fascinated by the scene of their crime and cannot resist returning to it. Has any lodger mysteriously kept to his room since Saturday morning under the excuse of an illness?
   c. Criminals are avid newspaper readers, particularly after they have committed an unusual crime. This desire for news is actuated both by fear and vanity. Has any lodger displayed any unusual interest in newspapers since Saturday last, by sending out for all editions, or going out to buy them?
   d. Has any lodger developed unusual symptoms of nervousness and anxiety since Saturday last, or been taking great quantities of alcoholic liquor? The lodger who remains in his room with the door locked all day while drinking freely, and shows great unwillingness to open the door, even for necessary purposes, is generally suffering from the fear of the consequences of some great crime.

There were many for whom the temptation to dob in difficult neighbours proved irresistible.

MAN KEEPS TO HIS ROOM
CHANGES HIS CLOTHES THRICE
Matter Reported To Police

... had it not been for the points enumerated in the Herald on Thursday for the help of investigators, in all probability no notice would have been taken of the man's actions.

The report was communicated to the police immediately.

And was discarded just as rapidly. As the *Argus* reported in a clipping Detective Piggott subsequently pasted into his personal scrapbook: 'So many improbable theories have been advanced that there is danger of essential facts being overlooked ...'

Notwithstanding, Piggott and Brophy encouraged the public to communicate with them about the crime through the press. They wanted to trace the child's movements on the day she was murdered, and hoped to hear from an informer or 'accomplice', ie whoever had interfered with the body, turning it over, after it had been dumped in the lane.

Pranksters were a complicating factor. As hundreds of people continued to visit the alley, the *Argus* of 9 January reported: 'Last night ... one of the numerous amateur investigators rummaging in the darkness excitedly declared that he had found some buttons and a piece of ribbon ... For several days shoe buttons have been strewn about the neighbourhood by sensation mongers with a perverted sense of humour ...'

The day previously an amateur sleuth had bounded into the CIB offices in Russell Street and dropped a small paper bag on the counter at Russell Street. 'I've just found this hidden behind a drain pipe in Gun Alley,' he said. 'Most likely it's the parcel of meat Alma Tirtschke was carrying from the butcher's shop.' It contained frankfurts, but placed in the lane by some practical joker. They had not been in the alley when it was searched by the police the morning the body was discovered. When told this their finder sadly put the frankfurts back into the bag and carried them off under his arm.

The press would not let up on the case—the desire for new information being a sure seller of newspapers. The *Herald* in particular battled hard to keep the murder story alive each night. The police were tight-lipped now, especially since Senior Constable Salts, first on the scene, had already given so many graphic details. Garrulousness was dangerous. Not only could it communicate police intentions to the perpetrator, but it could also expose details of police methods to public scrutiny and criticism.

By the end of the first week of January, a tacit strategy had been forged by the Melbourne press. They would push for an increase in the reward, as part of a larger campaign to either expedite an arrest or force the police to account for their progress, or lack of it, on the case.

It was a campaign waged on two fronts. First, newspapermen continued to badger government officials, reporting platitudes about no expense being spared and the police having a free hand. Secondly they undercut these comments by describing the actual circumstances of the investigation, asserting that the police were hampered by inadequate manpower and obsolete equipment.

The reports related cases where, for instance, Russell Street police searching in the city for a burglar were forced to explore dark alley-ways with the aid of safety matches, electric torches not being standard issue. Out-of-date handcuffs, the inadequacy and unavailability of police motor cars (there were only two, one for transporting the Chief Commissioner and one for general police work) were also mentioned. The *Herald* asked why more detectives were not assigned to the case and published critical letters.

The police investigation ended its first week without an arrest and with the detectives refusing to answer their critics. Then, at 9.45pm on 5 January, they received an urgent phone call: a resident in Little Bourke Street had some important information on the Gun Alley murder. The two detectives assisting Piggott and Brophy, Harper and Portingale, decided to take the police car, the rattletrap, which was sometimes also known as 'the suicide car' for its tendency to bolt forward unexpectedly.

They reached the corner of Lonsdale and Exhibition streets when a man staggered into the path of the car. In a desperate effort to avoid him, Constable Rand, the police driver, swerved, but the front wheels locked. The vehicle skidded and overturned, throwing Harper and Portingale from their seats. Rand was pinned beneath the car. Despite their own injuries—in Portingale's case a broken arm and in Harper's an injury to the pelvis—Rand's comrades came to his aid, extricating him from beneath the wreckage. Shaken and bloodied, the three limped back to headquarters and were taken to the Melbourne Hospital. The next day detectives Harold Saker, 29, and Clifford Lee, 31, were appointed to the investigation.

'NO LUCK FOR THE POLICE SO FAR!' blared the headline above a photo of the wrecked car. The accident compounded the wild-goose chase perception of the police investigation and the Keystone resonance was not missed by the *Herald*: 'Those responsible for the slowness of uptake on the crime ... cannot escape adverse criticism. A policy in keeping with the "thrift" which equips the police with a motor-car so old and slow that it is a joke—if a sorry one—may be favoured by the underworld, but it will not be approved by the public.'

Based on claims of government parsimony and indifference to public concern, Premier Harry Lawson's ministers faced demands from a clamorous press and outraged public for an increase in the reward. On Monday 9 January, with no new developments in the case over the weekend, the *Herald* announced it had decided to post its own reward of £250 to supplement the government's 'miserly sum'. But the government had decided to act, posting a £1000 reward. Such an amount had been offered only once before, in 1907, but nothing larger since 1879, when £4000 was the price for the whole Kelly gang. As the *Herald* did not back down from its offer, the total reward now stood at £1250. This was an enormous amount of money in an era in which a skilled tradesman might earn £6 for a 44-hour week. Now the paper had an investment in the case, it would milk its involvement for maximum circulation benefit.

6. The search begins

In 1921, the 38 metres of frontage running back from the corner of Exhibition Street along the southern side of Little Collins Street comprised: the unoccupied Royal Standard Hotel, a bootmaker, a laundry, a sewing machine repairman, a tailor, Henry Stanley's barbershop; then Gun Alley. Lane's Motor Garage was on the other side of the lane entrance and the side of the garage ran back from Little Collins Street and formed the west wall of the lane. It had a side door opening onto the lane at its innermost end. Right at the back of Gun Alley was a wide gate opening into Beamish's Livery Stables. Alma's body was found just inside the entrance of a 1.5-metre-wide brick-paved passageway which ran off from Gun Alley to the left.

This passageway, or easement, ran 19 metres to the east, toward Exhibition Street. On the right-hand side the passageway was flanked by a two-storey red-brick wall. On the left was a fence, made of corrugated iron and wood, from which opened the back gates of the shops fronting Little Collins Street. At intervals along the easement were rubbish bins, which the investigators emptied for any clues or traces of Alma's clothing. The easement stopped at a dead end: a closed corrugated-iron

GUN ALLEY: PLAN OF LOCALITY 1922

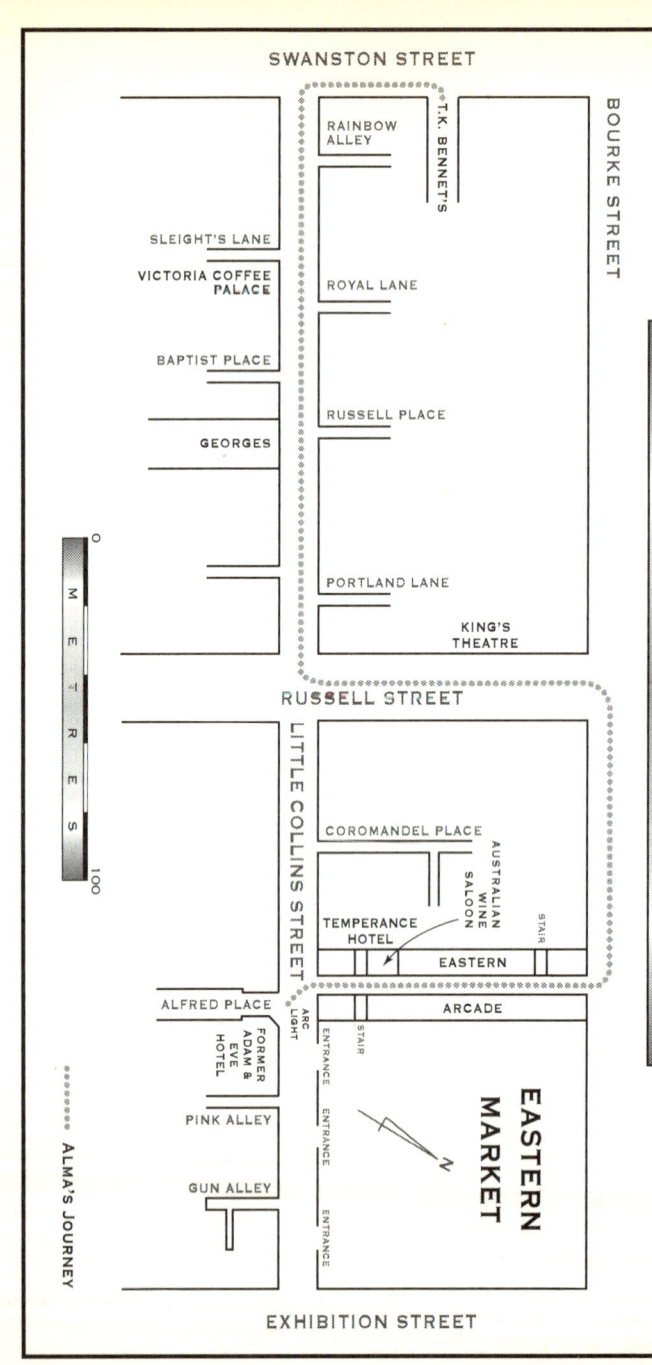

ALMA'S JOURNEY

Plan of Australian Wine Saloon
(Rooms 32 & 34 of Eastern Arcade)

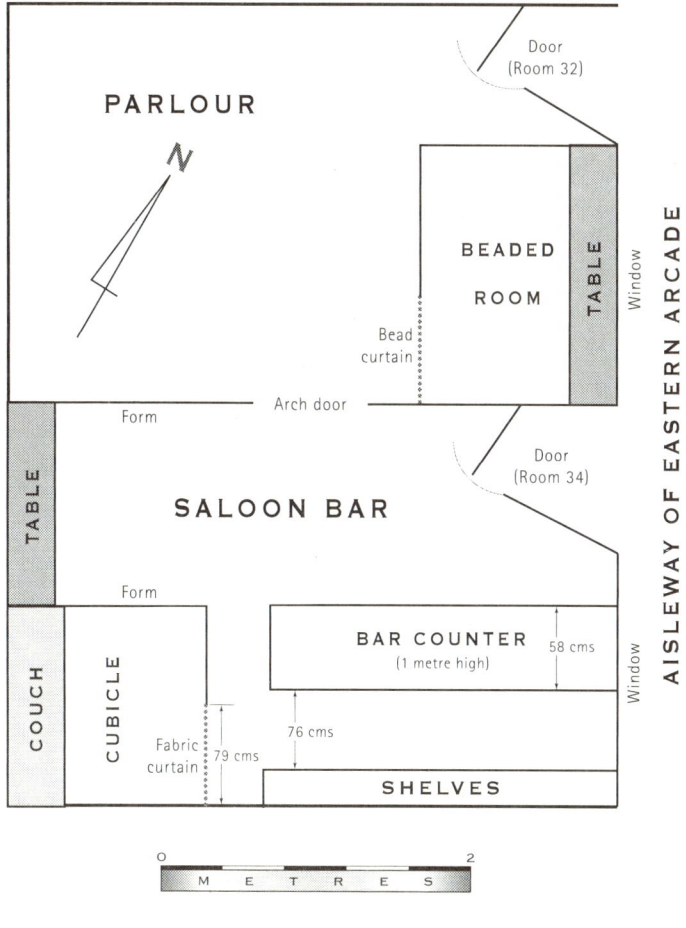

Door (Room 32)

PARLOUR

N

BEADED ROOM

TABLE

Window

Bead curtain

Form — Arch door

Door (Room 34)

TABLE

SALOON BAR

AISLEWAY OF EASTERN ARCADE

Form

BAR COUNTER
(1 metre high)

58 cms

Window

COUCH

CUBICLE

Fabric curtain 79 cms

76 cms

SHELVES

0 — 2
METRES

NOTE: This plan is only approximately to scale. Each of the big rooms was, over all, 4.82m x 3.45m. The cubicle occupied 1.82m x 1.65m of the one room, and the beaded room occupied 2.28m x 2.0m of the other room.

gate beyond which was the back of a laundry. Above the gate clotheslines were pegged heavily with petticoats and shirts.

Just inside the entrance to the easement was the cast-iron trapdoor of a drain, on which the body had been found partially lying. It couldn't be opened without a key from the Board of Works and wasn't inspected until several days later—on 4 January. Nothing was found.

By the time Piggott had arrived on the scene at 9am—three hours after Errington's discovery—if there had ever been any clues in the alley or easement, there were certainly none now. He turned his attention to the premises adjoining Gun Alley. The four detectives searched the stables and the shops and residences backing onto the easement, then the rooftops in the immediate vicinity of Gun Alley, in case anything had been thrown up there. As the morning progressed, the police extended west along Little Collins Street. It was plain, however, that Piggott and Brophy had not sufficient manpower to mount an immediate and comprehensive search of the whole neighbourhood. Their search would have to be undertaken in stages and would take many days to complete.

It was not until 4 January that inspection shafts at either end of Gun Alley and other apertures in the vicinity leading into the sewers were searched. The Eastern Arcade roof was not searched until that day, either. On 7 January policewomen were called in to visit a 'questionable house' in the neighbourhood and make a search for clothing. Days later, on 10 January, the Eastern Arcade cellars (each ground floor shop had a vault or cellar beneath it) were examined. By that stage, Senior Detective Ashton was assisting the investigation. But despite the careful examination of 'all nooks and crannies', the police 'failed to find a single garment of the dead girl'.

Armchair experts advised:

Sir,— ... if the police had surrounded the whole area bounded by Exhibition Street, Collins Street, Russell Street and Bourke Street, which would take in the Eastern Arcade, Eastern Market and the group of alleys in the vicinity ... as soon as the discovery was made, and had examined carefully every dwelling or shop and interrogated every individual within that area, they might have found the dead girl's clothing, and the actual murderer.

Such a search could have been accomplished ... but it would have entailed the service of at least 40 men, and not only four ...

FIAT JUSTICIA (St Kilda)

Even amateurs could see the investigation's deficiencies.

The police had made inquiries and searched houses along Little Collins Street until late on Saturday 31 December, the day after the murder. A bedroom at the back of the upper floor of a shop, at the rear of Lane's Motors, overlooked the lane and the easement. From this window it was only a few metres to where the body was placed. The murderer could have made little noise, for occupants of the bedroom were not disturbed—they told detectives they had heard nothing unusual during the Friday night. However, even if they had heard movements in the alleyway it is unlikely they would have troubled to look, since it was common for men to be in the lane at night. The easement provided shelter for tramps and drunks and was the recognised rendezvous for a streetwalker.

Piggott later recollected: '[Alma's] naked body must have been dumped in that cul-de-sac off the alley sometime after 1am. We were convinced of that because we knew a prostitute who had been at the spot just before one. Her information had always been utterly reliable, and she swore there was no sign of the body or a prowler at that time.'

George Ellis, keeper of Hopetoun House, formerly the Adam and Eve Hotel, on the corner of Little Collins Street and Alfred Place, would sit outside his premises on mild nights until the early hours of the morning, in the hope of encouraging customers, usually couples, who might be in need of a room for a few hours. At a quarter to one, Ellis, after bidding goodnight to some Italians who were leaving the Eastern Arcade's Cavour Club, went inside and closed the door. He told the detectives: 'At one or a little after ... I heard a very loud report and I came to the door to see what it was. I looked up and down the street but I could see nobody. I came right out into the street.'

Other residents confirmed the noise, some saying they heard 'two loud reports like gunshots'. Some suggested the sounds could have been a car backfiring or a car door slamming shut.

In 1935 when Piggott was 60 and retired from the police force, he gave an interview to *Herald* journalist Hugh Buggy, which was published over two successive evenings. It gives an insight into the workings of his mind and reveals the first inferences from which he forged his chain of evidence in the case.

That the child had been at least partially washed 'developed the theory', Piggott recalled:

> [that] the murderer had had plenty of time to dispose of the clothes and wash the body ... To be able to obliterate evidence in this way the murderer must have been in some house or room. He could never have done this

apparently at his leisure had there been the risk of other occupants of the house disturbing him. So at once we could rule out all thought of the murder taking place in a lodginghouse or a large house occupied by a family.

Nonetheless the detectives explored the possibility: 'We examined the adjacent cheap lodginghouses ... We failed to find a single garment of the dead girl.' However, the murderer's headstart in disposing of clothing was undoubtedly facilitated by inadequate police resources. According to the *Argus*, it took up to 48 hours to search 'practically' every house and room in the neighbourhood. There was also the likelihood that a family might be absent for the New Year weekend, or that there were some boardinghouses in which lodgers were required to vacate their rooms for certain hours of the day. If the detectives thought the risk of being disturbed was significant to eliminate family homes and lodginghouses, how can one account for their subsequent increasing focus on the Eastern Arcade with its seventy-plus tiny shops, all glass-fronted? Moreover, the arcade was a public thoroughfare and since the murder had taken place on the late shopping night just before New Year's Eve, many of these shops had remained open for business till late in the evening. The exception was the wine saloon which, because of the licensing law, had had to close at 6pm.

Piggott also eliminated the motor car theory: 'People who seek to get rid of the naked body of a murdered girl ... do not slam motor car doors with an emphasis that awakens sleepers half a block away ... It was absurd to suppose that had the murderer possessed a car he would not have tossed out the body miles from the city.' He went on to describe other police theories. 'Post-mortem examination showed that ... somebody had washed and sponged the girl's body after her death.' For *Herald* readers in 1935 this appeared to imply the body had been *entirely* washed. However, 13 years earlier Brophy had explained the limits of this washing to the coroner: 'On examination of the body I found a dry streak running down the front portion of the right leg ... This stain evidently came from some recess in the private parts and would run that way when the body was in an upright position. This gave me the impression that the private parts had been washed and that the body had been in an upright position and had ... been carried in that manner to the place where it was found.'

For the *Herald*, Piggott continued:

> [The girl's] body was carried upright ... A man who carries a heavily laden bag on his back in the city late at night is very noticeable. But if he encircled with his left arm the body of a twelve years old [*sic*] girl swathed in a blanket or overcoat his risk of detection is smaller. Assume someone comes towards him. He has only to step into some recess or doorway and conceal the bundle with his body. What does the passer-by think then? Merely that he has seen two lovers saying goodnight in a doorway ...
>
> But he would be a daring murderer who would carry a dead girl very far through the city in such a way.
>
> What is the natural tendency for a man desperately anxious to get rid of a corpse? To avoid all main thoroughfares. There, he might be obstructed by a passing taxi cab, be met by a policeman, or might walk into a group of home-going roisterers at any moment. Would such a man have dared to cross the wide sweep of Exhibition Street, with its arc lamps blazing all night, or Russell Street, also well-lighted?
>
> Would he blunder along looking haphazardly for a likely lane to drop the corpse?
>
> The psychological factor was strongly against such an hypothesis. So it was that two convictions were borne in upon us.

1. That the girl was strangled and her body washed not very far from Gun Alley.
2. That the person ... knew the locality well. [The easement] could not have been seen from Little Collins Street by a stranger. Such a man could not know that this narrow cleft existed behind those shops.

The latter theory had also occurred to George Ellis, keeper of Hopetoun House, who had told the *Herald*:

Anyone knowing the locality and the customs and habits of local residents and the policemen on the beat could have watched until, at an early hour of the morning, the street was deserted. He could then have reconnoitred for a dark place in which to hide the body. He would have found Alfred Place too well lighted to be safe. Pink Alley was the same, and moreover, at the back of that alley, in the newspaper office, men were working. Going further up the street the murderer would have found the very place he wanted in Gun Alley ...

This newsclipping was carefully retained in Piggott's scrapbook.

Fixing the time that the body was left in the lane was of great importance to Piggott. Having heard from the prostitute that Alma was not in the lane at 1am, Piggott obtained the report of the beat constable on duty in Little Collins Street that night. At that time, between 1 and 2am, the beat men generally called at the Town Hall police depot to have a quick cup of tea and something to eat before going back to their beats. Had the murderer known the movements of the beat constable and waited until the policeman had passed down Little Collins Street before abandoning the body?

In the beat constable's report, Piggott discovered an elementary policing fault. He did not confide this uncomfortable truth to Buggy in the 1935 *Herald* interview; it would take another 26 years before he would divulge it, and then only to Alan Dower, the son of one of Piggott's old police contemporaries, Robert Dower, a lowly constable at the time of the Gun Alley crime who later became a police sub-inspector. Alan, the police roundsman for the *Herald* during the 1950s, later planned a book on forensic detection. He interviewed Piggott in 1961 at his home some months before the old detective died. The subject of the beat constable in the Gun Alley case arose. Piggott said:

> Probably less than an hour after that prostitute left the cul-de-sac a beat constable came down Little Collins Street. It was his duty to check every lane and alley on his block. We did not doubt that he peered into the approaches of Gun Alley ... He was right enough in assuming that there was nothing in Gun Alley itself to warrant his attention, but because of this he just did not bother to walk only a few more yards up the alley and glance into the cul-de-sac leading to the left. Although I'm now an old man and forty years have passed since then, I still get angry when I think of it. If that constable had only done his routine duty properly, he could not have missed seeing Alma's body just round the corner.

If the body had been found so early, not only could the secondary interference have been avoided, but the original perpetrator might still have been close at hand. Due to the failure of the beat constable to perform his duty—to enter and walk down Gun Alley—it could never be confirmed conclusively whether the child's body was actually in the easement at that time. Piggott was so bitter at the missed chance that he allowed no excuses for the policeman.

'Nearby,' said Piggott, 'was an old street-lamp, good enough to show anyone passing along Little Collins Street whether someone was lurking up Gun Alley.' Piggott then said that the lad 'peered into the approaches of Gun Alley with his torch and saw the lighted lamp at the south end'.

But electric torches were not issued in 1921 as standard equipment and there was no lamp in Gun Alley, nor in its easement: both were pitch black. Few people knew that better than Piggott who, on oath, reported to the coroner: 'Gun Alley is a dark alley. There is no light whatever in that alley. And the ... easement off it is also absolutely dark.'

Moreover, in the 1961 interview he suggested that the constable might have caught the killer red-handed: 'And we realised later that the killer ... was actually kneeling or standing beside the naked body with his heart in his throat while the constable was walking just a few yards away!'

No evidence can be found to support this claim. Had the constable, for instance, reported that he had heard someone in the darkness of the lane? If so, there is no record of it and Piggott himself offers no evidence for his remark.

More disconcerting than his unwillingness to acknowledge a young constable's fear of the dark is the contradiction of what, in 1935, Piggott remembered as being one of his most important primary deductions: that 'for a murderer to place the dead girl in Gun Alley without risk of detection he had to be acquainted with the movements of the beat constable ... To have had that knowledge he would have to be a resident of the neighbourhood, or a person who had a business place somewhere near.'

The claim was, perhaps, defensive: from a proud and defiant ex-policeman, nearing death, anxious to dispel any doubts in the public mind. If only it could all have been laid to rest long ago. For the Gun Alley case and the way it was investigated would haunt Piggott to his death.

7. Raising the stakes

At first, neither Piggott nor Brophy had time to talk to reporters, beyond appealing for anyone who might have seen the child to come forward. In an effort to quash rumours and to exert some control over what was being published in the newspapers, a formal meeting was arranged. On 3 January, Superintendent Potter, Piggott and Brophy met with the press; as a result, they decided to hold daily meetings updating the press on the investigation. Unfortunately, as the investigation continued without an arrest, patience began to wear thin on both sides. From the end of the first week, there was friction.

Adding to this tension was the press's, notably the *Herald*'s, own investigations. In a short statement to the *Herald* on 2 January, the detectives revealed that Alma had been seen in the Eastern Arcade. The *Herald* interviewed residents in the neighbourhood, including George Ellis, and reported the next day: 'During inquiries made this morning it was suggested the murder was carried out in the vicinity of the Eastern Arcade ...'

By 4 January, the police investigation was focusing on a small group of individuals associated with the arcade. The crowd of Gun Alley sightseers that afternoon was so great, according to the *Herald*, that 'business people in the locality were greatly inconvenienced ... Women were particularly troublesome and threats to turn a hose on them were unavailing.' Police reinforcements were sent for.

Thursday 5 January 1922 was the last day on the case for Detectives Portingale and Harper, before their accident. At 8 o'clock that morning they accompanied Piggott and Brophy to Footscray. There the detectives interviewed the former proprietor of the wine saloon in the Eastern Arcade, and arranged for his brother to go to police headquarters. In the meantime detectives Ashton and Walshe went to the Eastern Arcade and interviewed a shopkeeper, a man named McKenzie. Detective Holden questioned a fourth man, Williams, and subsequently the detectives met with the former barmaid of the saloon. All five persons were questioned at length at the detective office.

McKenzie and Williams rented room 33 of the arcade, opposite the saloon. According to Piggott, they were, with an unnamed newspaperman, 'belting up a really hot life in a room of the arcade and trying to keep it dark ... We had a fair idea what they were up to. Homosexuality with all sorts of twists.'

Each person was subjected to searching interrogation. Indeed Mrs Ross, the mother of the saloon proprietor, went to the *Age* to complain at her sons' treatment and at the length of time—eight hours—that the elder, Colin, was held at Russell Street. The *Age* ignored her.

Though the men taken to Russell Street were merely being questioned, the rumour was that they had been arrested. By 2 o'clock that afternoon, over 3000 people packed around the Little Collins Street entrance to the arcade. Police were by now placed on guard but many people bypassed them and walked into the arcade and the market. Finally the large iron gates at the Little Collins Street ends of both premises were locked, to the crowd's annoyance. Another rumour spread: that one of the arrested men remained in the arcade.

'Bring him out! Bring him out!' screamed a woman.
'We'll tear him to pieces!' shouted another.
'Pull the place down!' cried others.

The police appealed for reinforcements, and mounted troopers were sent to control the crowd. With the arrival of the troopers the street began to clear, although groups of people remained in the locality until late into the night. As a result it was decided to close Gun Alley and place a constable on guard.

When the main crowd had melted away, a young returned soldier carrying a bunch of flowers walked up to the constable at Gun Alley. He asked if he could see the place where the dead child was found. At first the constable refused, but the young man assured him that it was 'for a matter of sentiment and not curiosity'. The constable relented and the man was allowed to enter the alley. Near the end of the alley he bared his head and placed the flowers where Alma's body had lain. They remained there the rest of the day.

Meanwhile, at Russell Street, three of those being questioned, including the woman, were permitted to leave the detective office. The other two were detained until after 7pm. After a day of solid interviews, Piggott and Brophy now had to face a throng of newspapermen. Despite the fact that the detectives were exhausted and had had nothing to eat since breakfast that morning, they were optimistic. This marked the turning point between press and the police in the Gun Alley case, the sixth day of the investigation. To the public and the press it appeared that the police had failed abjectly. There was no cause for confidence, yet Piggott and Brophy insisted on it. Piggott, a rosebud in his lapel, drew appreciatively on a sixpenny Havana and asserted that yes, he was still confident of an arrest.

Reporters asked why. It was suggested that some found the reward of £250 'miserly'. The detectives replied that it was satisfactory. They were next asked about the 'lav theory', which was news to them. A reporter explained that Alma's grandmother had told the *Herald* that the young girl had a bladder weakness, which perhaps had led her to the arcade.

On that note the meeting was concluded. The detectives consulted the Late Final Extra of the *Herald*, which had an interview with Mrs Tirtschke. She had said: '... We do not credit any theory of her having been lured away for any purpose whatever by a stranger. I and other members of my family are all agreed that it would be only a physical need overcoming Alma that would account for her deviating one yard from her path.' The detectives went straight to Masonic Chambers to see Mrs Tirtschke again.

The next night's *Herald*, 6 January, finally corrected the strangulation theory. Almost certainly Dr Mollison had insisted on it. The clarification had implications for the police in how they envisaged the murder—eliminating the cord theory made premeditation less likely, with a manual strangulation suggesting it may have been unplanned, perhaps from trying to silence the girl. Now the detectives appealed through the press if anyone near the arcade or market had heard the child's screams.

A few days later Piggott told the *Argus*: 'Any day now we expect to get our man.' The newspaper's editor disagreed: 'As each day passes, the grievous disappointment of the public at the failure of the police to track down the murderer of the child Alma Tirtschke grows more profound. The detective and police forces of Melbourne are on ... trial, and no matter how exacting they may find the ordeal they must realise that the public will not tolerate failure on their part.'

Recognising that its neglect of police services was being exposed and that the death of Alma Tirtschke had the power to bring it down, the Lawson Government needed a face-saving strategy. On Wednesday 11 January, the increased reward was approved: £1000 to any person giving information that would lead to an arrest and conviction, and the offer of a free pardon 'to any person implicated in the murder ... who will give such information ... provided such informant did not actually commit the murder'.

Within hours the police were ready to make an arrest.

8. 'A great country'

The most direct route to the Australian Wine Saloon from the street was via Little Collins Street, the rear entrance of the Eastern Arcade. The premises comprised two identical shopfronts (rooms 34 and 32) with two windows painted over with whitewash and doors. The room 32 door was permanently locked. Patrons entered the saloon via room 34's door—the door closest to Little Collins Street—through which was the saloon bar. Immediately to the left was the bar counter, one end up against the window. Bottles lined the wall on shelves behind the bar. At the other end of the counter, in the south-west corner of the room, was an entryway with cloth curtains hanging over it, which led to a cubicle made of framework. Even when the curtains were open, it was impossible to see into this cubicle from anywhere in the saloon, except from behind the bar counter. In the cubicle was a couch and on it lay a pair of dark, grey–blue military blankets. There were two chairs, a small gypsy table and a cellar-opening which led down from the cubicle to a vault.

The saloon was connected to room 32 by an arched door in the wall. Through here was the parlour, a room for the public, with a smaller room behind a beaded curtain. The saloon staff referred to these rooms as the big and small parlours.

Behind the beaded curtain a table stood against the two panes of the white-painted window. The upper portion of the window was a screen of perforated metal for ventilation. Any sound would carry into the arcade. If someone were to scream here it would be audible outside.

This is how the Australian Wine Saloon appeared until 7am on 2 January 1922—after which, due to the expiration of its licence, its interior was cleared out and the partitions forming the cubicle and the small parlour dismantled and removed. Only the bare walls remained.

At about midday on the last day of the saloon's licence, the same day Alma Tirtschke's body was discovered, Piggott went into the wine saloon. He went up to the bar counter and purchased a glass of wine as a pretext for having a look around. He was served by Stan Ross, the brother of the proprietor, Colin Ross. Just after noon Colin came into the saloon.

'My name is Piggott. Senior Detective Brophy and I are investigating the murder of little Alma Tirtschke—were you here yesterday?'

'Yes,' said Colin Ross. He had had some experience of the police and was wary yet cooperative.

'Did you see a little girl about the arcade?'

'Yes.'

'What was she like?'

'Oh, she was about 14 years of age.'

'Where was she?'

'She was walking up and down as if she was looking for somebody.'

'How was she dressed?'

'She had a black skirt, it was pleated; and a white hat. She was a college girl. There was a band on her hat with red.'

'What sort of blouse?'

'A white blouse.'

'What else?'

'Well, she had black stockings, and boots or shoes—I think boots.'

'What made you take such particular notice of this girl?'

'Things were very slack and I was standing outside for some time and I saw her come up and down the arcade. She was looking in the windows.'

'But what was your reason?'

'Well, business was slack and I was simply standing out there.'

'Any other description?' Piggott probed. 'About her hair, can you tell me about her hair?'

'Her hair was golden-coloured and hung down her back.'

'Did she carry anything?'

'Yes, a brown paper parcel.'

With a wave of his cigar Piggott indicated McKenzie's room across the arcade. 'Do you think there is anything wrong there?'

'I do not think you are far out. That fellow there is always getting young tarts in there. He can catch them and I cannot. I often wonder what is wrong.'

Piggott asked: 'How much do you know, Ross?'

'I do not know anything at all.'

On 5 January, the detectives went to Colin Ross's home in Footscray and brought him and his brother Stan to Russell Street for questioning. The two brothers were interviewed separately; Colin was detained for eight hours and made a statement. Because it demonstrates how consistent Colin would be in this and all future interrogations, it is quoted in detail:

> I am at present out of business. I was the holder of the Australian Wine Shop licence in the Eastern Arcade for about nine months past. The licence expired on the

31st December, 1921. I reside at 'Glenross', Ballarat Road, Footscray. On Friday the 30th of December I came into the shop about 2pm. It was a very quiet day. Between 2 and 3pm I was standing in front of my shop and looking about. I saw a girl about 14 or 15 years of age in the arcade. She was walking towards Bourke Street and stopped and looked in a fancy dress costume window. I later saw her walking back and she appeared to have nothing to do ... I went back into the cafe. I can't say where she went. I was about the cafe all the afternoon.

About 4 o'clock, a friend of mine, Miss Gladys Linderman, came to the saloon front. I spoke to her for about one hour. She came into the private room, and we had a talk in the room off the bar, the one where the cellar is and which is unused. She and I went into the arcade at 4.45 and remained talking for about ten minutes. I then saw her out into Little Collins Street. I made an appointment to meet her again at 9pm ... I went back into the cafe. I remained until 6.10 then I left for home. Got home about 7pm, had tea, left home at 8pm, came into the city, waited at the corner of the arcade in Little Collins Street. Miss Linderman came to me at 9pm. We went straight into the cafe. We remained in there till 10.45, then left, locked the place up, went to King Street. She went to her home, 276 King Street. After leaving her I went to Spencer Street Station, took a train, arrived home 11.50pm, and remained there all night ... I have two keys of my wine saloon. I had one and my brother Stan had the other. ... No person could enter that wine shop unless let in by my brother or myself ...

On the Saturday I was again at the saloon. It was the last day of the licence. I saw Clarke, manager of the arcade, about 11am and arranged with him to get me a key of the back gate of the arcade which is locked by means of a chain and padlock. He gave me a key about noon. I left there at about 6.15pm. I came back to the arcade at 6.45am Monday and a van came at 7am and then took my effects from the saloon ... My brothers Stanley and Tom were with me. I left there at 8.30am and went home. I handed the keys to the caretaker. I cannot say what goes on inside No. 33 in the arcade but I have seen several women going in and out and in the company of McKenzie ... The ages of the women would range from about 20 years and upwards.

I cannot say if any person saw me with Gladys Linderman while at the arcade. I was not in the company of any other women that afternoon or evening at the saloon.

Close to the saloon and about 36 feet distant is a men's lavatory, the door of which is generally locked. At night time it is occasionally left open. I had a key of that lavatory ...

As per police procedure, this statement was obtained by question and answer. Further questions were put when it was concluded. The supplementary statement follows:

I admit I did walk up and down Little Collins Street in front of the arcade from about 8.45 until 9pm. I say there was not a light in my saloon after 10.45pm unless my brother was in there. My brother was first to enter my saloon on the Saturday morning. I came while the detectives were talking to my brother ... I did have two blankets in the saloon; they were used as a rug or cover for the couch to lie down on in the afternoons ... I remember, before Miss G Linderman came to the cafe, there were two young women in the bar. They would be 19 or 20 years of age. They left the saloon in company with two men. That was on Friday the 30th. In my opinion No. 33 is a brothel. Several men have keys of the room.

More questions were put to Colin Ross that day, but his responses were not taken down in writing. Instead they would be recollected by Piggott and submitted in his deposition at the inquest.

'What time did you get into the wine bar in the afternoon [of 30 December]?'

'About 2 o'clock.'

'Who was with you in that bar that afternoon?'

'A man named Allen and a woman was there. Detective Lee called and ordered the woman out.'

'What was her name?'

'I do not know.'

'What time was Gladys Linderman there?'

'About 4.45,' Ross answered, but Piggott made an error here: by comparing this question and answer with Ross's written statement, it is clear what Ross said was that he and Gladys left the saloon at 4.45pm.

When he had answered all of their questions, the police found there was nothing to warrant Ross's arrest or continued detention. They had earlier released his brother Stan, the barmaid Ivy Matthews, and the two men associated with room 33.

Years later, in his interview with Hugh Buggy in the *Herald*, Piggott recalled: 'After detention for questioning we released Ross. There was method in that step. I had questioned him about his relations with women.' Indicative of these questions about Ross's sexual relations were those in the following exchange. It was made public by Piggott at the inquest, and damaged Ross's character.

Piggott had asked Ross: 'Is it a fact that you state that you never have intercourse with a female unless she is naked?'

'That is a lie,' Ross answered.

'Is it a fact that you have said if they do not do what you want them to do you would strangle the bastards?'

Ross: 'That is a lie.'

'Is it a fact you have boasted you were the largest sexually made man while at Broadmeadows [army hospital]?'

'That is a lie.'

The questions in themselves, however strongly denied, were enough to suggest Ross was perverse.

T Gurr and HH Cox, who use Piggott as a source for the Gun Alley murder in their *Famous Australasian Crimes*, state that: 'Piggott and Brophy were working on the theory that it often pays to let a murderer play about—it gives him a chance to talk.'

Piggott knew confronting a suspect with sleazy allegations, however false, could be useful. They might lead a suspect to disclose guilt by acting defensively—or offensively—when approaching former confidants or possible informers. Yet it seems that Ross really did not know who would say such things about him.

On the morning of Friday 6 January, the following day, Ross boldly returned to Russell Street and asked for Piggott.

Ross: 'Who has been saying these things to you about me?'

Piggott: 'I won't tell you.'

'I want to know.'

'Well you won't know. I never divulge where I get my information. But why are you so anxious to know?'

'Because,' said Ross, 'I will warm them up.' He told Piggott that he did not believe anyone had told him.

But it was exactly this 'warming up' that Piggott had been looking for—'Very good,' he urged, 'try it'—hoping that Ross might do or say something incriminating.

The source of Piggott's allegations is unknown, though the detectives had been interviewing prostitutes regarding the sexual predilections of their clients.

Stanley Ross's statement corroborated that of his brother:

I am a labourer; I was employed by my brother, Colin Ross, who was the licensee of the wine saloon in the Eastern Arcade.

On Friday 30th December I was at the saloon. I think my brother came in about 2 o'clock ... he was about during the afternoon and a woman named Gladdie was in the saloon. She came after he did. She remained about 10 minutes in the little back room with my brother. I did not see her leave but when I came back she was gone. There was another girl came in, she was absolutely the only one in the premises. There was a man there named Darkie. I closed the saloon at 6 o'clock, Colin said I must get home. He left a few minutes after 6 o'clock. I did not see him again that night. I had tea at the Commercial Cafe, Elizabeth Street, took a walk up Bourke Street, came back to the saloon about 7pm. Went to the lavatory, returned to the cafe and put key through letter box. I then went to Flinders Street and there met my mate, Lou Porter, and Joe Bolan of Footscray. We walked about Swanston Street and Bourke Street til about 10pm. I then went to Footscray. There are two latch keys to the saloon no other persons have keys of the shop. When I left the shop all lights were out and the interior was in the same condition when I returned on the Saturday morning. The key of the lavatory I found on the floor where I had pushed it through the night before. I am not acquainted with Mr McKenzie from the shop No. 33 opposite. Nor do I know a man named Williams.

Of the two men from room 33, McKenzie and Williams, Piggott stated that both he and Brophy 'satisfied ourselves that they knew nothing whatever about the crime'. Sometime afterward, however, it would emerge that McKenzie had lent his room in the arcade to a friend who had indeed entertained a girl there on the night of 30 December, the night of the murder. But this girl turned out to be the daughter of a former police officer.

In her interview of 5 January, Ivy Matthews, Ross's former barmaid, told the police she knew nothing. Moreover, she met members of the Ross family outside the detective office that evening and protested indignantly to them about being questioned. She waited for Colin and reiterated her indignance when he was eventually released. Stanley went back to the detective office that evening at about 6.45. He found that Colin was still being interrogated. Stanley then went by train to Footscray from whence he came back to the Ballantynes' home in West Melbourne (the family of his sister-in-law, Mrs Tom Ross), arriving there at about 9.30. There he met up with Colin and several other persons, and at about 10.30 he and Colin and two others left for Footscray.

The confidence Colin displayed in police interviews seemed indicative of a man whose conscience was clear. Though the Ross family must have realised he was a suspect, nobody sought the aid of a solicitor. Even up to the day he was charged he went quietly with the police—cooperative though indignant—as if feeling that this was all some kind of a misunderstanding, a mistake that the police themselves would shortly clear up.

At 10am on Thursday 12 January, six detectives—senior detectives Piggott, Brophy, Ashton and Walshe, and detectives Lee and Saker—drove out to 'Glenross' in Ballarat Road, Footscray, the home of Colin Ross. 'Glenross' was a weatherboard house surrounded by a flower garden. At the back were cinder-surfaced yards, a stable and outhouses. Open land belonging to the family adjoined the premises where their horses grazed.

The police had watched to ensure that Mrs Ross, accompanied by her son Ronald, had departed the house, leaving only Colin at home. Ashton took Saker and Lee to the rear of the property: the two younger men vaulted the back fences. They found Ross in the backyard lavatory. Ashton brought him inside, into the kitchen, where Piggott explained that he was again wanted for questioning at Russell Street. Ross put up no resistance but asked if he might first change into some better clothes.

There are two versions of what happened next. The first is Piggott and Ashton's, recounted at the inquest and trial.

Piggott asked Ross: 'What did you do with those blankets that you had at the wine shop in the Eastern Arcade?'

Ross: 'They are out in the vestibule on the sofa.'

Piggott watched as Ashton went to the sofa and pointed to two blankets folded up under a pillow. 'Are these the blankets you had in your wine shop?' Ashton asked.

'Yes,' Ross answered.

Piggott and Brophy together began to unfold a brown blanket. 'As we opened it,' Piggott would later testify, 'I could see the sheen of what appeared to me to be golden hair.' He gave Ashton the blankets, saying: 'Fold them up again and put them in the motor car and we will take them to the detective office.' Ashton heard Piggott say: '... remove them carefully, they are to go to the Government Analyst'.

One of the detectives then accompanied Ross to his bedroom where Ross changed.

The second version is given by Ross himself, under oath in the Melbourne Supreme Court. The account varies slightly, but crucially, as it suggests he did not make a visual identification of the blankets when they were impounded:

> While I was dressing to go to the detective office they asked me the whereabouts of the blankets that had been

in the saloon. I said they were out on the couch. One of them went out and called out, 'Are these the blankets out here?' I replied that I supposed they were.

Ross's version, that the conversation occurred while he was getting dressed, is supported by Ashton's admission under cross-examination. He was asked: Where were you standing when Piggott said [to Ross]: 'What did you do with the blankets?'

Ashton: 'I was inside the house, in Ross's bedroom.'

Ross put on a dark-grey tweed suit, a stand-up collar and a blue tie. He gave his tan boots a quick brush and combed his hair. He then went in the police car to Russell Street.

Outside, Mrs Ross saw the detectives pass with Colin. She and Ronald immediately followed them. It is not difficult to imagine her distress. She had been a widow for 22 years, her husband the son of Donald Ross who had been a prominent Justice of the Peace for the Sunbury and Bulla districts. Interestingly, Piggott's mother had attended school with Thomas Ross—Colin's father. Before their families moved to Melbourne the Piggotts and the Rosses were close neighbours, both families being highly regarded in the little farming village of Bulla, 25 kilometres north of Melbourne.

The detectives told Mrs Ross she could wait with Ronald in an anteroom at the detective office while her son was being questioned. Meanwhile, Colin had been brought into the clerk's office and told to take a seat. The waiting game was part of the interrogation strategy and was intended to make suspects anxious and uncomfortable. Ross's attitude, however, was pragmatic: he was allowed to smoke so he took out a cigarette. Constable McGinty, the clerk on duty, had the job of keeping an eye on Ross until the detectives were ready to question him. McGinty was also given charge of the two blankets, and simply left them on his desk for the next two hours.

At the trial the Crown would cite an exacting scientific examination of these exhibits, and yet ignore the myriad opportunities for their contamination: while being transported in the police vehicle, or lying on McGinty's desk (let alone anything else that might have occurred since the blankets were removed a fortnight earlier from the wine saloon). This makes a mockery of the detectives'—and the Crown's—presumption as to scientific method. Indeed, Ross's defence team would challenge the validity of the blankets as evidence, in addition to the analytical results derived from the hairs found on them, on the grounds of improper police handling.

While Ross waited in the clerk's office, the detectives questioned his friend Gladys Linderman (Wain). Where possible, they turned her replies subtly to their advantage. Like Ross, she had little education. She was married and plainly embarrassed to be asked about her association with Ross:

> I am a married woman and reside with my husband at 276 King Street, Melbourne. I do not go under the name of Gladys Linderman. I can give no reason why Mr Ross should give that name to the detectives ... The Ross family are friends of mine and my mother's. I remember Friday the 30th of December 1921 ... I visited the Eastern Arcade at about 4pm or a little afterwards. As I passed his saloon [Ross] was standing at the door talking to a woman. I did not know her. Ross said to the woman, 'Excuse me.' He walked after me ... We stood talking at the foot of the stairs for about three-quarters of an hour. I asked him for a glass of water. I may have said lemonade. He said, 'Oh you had better come in and have it.' I then walked into the bar part of the saloon, passed the end of the counter and into a room in which was three chairs, a couch and a small table. I was in there about ten minutes and while there I had a glass of

lemonade. I never drunk wine. While I was in that room no other women or man came in. I saw Stan Ross, Colin's brother; he came and spoke to me. When I went out I saw several men in the bar drinking. I did not go into the other room. I have no idea who was in there. I do know that there is a curtain made of beads in that room and it is really divided into two rooms but I am sure I was not in there. I left the saloon about 5.20pm and left Colin Ross at the Little Collins Street entrance of the Eastern Arcade. I agreed to meet him again about 9.00pm at the arcade entrance. I met him about 9.00pm. A Mrs Kennedy of Port Melbourne was with me ... I spoke to him there for about 10 minutes then ... went back into his saloon. This time we went into the large room which is divided off with the beaded curtains. Colin Ross went into the bar and turned on the lights. I had nothing to drink. We stayed there until about 10.20pm ... I did not go down any cellar in the saloon. When we left, Colin Ross put out the light and slammed the door which locked itself. After leaving, we both walked down Little Collins Street into Russell Street then down Lonsdale Street to the corner of Lonsdale and King Street. We remained there talking for sometime. He handed me a bottle of champagne to take home. I got in home about 11.15 no earlier. After leaving, I saw him go in the direction of Bourke Street. I believed he was going home ...

After some time Senior Detectives Piggott and Brophy directed Ross to accompany them into the windowless interrogation room. 'The same old dug-out,' said Ross—he had been questioned here on 5 January. He had had no lunch. During the interview he chewed gum.

Brophy shut the door. Ross sat down on a wooden chair.

Piggott: 'You told me that the woman who was with you was Gladys Linderman. She now tells us that her name is Wain, and she can give no reason why you should call her Linderman.'

Ross: 'I suppose she can say what she likes.'

'What time did you say you left that woman on that night?'

'About 10.45.'

Piggott made Ross give precise times for his movements on the Friday night. Ross answered that he caught the train from Spencer Street at 11.32pm, arriving in Footscray at about 11.50pm. He then caught the tram to the terminus at Ballarat Road and was home 'about midnight'. He said he went straight to bed and that his brother Ronald slept in the same room with him.

Then, more sexual questions.

Piggott: 'Is it a fact that when you have drink taken [*sic*] you are addicted to exposing yourself?'

Ross: 'That is a lie and I do not believe any person told you that.'

'Do you think that I am lying?' asked Piggott.

Was this a dare to challenge Piggott's authority? Ross was wary of being baited—he didn't want to give either detective an excuse to lay into him. He still had no legal representation, only his wits.

'Do you think that I am lying?'

Ross refused to buy in. 'I won't say that,' he replied. His refusal to answer was unfortunately worded. When reiterated by Piggott at the inquest, it would be construed as an implied assent to Piggott's allegation.

Piggott: 'It will be proved that that wine bar of yours had a light burning in it on the morning of the 31st at about 12.45.'

Ross: 'That is a lie. A deliberate lie.'

'It will also be sworn that the little girl was seen inside your wine shop with a glass in front of her.'
'That is a lie.'
'It will be corroborated.'
'You can get nothing on me.'
'Have you anything to say or any explanation to give now?'
'No. Only that you have got nothing on me.'

Shortly after 5 o'clock several detectives escorted Ross across the road to the city watchhouse, where he was formally charged with murder. While Ross was crossing Russell Street, a *Herald* photographer tried to take a picture, but a detective waved his hand. Stepping in front of Ross, he obscured the view. That evening, the *Herald* made reference to the detective's obstruction with a paragraph captioned: 'Detective Sympathetic'. It was the last time a police officer would prevent the press photographing the accused.

Arriving at the watchhouse, Piggott filled out the charge sheet. Ross was then directed to place the contents of his pockets on the counter. Only when he refused to sign the inventory of his belongings, because the murder charge was mentioned on the same sheet, did Ross exhibit any emotion. As he was taken away he became more animated, calling out something about 'a frame-up'.

Outside, Piggott and Brophy were ringed by reporters, and Piggott answered some questions. A young lad on a bicycle, a copy boy, waited by the *Herald*'s man. When Piggott finished, the reporter tore the shorthand from his book and told the copy boy to go for his life—the front page of the *Herald* was being reset.

Across Russell Street, police broke the news to Mrs Ross that her son had been charged with murder. She protested loudly that he was innocent and begged hysterically for his release, then fainted.

The Ross family now knew they needed to consult a lawyer. That night they contacted Naphtali Henry

Sonenberg, barrister and solicitor, arguably the finest criminal lawyer then practising in Melbourne. Colin would appear in the City Court the next day, where he might appeal for bail. Sonenberg said he would be there. Ross was listed as seventh to appear on the morning of Friday 13 January.

In the meantime, police authorities, anticipating that a huge and unruly crowd might try to enter the City Court for the hearing, altered the timetable: the charge against Ross would be heard first. This information was not communicated to Ross's family, and thus no one was able to tell Sonenberg. With no legal counsel, Ross stood alone before the law.

From an early hour mounted policemen were on duty near the courthouse. The gates of the Eastern Arcade were locked and barricaded, and foot constables were placed on guard. Outside the Russell Street watchhouse and City Court buildings a large crowd assembled.

The *Herald* that evening reported 'all sorts and conditions of people' tried to get into the courthouse. They were excluded: the police had orders that nobody other than press reporters, solicitors, police and persons having business at the court should be allowed inside.

In the meantime, in his cell, Ross waited for the morning's appearance. He was genuinely optimistic. A constable supplied tea to the occupants of the cells; Ross said he was unable to drink it. When he got out of the place, he said, he intended to subscribe 5 shillings weekly for the purpose of providing watchhouse detainees with better tea.

As the number of those waiting outside swelled to almost 500, a strong detachment of police arrived to start enforcing the 'move on' regulation. Since none but police and court officials were allowed to stand anywhere near the court buildings, onlookers had to keep continuously on the move, passing up and down in front of the court. It seems they believed that Ross would have to be brought out of the watchhouse into Russell Street. In fact there was a passage direct from the cells to the dock in the City Court.

The court was crowded to the doors long before 10 o'clock when Police Magistrate Mr TB Wade punctually entered with seven of his fellow magistrates to take their seats. Sub-Inspector Kane directed Sergeant Kinleyside to call the accused. Ross had groomed himself: his hair was neatly brushed back and his face appeared to be clean-shaven. He was nervous. Shortly before his appearance, Colin had been permitted an interview with his mother and when they parted he had wept.

'Colin Campbell Ross,' declared Sergeant Kinleyside, 'you are charged with that, on December 30, at Melbourne, you did murder one Alma Tirtschke.'

Piggott then described Ross's arrest on the previous day. He stated where Alma was identified: '... passing half way between Swanston Street and Russell Street, and at the intersection of Russell Street and Little Collins Street she was seen turning around towards Bourke Street ... [A] woman and her daughter [who were present this day in court] were immediately behind her [and had reason to] look into her face. The child went into the Eastern Arcade ... moved along the eastern side. While she was there Ross—'

Piggott checked himself. 'Or, I should say, a man like the accused was there standing in front of his wine shop ... Ross was questioned by myself on the morning of the 31st, the day after the murder, and he admitted that he had seen the little girl, and described her to me.'

After relating the finding of the body, Piggott concluded: 'There is other evidence which, at this stage, the police do not wish to disclose, and I ask for a remand to this court on January 21. When the evidence is ready for the coroner we shall ask that the accused be remanded to that court.'

'Ross,' said Mr Wade, 'have you any objection to a remand until the 21st?'

'Yes,' replied Ross firmly. 'I would like some of my witnesses to come up and prove my whereabouts on that night.'

Mr Wade: 'Then it seems to me you do require a remand.'

Ross: 'But there is no reason why I should be here.'

At this point Mrs Ross stood up in the court and said: 'I can prove where he was.' But Ross's brother Ronald pulled her back into her seat again.

Ross continued: 'I can prove my whereabouts on that night. I strongly object to the remand. I have all of my witnesses here in the court.'

Mr Wade: 'You are remanded till the 21st.'

Ross stared at the bench, stunned. After a few moments, he muttered, 'That's the country's law ...' Then as he turned to leave the dock, he added in a louder tone: 'This is a great country! There's no doubt about it.'

Ross was taken through the watchhouse to the door cut into the wall of the Melbourne Gaol, and passed into the custody of the gaol's authorities.

That night, under the *Herald*'s masthead was a court portrait headlined: THE ACCUSED MAN. Beside the picture was, in large capitals: COLIN ROSS IN COURT—CHARGE OF MURDER. The next evening, a photograph of Ross appeared on the front page. Everybody could now view the accused killer and read the allegations—and the rumours.

Today, the publication (or other dissemination) of a picture of an accused person prior to, or during, their trial, would result in a prosecution for contempt of court, because witnesses could make an identification from the photograph rather than their memory. If the *Herald* acted today as it did in the Ross case, Australian law would recognise that a fair trial of the accused was impossible and the charges would have to be dismissed. In 1922, however, while a newspaper's capacity to prejudice a fair trial was recognised by judges and lawyers as possible, it was not upheld by the law.

The *Herald* continued to publish photographs of Ross, thus compromising justice for this prisoner. No newspaper pursued the Ross case as assiduously. The *Argus* and *Age* were less sensational, largely because they failed to grasp the emerging power of photojournalism. While these papers soberly continued laying out columns of classifieds on their front pages, the pioneering *Herald* was, by contrast, nightly offering a broadsheet front page with dramatic reports and photographs.

Arthur Walcott, the photographer attached to the Government Printing Office, also took Ross's picture—for the prison register, as he had for hundreds of other felons. In Walcott's photograph, Ross is no longer clean-shaven, as he was not permitted a razor: he has a noticeable stubble. He frowns. His dark hair is brushed back neatly and parted in the middle. Required to surrender his collar and tie, Ross has buttoned his shirt at the throat. He is still wearing his tweed jacket. His build appears sturdy and fit, his face not unhandsome. Ross had become prisoner number 36267.

Piggott obtained a copy of Ross's prison photos and pasted them like trophies into his personal album.

9. Crime chemist

The Government Analyst in 1922 was Charles Price. After his death in 1924 the job went to his young deputy, Charles Anthony Taylor. In his book *Crime Chemist: The Life Story of Charles Anthony Taylor, Scientist for the Crown* (1965), the *Herald*'s former police roundsman, Alan Dower, related how:

> On the stroke of ten on January 13, 1922, the day after Ross was arrested ... Piggott ... strode into the Government Analyst's bureau of the Health Department in Queen Street, Melbourne. Thankfully he dumped a bulky brown paper parcel on a table. He was inscrutable as usual as he untied the bindings, withdrew three blankets, and laid them out before Price and Taylor.

However, at that time Piggott was in the City Court deposing as to why Ross should be remanded; something Dower could have ascertained by a quick check of any of Melbourne's contemporary newspapers. Moreover, after saying that Piggott brought in three blankets, Dower thereafter refers only to two blankets. Of these, Dower claims Taylor told him only one bore all the evidence. Court transcripts show this information to be erroneous:

two blankets were seized by the police (not three), and both surrendered evidence.

A fire at Dower's home in the 1970s destroyed his papers, including all his notes and records of interviews. As he died in 1985, prior to the commencement of this book, it has not been possible to challenge his version of events. It is difficult therefore to gauge accurately the extent of Taylor's involvement in the Gun Alley case. As he was Price's deputy, it is probable that he was present when Piggott brought in the blankets, and that he assisted with the hair examination. Dower did not check the official record, and thus amplified Taylor's involvement with a celebrated case. Nevertheless, as Dower was certainly the last person to whom Piggott and Taylor gave interviews before their respective deaths, he cannot be ignored. This author has adopted the premise that Dower did get his principal quotes right, but that he then failed to cross-check and verify the factual information given to him by his interviewees. This means much of Dower's information can be confirmed—or discounted—by comparison with primary sources.

It must have been in the late morning or early afternoon when Piggott and Brophy walked into Price's office. It is not known how they transported the two blankets, though it is possible they had the use of the police car. There is no evidence that the blankets were parcelled up together for transport.

There were two blankets only; one was described variously as the 'brownish-grey', 'brown' or 'red–brown' blanket, the other as the 'grey' blanket (also described by the former barmaid of Ross's saloon as 'grey–blue').

At the inquest, Piggott stated: 'On the 13th January, Senior Detective Brophy and I went to the office of Mr Price, the Government Analyst, and there handed over to him those two blankets. We spread the brown blanket over a wooden screen ... and we picked off twenty-two what appeared to me to be golden hairs. They were handed to Mr Price separately and he placed them in a bottle. The other blanket was then examined and on one side we saw two smears which appeared to us to be seminal stains ... I saw Mr Price make a microscopical examination of the seminal stains on the blanket and he allowed me to look and he pointed out to me the spermatozoa. Those exhibits were left with Mr Price.' Piggott also left an envelope containing hairs from Alma Tirtschke's head.

At the inquest Price confirmed receipt of the blankets and hair. He went on to say:

... (a) I made an examination of the dark auburn coloured hair contained in the sealed envelope handed me by the Detectives. The hairs had an average length of 6½ inches. They were not whole hairs, the root or bulb being absent.

(b) Twenty-two distinct hairs in all were removed from the brownish-grey blanket ... in my presence by Detectives Brophy and Piggott. The hairs were of a light auburn colour, the longest measuring 15 inches and the shortest 1½ inches and the average length was slightly more than 6½ inches, although the root or bulb was absent from all but one of the hairs.

The gradation of pigment in the medullary canal of the majority of the hairs showed that they had not been cut away from the scalp but were about to be cast off in the ordinary process of nature. From the results of my examination ... I am of the opinion that although there are slight variations in colour, length and diameter with the hair removed from the head of the deceased,

Alma Tirtschke, the two specimens of hair are similar and were derived from the scalp of one and the same person. I have mounted on glass specimens of the hair taken from the sealed envelope and the hair removed from the blanket and [have] also prepared an exhibit of the remaining hairs. (Exhibit produced and handed to court.)

(c) I did not detect the presence of any seminal stains on this blanket.

(d) On the grey blanket ... I noticed two irregular dirty white stains ... I removed portions from each of the stains and after suitable preparation submitted them to microscopical examination, with a result that I detected the presence of ... human semen ... I also found on this blanket 5 human hairs similar in colour to those removed from the brownish grey blanket. I have mounted that specimen on glass also and now produce it. (Exhibit handed to court.) Those hairs were similar to those that were present on the other blanket and I would say that they were derived from the same head of hair.

Price's deposition may well have stunned the court. It was evidence of a type not previously seen in Melbourne.

10. Coroner's Court

In 1922 there were no official police photographers and it was often a delay of days until Walcott, the government photographer, could attend a crime scene. With his commitments shared among all government departments, particularly railways and agriculture, it was not uncommon for the police to be told, on making application for his services, that Walcott had been despatched to country Victoria to photograph new fruit-picking techniques or new harvesting equipment and that he would not be back in Melbourne for several days. This meant that it was impractical for the police to use photography as an aid to crime detection or as a means of recording evidence at a crime scene. The notion of the photograph as a record of crime scene evidence had still to evolve.

Walcott probably photographed Gun Alley on 17 January, the same day as the Government's surveyor, Bill Sherrard, prepared a scale map of the locality. The photographs were intended to complement Sherrard's map and today survive as fine-grain, crystal-clear windows upon a time and place that have gone forever.

On 19 January the coroner, Dr Cole, announced that the inquest into the death of Alma Tirtschke would be held at the city morgue on Wednesday 25 January at 9am. On

21 January Ross was further remanded to appear at the Coroner's Court for the inquest.

During Ross's remand, lawyer Naphtali Sonenberg visited him at the gaol. On one occasion prior to the inquest, the door admitting Ross to the area of the visitors' boxes opened sufficiently that Sonenberg could glimpse the gaol's gallows. When Ross joined Sonenberg, the lawyer indicated his client should look back through the still-open door. It seemed to Sonenberg that the sight dismayed Ross. Stern-faced, Sonenberg gripped Ross's arm. The chief warder glared, but allowed the contact since Ross was still only a remand prisoner. In Ross's ear Sonenberg said: 'Open your mouth while you're in here and you could end up on that platform. Say nothing. They'll plant people in here to testify against you.'

For a long second Ross looked at the gallows. But then the door closed, shutting it off from view.

The old morgue and its adjoining Coroner's Court in Batman Avenue, just south of the city centre, were cold, drab buildings. Beyond the tall iron gates their appearance was oppressively Gothic. At their rear were the railway yards and electric trams wailed as they took the Yarra-bend curve. Gusts of wind caught the gritty traction sand, flinging it into the eyes of passers-by.

At 7 o'clock on the morning of Alma's inquest, a heavy rain began to fall on the crowd gathered to secure seats in the small courtroom. Very few would gain admission. Under the direction of Sub-Inspector Byres, 11 uniformed police were on hand to keep order. Two troopers on white horses waited on the other side of the road in case of any emergency. The gate itself was guarded by two constables who examined the credentials of all who sought entrance.

When the limited public accommodation had been filled, the gates closed. Several hundred people now gazed through the iron railings, the largest crowd seen at the Melbourne Coroner's Court for an inquest.

By 8.30am the sky had cleared. Piggott and Brophy arrived by motor car. Several witnesses came in taxis, the women pulling their furs and veils about their faces to avoid being photographed. Pressmen were, as reported in the *Herald*, 'thick as fallen leaves in autumn'.

Ross's mother, sister and two brothers had arrived earlier. They hurried into the inquiry room, avoiding the photographers.

'Here comes the Black Maria!' was the cry at 8.45am. The crowd pushed forward, jostling the police officers at the front gates, but the prison van passed through the side gates to the morgue and stopped close to the front door.

Colin Ross stepped into the morning sunshine. His wrists were manacled and his face looked drawn. Cameras clicked and snapped. That evening's *Herald* showed Alma's last photo under the masthead; a portrait photograph of Ross just below; snapshots of Errington and Alma's uncle John Murdoch. Another photograph of Ross, manacled and walking between two constables, appeared on page five.

Inside the courtroom Ross's chair was on a dais behind the counsels' table so that he and his solicitor could, when necessary, consult. Two constables were seated nearby.

On the exhibits table were plans of Gun Alley, photographs of the locality, a college hat-band, a lock of light auburn hair and a photograph of the deceased. Judging from the comments of witnesses, it seems this picture was Alma's last school photo. No mortuary photograph had been taken.

The interior of the courthouse was sombre, the muted light filtering through tall coloured-glass windows and onto the pale green walls.

'Silence!' called the orderly a few minutes after nine. As the coroner, Dr Cole, strode in, the court stood. Cole was a serious-looking man with thinning white hair and a near-skeletal physique.

The witness box was on the coroner's right and the two chairs to his left were occupied by JPs A Phillips, Deputy Coroner, and Dr J O'Brien. At the counsels' table sat RL Scott Murphy, who appeared on behalf of the Crown Solicitor to assist the coroner. Next to Scott Murphy was Sonenberg.

Sonenberg asked that all witnesses be ordered out of court, to prevent contamination of evidence. Such was common procedure in other courts but the Coronial, where, as Dr Cole pointed out, 'the coroner is master of his own court'. Sonenberg and Cole argued the matter, Cole conceding that all witnesses bar Piggott and Brophy, and the medical and technical witnesses, should go.

It was a precursor of exchanges to come: did the elderly Cole feel his authority challenged by Sonenberg, whose reputation as an 'absolutely unplayable' criminal lawyer was awesome?

The first witness called was John Murdoch, who testified that he identified his niece at the morgue. He spoke in very low tones and his hand shook perceptibly as he signed the deposition of his evidence. Next came the post-mortem evidence of Dr Mollison. A number of other witnesses appeared and were dealt with rapidly: Errington, Maie Murdoch and the staff at Bennet and Woolcock's.

Alma's movements through the city on the last day of her life were gradually retraced. Bill Tate, a porter at the Victoria Coffee Palace, testified that while crossing Little Collins Street at 2 o'clock that afternoon, he saw a little girl dressed in college clothes. 'She was walking along looking up at the buildings very slowly. There was nobody about in the street and she seemed such a little girl there that I wondered what was wrong. Whether she had lost herself or was looking for somebody ...' In response to questioning by Sonenberg, Tate specified that he saw the girl at the back of department store George and George's in Little Collins Street walking towards Russell Street very slowly.

Alma was seen in Bourke Street not long afterward by Blanche Edmonds and her 19-year-old daughter, Muriel. Mrs Edmonds had weekly appointments with Mrs McKay, a therapeutic masseur, who occupied a room on the gallery level of the Eastern Arcade. She said:

> ... It would be about half past 2 when we were in Bourke Street. I saw a little girl just close to the entrance of the Eastern Arcade ahead of us, that is, just below the entrance ... on the Swanston Street side ... She had bright golden hair with a ruddy tinge through it ... she was wearing her hair flowing. She looked to me to be about 12 and a half years of age. She was dressed in a box-pleated pinafore dress over a light blouse [with] a mushroom shape hat ... trimmed with blue and a dark red band on it ...
>
> She walked into the Eastern Arcade ahead of us about 10 yards. We walked in and got opposite the entrance to the steps at the Bourke Street end and she turned round twice as if afraid or nervous. I noticed the child's face and it was a very freckled face. Looking at the photograph produced I would say that that corresponds pretty well with the girl that I saw. The only thing is that she is smiling here ... She was not smiling when I saw her. She looked scared, she looked very nervous. She was carrying a parcel ...
>
> I did not go through the arcade. I walked up the steps which are just in the entrance. She was just about [in] the centre of the arcade then and I noticed a gentleman standing further up the arcade at the entrance of the wine shop just a step or two from the door. I know that man ... I recognise the prisoner here as the man.

... Looking at the exhibit of hair produced, I say that the girl I saw had hair similar to that. It shone very much in the light. Looking at the photograph [of the arcade], the little girl was just opposite the scales, that would be about six doors up ... Ross was standing just outside his wine shop door ... as if he just stepped out of the door and stepped back and when I looked round again he was gone. When I got upstairs I looked over the banisters and I could see no sign of the child or the man.

Daughter corroborated mother almost entirely.
Close to 3 o'clock Alma was seen by Mr and Mrs Stanley Young.
Stanley:

... On the 30th December 1921 I was in company with my wife in Little Collins Street between 2.30 and 3pm. We were coming from the Eastern Market into Little Collins Street and when we got there we noticed a girl coming out of the arcade into Little Collins Street. She was dressed in a blue-like overall skirt, a white blouse and a white hat ...

May Young's account describes the girl in more detail:

... I would take the girl [we] saw to be between 10 to 12 years of age and she had auburn hair ... She had a box-pleated pinafore on, a blue thing, and a white blouse it seemed to be ... She came out of the arcade and looked back and then she stood and dropped her parcel. It was a brown paper parcel with a piece of string around it ...

Stanley Young:

... I noticed her walk across the road from the arcade to the Adam and Eve Hotel which is now delicensed on the corner of Alfred Place and Little Collins Street. And whilst there she dropped her parcel and stopped to pick it up and she stood there until we got as far as Russell Street ... She stood there during the whole time. But when we looked around again from Russell Street she was gone ... From the time we last saw her until we noticed her absence I suppose it would be 2 to 3 minutes. She seemed to be waiting for someone at the corner. She appeared to be frightened when we first saw her come from the arcade. She kept looking around behind her ... looking back towards the arcade when standing on the corner.

Alma had been within 10 minutes of Masonic Chambers, and an easy 10 minutes' walk from Bennet and Woolcock's. Yet she had taken an hour and a quarter to cover this distance.

While these accounts were being given, Ross sat calmly. But the next witness he knew and he focused his full attention on her. Olive May Maddox, a married woman of Collingwood, said she was 20 years of age. She was fashionably attired in a dress of white serge, with black silk stockings, black suede shoes, and a large drooping hat of flowered material, which periodically hid her face. Her cheeks were flushed: rouge, TB or alcohol? She was shaky enough to be allowed to sit down in the witness box.

Maddox deposed that she had known Colin Ross for about nine months and had visited his wine saloon frequently, even daily.

> ... Looking at the sketch plan produced I say that is the layout of the interior of the two shops that form the wine cafe but there is a bit of a curtain over the doorway

leading into the second room. In the shop nearest to Little Collins Street there was a counter and at the Little Collins Street end of the counter there was a small room. That is shown on the plan. That was a private room used for the proprietor Ross. You would have to get behind the bar counter to get into that room. I think there was a curtain over the door but I am not positive. In the remainder of the shop there were benches—that is, in the bar. That is where people, men drinking over the counter, congregated. The other shop was divided. There was one full room divided off into a parlour. You came in, out of the bar, and you could walk into it. There is no door to open—there is a beaded curtain that is all. You go into the large room and there is the small room ... The little room is taken off from the big room: that is the second shop nearer to Bourke Street.

Thus Maddox demonstrated she knew the distinction between the little room behind the bar counter—the cubicle, as it will later be designated—and the little parlour with the beaded curtain, which will later be designated the beaded room.

On Friday the 30th December last ... I went to that saloon at 5 minutes past 5 ... I walked straight into the bar. I was with another girl, Jean Dyson, and I ordered a drink for the two of us ... you walk through [and] you must see in the little room and there were two men sitting here (indicating) and a young girl over in the far corner, she had a glass in front of her. It was in that little public parlour, the beaded curtains were not screening her; you could see right through.

There was no light at all in that room. I saw a little girl there. ... To me she was dressed—of course you know it was only a matter of a few seconds' look at the girl—she had a white affair here (indicating upper part of body) and looked to be dark down here (indicating lower portion of trunk). And what took my eye was the college hat ... The girl had gingery coloured hair ... This girl looked to me a girl of 14 or 15. There was a glass in front of her. It may have been empty or there may have been something white in it; I cannot say I saw nothing in it ...

After walking through ... I walked into the bar to have my drink. It was, it has always been, my custom to talk to Col Ross and when I returned to the bar I first saw [him].

... He spoke to me first. He said, 'Hello Ol.' I said, 'Hello Col.' I said, 'That is a young bit of a kid to be drinking there.' I said it just slangy, pointing like, and he turned around with a smile on his face, a bit sarcastic, and he said, 'Oh well if she wants it she can have it.'

There was nobody in the girl's company at the time. She was alone. There were two men in the room but they were not sitting with her. They were sitting against the wall conversing. I left the cafe sometime about a quarter past 5 ... When I went out ... the girl was still there. I went down Bourke Street to Swanston Street ... and I returned to the cafe at 5 minutes to 6. I went into the bar just the same as previously and ordered a drink ... I did not see the little girl there. I looked. I did not see Colin Ross there. I left at 6 o'clock; it might have been a few minutes after ...

Maddox now made reference to 5 January. On this day, Ross had spent eight hours, to 7pm, in police custody.

I next saw Ross on the following Thursday night ... down Jolimont, where the Repatriation Building used to be on the corner. He was standing talking to some people I know; and a girl, Florrie Dobson, turned around and said, 'It is alright Ol, it is not the d[ick]s'—because I thought it was the police on the corner.

... we started talking then. And he said, 'What do you think about this murder?' And I said I did not know, if I knew anything I would not tell the police. He said, 'No you don't want to tell the police anything if you know anything,' and he looked at me. He said, 'The papers make out she is a goody-goody, that is only for the sake of the public.' And he said, 'She was a cheeky little devil.' And there was something else but I would not like to say it. He said, 'She was just at the age she would feel like as if she wanted a man.' He put a proposition to me then—not about the case though. He offered me £2 for something unnatural.

He said something more in regard to the murder. He said, 'I tried to pool that b[loody] b[itch] Madame Ghurka.' He said, 'The police came and asked me and I told them I saw a little girl looking in Madame Ghurka's window.'

This reference to Madame Ghurka does not appear in any police record of interview with Ross. Maddox was then handed Alma's photograph:

I do not know if I could recognise the photograph of the girl if it was shown to me. Looking at the photograph produced there is a likeness but it does not look the image of the girl. She seemed to have a little face—you must remember the room was not lighted and it was a little bit dusk. But what I noticed particularly was the hat and the hair over her shoulder but I could not identify the girl exactly by that photograph ...

Sonenberg cross-examined. Having ascertained Olive Maddox was separated from her husband 'since 31st July 1919', he asked: 'Do you follow an occupation of any kind?'
'No.'
'Then how do you live, Mrs Maddox?'

'I think everyone knows how I live.'

'Pardon?'

'Everybody knows how I earn my living.'

'Well, I won't pursue that, if everyone knows ... [But] so far as you and the police are concerned ... you apparently have had a little bother with them in your time?'

'I have.'

'For street offences?'

'Yes.'

'And you have no special love for them apart from this particular case?'

'No, I have not.'

'You are not the class of girl to go and give information to the police?'

'No. But I would on an occasion like this.'

'You say that you have been going into [the wine saloon] from day to day and stopping there for some hours?'

'Mostly of an afternoon.'

'Are you a hard drinker?'

'Oh, no!'

'What do you drink mostly?'

'When I frequented the wine cafe, only on one occasion have I ever had anything but wine shandies. I never drink wine straight, I put port wine in lemonade.'

'But on occasions, I suppose, you have been a little under the influence?'

'On many occasions.'

'And has there ever been anything between you and Ross—anything more than his calling you "Ol" and you calling him "Col"?'

'No.'

'I mean you have never pursued, apparently, your business calling with him?'

'No. It is not his fault though. He has suggested on more than one occasion I should have intercourse with him. I have always refused ...'

'Have you had a row?'
'No.'
'No bother at all?'
'We have had no row or bother at all. The last time I saw him we were the best of friends.'
'When did your present feeling against Ross arise?'
'That arose first when I thought it all over and this case and one thing and another. I did not get exactly bitter but I think it is a dreadful thing.'
'And you have got nasty towards him?'
'I did not get nasty towards him.'
'But you have a hostile feeling?'
'I have no hostile feeling towards him now. I feel that justice should be done. I want justice to be done.'
'... I suggest that you and Ross have fallen out over other matters and that you have a hostile bitter feeling towards this man?'
'Would you like me to tell my feeling? I say I am acting solely in the interests of justice and that is why I had the feeling to come here today and give evidence.'
'On the 30th December had you been to the wine shop in the morning?'
'No.'
'... how many wines did you have in the saloon?'
'Altogether I had two wine shandies.'
'... How long did you look into the small room?'
'... I glanced into the little room and saw the girl and I walked straight on. That is the only glance I got of the girl.'
'What time did that occupy—a little less than a second?'
'... a little more than a second ... I had a good look to see if there was anyone I knew in the room. I suppose it was only a matter of about three or four minutes I looked there.'
'Are you serious in telling us you went from the bar into the big room and you stood at the entrance of the room guarded by beaded curtains and looked into there for three or four minutes?'

'I did not have a watch to estimate the time.'

'... Do you estimate the time you were looking into this room as three or four minutes?'

'I suppose it would be about that.'

'And you say that after having a look at this girl for that time, you cannot say now whether the photograph is the same face as you saw in that room.'

'I say having looked at this girl for three or four minutes I feel certain the face in the photograph is the same as the girl in that room because there is a likeness.'

'You have said that "There is a likeness but it is hard to say. I could not identify the girl by the photo"?'

'That is correct; that is what I say.'

'Tell us, Miss Maddox—'

'Mrs!' (Laughter)

'Mrs, I beg your pardon ... When for the first time did you give this evidence?'

'I gave this information the day that I wrote the statement.'

'And when would that be?'

'I do not know the day, the police know; I forget the day.'

'You do not know when it was?'

'It was sometime about the Monday—no it wasn't, it was the Tuesday, I think, because I was pretty potty the day before I wrote the statement ... How I remember was because I saw Ivy Matthews and I had to go up to see her. She was barmaid there before, who was employed by Ross as manageress.'

'And was it before or after you saw Ivy Matthews that you made the statement?'

'It was after ... I said to her, "I am frightened to give evidence because the police do not like me. I have been in their clutches and there are my convictions and that, so I am not sweet with them." I was a bit scared. And she turned around and said, "Have you any doubt, do you really think it was the little girl?" And I said, "I am positive it was the little girl." I said, "If I tell the police ... and if I write a statement I wonder will I get into trouble?" She said, "The police cannot touch you." And I turned around and said, "I will chance it and go and do it."'

'That was after Ivy Matthews advised you to do so?' questioned Sonenberg.

'She did not advise me to do so. I asked her advice. I will put it: after I had advice taken [sic], I wrote the statement out myself.'

'You wrote the statement yourself?'

'Yes.'

'And when was this?'

'That would be about the Tuesday. I do not know the date. It would be about the 3rd January—more than a week afterwards—[when] I saw Ross at Jolimont on the Thursday. It was after that ... A good while after that. I think it was in the next week following the Thursday I am speaking about. I do not know about the date. It was 2 or 3 days before he was arrested, 2 days I think, no, 3 days.'

'Have you been promised anything for giving all of this evidence?'

'No, and I do not expect anything.'

'You know there was a large reward offered?'

'Yes, I know.'

'Has anyone spoken to you about the reward?'

'No.'

'Do you expect anything?'

'... I never count my chickens before they are hatched.' (Laughter)

'This is serious. What do you mean by saying counting your chickens before they are hatched?'

'By that I mean ... when I do not expect anything I do not look forward to anything.'

'But if anything came your way you would appreciate it?'

'If anything did come my way I would appreciate it certainly, but I do not look for anything all the same. I do not see why I should get anything because I am only doing the right and proper thing. I am doing my duty as a woman ...'

Sonenberg: 'Did you mention you were a bit "potty" the day before you sent the statement to the police?'

'No, I did not say I was a bit "potty" the day before I sent it.' [Actually, Maddox had said 'pretty potty'.]

'How did you send the statement to the police?'

Reticent at this stage to admit she could not read or write, Maddox hedged: 'When I sent the statement to the police I did not write it out as if I was sending them a letter ... It was not in my handwriting. Mr Brophy wrote it out. I told him exactly what I had seen and he wrote it out and I signed it.'

'In your statement you said the girl you saw appeared to be 16?'

'[Today] I stated the girl appeared to be between 14 and 15 ... You cannot tell when a girl is sitting down. I said in [my statement that] she looked to me at first sight to be a girl about 16 years ... As to what I think now I think it was the little girl that is what I think ...'

'When did you first hear about the murder?'

'I did not hear anything about a murder until 4.30 on Saturday 31st. I was arrested on the same day.'

'Did you go to gaol?'

'I remained in the watchhouse until about 1 o'clock on Sunday.'

'And after that you remained silent for 10 days before giving this information to the police?'

'... I told other people.'

'But where the police were concerned, you remained silent for 10 days before giving them this statement?'

'Yes.'

Sonenberg finished, confident that Maddox's testimony was so equivocal and confused that it could no longer be turned to the advantage of the police. In an effort to preserve the witness's credibility, Scott Murphy stood up to ask, 'It has been brought up by Mr Sonenberg that you were arrested on the 31st December. What was that about?'

'That was for absconding from my own bail for soliciting about four months previously.'

'Did that have anything to do with this case?'

'No.'

'You said that before you told the police you had told other people what you had seen?'

'I had mentioned it before the murder was known on the Friday night when I came back to Col Ross's wine bar. I mentioned it to a girl I know, her name is Mrs Bremner. I only mentioned it to Ivy Matthews before I got into trouble and to my mother and to a boy-friend of mine all before I informed the police.'

'What was your reason for informing the police?'

'My reason ... was I had heard people speaking of it and I am only young. I am only 20 [but] I always knew enough to keep my nose out of police affairs. I have been afraid of them. I did not want to get mixed up with them but I have heard people talking and saying it was a dreadful thing, that there were plenty of women of my sort about the street without treating a little girl like that. And I thought I would do all I could to get the guilty person and get them the punishment they deserved ...'

Reportedly Ross dropped his 'listless air' and stared straight at Maddox throughout her testimony. Occasionally he lifted his lip in a contemptuous smile. When she concluded, the coroner adjourned for lunch. Shortly before the court resumed at 2.30pm, Ross was described by the *Midnight Sun* reporter as 'idly reading a paper', seemingly 'the picture of contentment'. But the *Herald* of that evening, under the caption 'Ross Reads the *Herald*' pointed out it was the early edition he was reading, which contained not only photographs of the deceased and of him (including one as a handcuffed prisoner) but also an account of the morning's evidence. Perhaps he had good cause, then, to be examining the paper.

The first witness after the lunch adjournment was David Alberts, aka comedy actor David Stirling. He said that between 7.30 and 7.45pm on 30 December he entered the Eastern Arcade through the Little Collins Street entrance and a man, whom he identified as Colin Ross, approached him and asked for a pencil. Alberts replied he did not have one. He had never before seen Ross but recognised him now because 'When he spoke his mouth seemed to illuminate. He had gold teeth in his mouth and his hair was pretty shiny, very neat ...'

Next up was Alexander Olsen, a phrenologist at the Eastern Arcade, who said he saw Ross in Little Collins Street between 9.00 and 9.15pm on 30 December. George Arthur Ellis, lodginghouse keeper, said that on the night in question he was sitting outside the door of his premises, formerly known as the Adam and Eve Hotel, at the corner of Alfred Place and Little Collins Street, from about 8pm to 12.50am. There was a light between where he was sitting and the entrance to the arcade. Between 9 and 10 o'clock, and again at 12.50am, he saw a man walking in and out of the arcade, 60 feet away. That man, said Ellis, was Ross. At about 12.45am two Italians came out of the arcade and bade Ellis goodnight. About 5 minutes later, Ellis went inside but came out again at about 1am after hearing a loud bang. He looked up and down the street but it was empty. The next time Ellis saw Ross was at a line-up of men at Russell Street.

Cross-examination on the point of the old man's eyesight was predictable though necessary, and not without a qualified result. Ellis: '... I never saw Colin Ross in my life before [the night of 30 December]. I am not short-sighted, I wear glasses but I can see very well. I cannot read without glasses ...'

When Ellis declared that he had never seen the man he identified at Russell Street before, Sonenberg remarked: 'That's just what we say!'

There was a general laugh, including Ross. Ellis subsequently corrected himself. Sonenberg then extracted two interesting disclosures about the way the police gathered his evidence—

Ellis: '... I heard of the tragedy the next morning, that is, the morning of the 31st. As to when ... I spoke of the existence of the man in Little Collins Street ... it was after I saw Mr Nicoli, the man who bade me goodnight, that I gave information ... to Detective Brophy. That would be the next day or the ... Sunday. I described the man and I described all the clothes he was wearing. [Detective Brophy then] went over and interviewed Nicoli. As a matter of fact, when I described the man I say I saw, Mr Brophy did not take the description in writing. He went straight away over to the Italian Club. No memo in writing was made in my presence. I went up to the detective office to identify Ross when he was arrested. That would be about a fortnight afterwards ... It did not strike me as peculiar that I was not called upon to identify the man until he was arrested ...'

The next witness was Michelucci Nicoli, 55, plaster modeller. He declared that on the night in question he left the Italian Club at about 12.45am. He and his friend, Frank Anselmi, came down the staircase and noticed a light 'inside the wine shop and the next shop'. Both men were in high spirits.

'The place is alight!' Nicoli jested. But Anselmi had to visit the lavatory (situated under the stairway beside shop 33). Nicoli stated that when he went out into Little Collins Street he saw a man walking away from the arcade down towards Russell Street. He said he did not see anybody else except an old man sitting outside in a chair, to whom he said goodnight.

The man Nicoli saw walking toward Russell Street from the arcade would never be satisfactorily accounted for.

Baptisti Rollandi, who lived on the premises as caretaker of the Cavour Club, confirmed that Nicoli and Anselmi left the club at 12.45am. Rollandi stayed on tidying up the club rooms for about another 15 or 20 minutes, then went downstairs to lock up the back gates of the arcade. Rollandi: 'I went near to the wine saloon but I did not see any light or anything of the kind.'

11. 'Miss Matthews'

Ivy Florence Matthews was now called. An attractive tall blonde woman entered, to a buzz of excitement. There had been many rumours about the ex-barmaid at Ross's saloon, including that she had been an accomplice in Alma's murder. Some in the courtroom thought Matthews to be in her mid–30s, though she herself later claimed to be 27. She stood confidently, attired in a royal blue dress with gold embroidery on the bodice. She had a smart blue toque on her head, and, according to the *Herald*, her eyes were 'deep blue—to match'.

Until now, the Matthews deposition, as part of the Crown's prosecution file, has been subject to public closure for 75 years and never fully revealed. Yet it contributed substantially to the Crown's case, along with the testimony of another witness, Harding, who appeared on the inquest's second day.

Ivy Matthews, barmaid, of Rathdowne Street, Carlton, said she knew Ross and had been employed in his wine shop as manageress until the previous November. Referring to a plan of the saloon, Matthews accurately described the layout of the rooms, making a clear distinction between the two small rooms—one with cloth curtains at the end of the bar ('the cubicle') and one with beaded curtains partitioned off in the second room, making a small parlour ('the beaded room') up against the window of the northern shop. It is important to note that the designations 'cubicle' and 'beaded room' had not yet been used to distinguish between the two little rooms. It was in the little parlour (the beaded room) that Maddox said she saw the schoolgirl.

Matthews described the furnishings in each of the rooms, mentioning the two blankets (grey–blue) in the cubicle. She was then shown the blankets held as exhibits, one being grey–blue and the other, from which the 22 hairs were taken, brown. Government Analyst Charles Price was yet to give his findings.

Matthews: '... The brown one is not one that was in the place.'

Scott Murphy: 'Were you in the bar on December 30?'

[No, but] I was conversing with [Colin's] brother Stan at the door at 3 o'clock [and] I saw Colin ... He was in the little room partitioned off the bar. I was in the habit of coming into the arcade ... to visit a friend of mine ... I was standing at the door conversing when Stan beckoned me to come up. ... my first question was, 'Where is Colin?' ...

Colin Ross did not speak to me when he came past. ... There are cloth curtains hanging down ... and you could not see unless they were thrown back. ... When he came out he parted those curtains and I saw in the room and I saw a little girl sitting on a chair ... she was but a child.

She had her hair about down to here (indicating) ... It was not exactly red hair ... Looking at the exhibit of hair produced, I say it was hair of that colour. The girl had a hat on, a white hat like a little mushroom-shaped hat ... I saw a ribbon around [it] ... I noticed the child again after Ross went in ... she parted the curtains and looked out ... I had a good view of her face then. Looking at that photograph produced ... the general features resemble that child with her hat on. I should think she was a child about 13 years of age ... She had a little light linen sort of jumper or blouse on and straps came down over the shoulders. I could see at once of course, the child was a little college girl..

When Ross came out of that room he went to get a drink of some sort ... After [he] returned to the little room it was after that the child peeped out. I did not take very much notice because very often myself if a woman has come in with a child or a refined woman or man came in, instead of their going into the big room where there was a crowd I would ask them to come in and have a drink in that small room. I did not know but that perhaps her mother was with her. I was there perhaps 5 minutes ... I just said goodbye to Stan and walked up the arcade.

I next saw Ross on the Saturday afternoon ... I left home about 2 o'clock and went to the Melbourne Hotel and while there the barmaid [handed] me *Truth* [in fact, the *Herald*] ... with a report of the tragedy in it ... she said, 'What do you think of that?' ... I made up my mind to ... speak with Ross. I came up through the arcade and passed his bar. I looked in and saw he was serving. I walked back again and then went to a shop a little bit further down and back again to draw his attention. That would be about half past three ... After I passed the third time he came out and I spoke to him in Little Collins Street.

I said, 'Why did you do it?... You know that was the child that was in your place, she was in there yesterday.' He said, 'Not on your life, I would not do anything like that.' I said, 'Colin, I know you too well, I have told you all along this is how it would end.' Then he told me to walk along a little bit as people were looking at me from the arcade ... He then told me, I do not like to say what he just told me in reference to the little girl. He just said that the child was not—meaning in his own phrase, I could not use the expression he used—meaning that the child had been tampered with by men before. That is the impression he gave me ... I said, 'Even so, what a terrible thing, why do you not get a woman?' ... It was always these young children passing he seemed to be after ... He told me she came to the door while he was standing there and asked for a drink. He said that he took her into that room, gave her drink ... and fully intended her to go at 6 o'clock but she stayed on.

He said, 'Ive, you know the disease I am suffering from, the moment I am in the presence of a child I seem to lose my head and I did to that child what was all over in a few minutes.' And he said the child was dead. He also said that he did not tie a cord around her neck. He said he ravished her but did not choke her. He did not intend to kill her ... I have lived with this man in this bar and I have known his weaknesses ... and he has appealed to me and told me how this disease affects him. I have appealed to him to get a woman and leave the children alone ... He said, 'You know I got her and she was dead before I knew where I was. After that I felt just like getting hold of a knife and finishing herself and me too. I should have slashed her to bits.'

... He said '... I know they will all suspect me.' I said, 'I suspected you the moment I read it in the paper.'

He told me he had put the body in the blankets, that he had gone home to Footscray that night and come back in the early hours of the morning and removed that body from the wine cafe into an alley ... He said he came in by car from Footscray ... He has told me himself that he would not touch a woman but rather a child—I cannot exactly say what he said to me. [The words] are too loathsome and too filthy ...

The witness wrote on a sheet of paper the words *I would rather have one that is not feathered*. The paper was passed to counsel but not read out to the court nor made available to the press.

> I knew Ross for about 8 months ... He had uttered sentiments such as that all along. I have not seen any sexual offences committed by him. If you mean have I seen him follow children from the door or call out to children passing, yes I have. I have known him to have young girls in there. Perhaps not childish looking children as that but girls of very, very tender years ...

Sonenberg: 'Objection. Your Worship, in a charge of a distinct kind—of murder—the fact of other offences akin to murder having taken place, if they ever did, is surely not relevant to the charge in this case.'

Dr Cole showed his authority: 'Technically, no person is accused in this court.' He was not about to be dictated to by Sonenberg. Rather, Cole would now make the worst misjudgment of his long career, by allowing as evidence statements designed to show Ross was a pervert. Cole: 'This is a court of inquiry, and we are not bound by the ordinary rules of evidence ... I don't think I ought to exclude this evidence ... This is a case where a child dies from strangulation and has been raped ... and I take it that you, Mr Scott Murphy, are trying to show that cases of rape or attempted rape have occurred before?'

Scott Murphy agreed.

Sonenberg: 'You see how unfair it would be to admit this evidence.' He held up the *Herald* with its photographs of the accused and the murdered girl on its front page. 'Every word of this inquiry is being taken down and will go broadcast to the country. The Crown, if it desires to do so, may use the evidence at the trial, if there should be a trial.

But today we are only to decide whether there is a prima facie case to go to a higher court, and I put it to you that it would be unfair to induce [*sic*] it at this particular stage.'

Cole: 'In these cases, unless specially forbidden, the press is at liberty to publish the evidence.'

'I admit that,' said Sonenberg, adding with a hint of irony, 'and you know that every word goes out and it neither reflects in favour of nor against the accused.'

He was being sarcastic. In 1922 there were few legislative restraints on newspaper coverage of court cases. It was not yet recognised in law that a jury might be prejudiced subliminally by the pre-trial reading of crimes and court hearings in the press.

Sonenberg persisted: 'The Crown has all this material and can use it, but we are trying whether this man should go for trial for murder ... we ought to be guided by the strictest evidence and nothing arguable at this stage should be allowed to go in against him.'

Cole: 'Overruled.'

Scott Murphy (to witness): 'You were about to give evidence of having seen girls of tender years in the cubicle next to the counter?'

> I used to come on duty at 1 o'clock and very often I used to see the girls in there but he very seldom allowed them to stay there after I came ... [There] was a key belonging to a man named Jack McKenzie. He had a room opposite and he and Ross were fairly friendly and very often he used to lend the key to Ross and it used to hang on a nail in the bar. And sometimes he used to come and ask me for that key ... I have known Ross to use that room in connection with young girls ...

Sonenberg faced the witness. He had defended Ross the previous November against a charge of shooting. By what she said and did not say on that occasion, this woman had proven herself an ally to Ross. Now, as his opponent, how formidable was she? 'Is Ivy Matthews your proper name?'

'I think "Miss Matthews" is my proper name.'

'Is it your full name—are you married?'

'I am married. Ivy Florence is my name.'

'Your married name?'

'My husband's name is not Matthews.'

'Are you living apart from your husband?'

'I am not in the meaning of the word apart as you may try to suggest it ... My husband is an invalid in Queensland but the way you interpret—am I living away from my husband—is, am I apart from him. Certainly I am so far as distance is concerned but not in any other way.'

Sonenberg had heard from Ross that Matthews drew pensions under several names. He asked: 'Do you draw pensions under the name of Matthews?'

'No.'

'Have you ever drawn pensions?'

'I have drawn my brothers' three pensions under my ... own married name.'

'Was your mother's name Matthews?'

'I suppose so.'

Sonenberg pursued the question of her livelihood. How credible was this witness? Could she be of honest means? Matthews responded with the information that her husband had been in Queensland for seven years and during that time she had not seen him.

> ... I have maintained myself through money sent by my husband to me, and by [my] employment ... I absolutely decline to tell you my husband's business at all. Why should my husband be dragged into this court ... The last occasion I received any money from my husband was ... three weeks ago ... You ask me now how much I got and I decline to tell you ... That is my business ... I decline to answer anything to do with my husband ...

Matthews' forceful replies under cross-examination would win her admiration and sympathy. Sonenberg then asked about her employment with Ross.

> I had been at Ross's twelve months. I was there prior to his coming into the business ... after Ross came into the place ... I noticed his particular liking ... for little children. I never said anything about tampering—I said Ross had a weakness for young children and he knows it is the truth ...
>
> I did not say he has told me he had ravished little girls ... The word 'ravished' only passed my lips in connection with this child ... He has used that expression I have written down dozens of times.

Sonenberg: 'I am presuming you are putting yourself before this inquiry as an honest moral woman?'
Matthews: 'I am.'
'And I take it that you can earn your own living in an honest calling, without Ross or anybody else?'
'Yes ...'
'Why did you remain in that employment for one minute after that man used that expression ... as I term it: a filthy low expression?'
'Mr Sonenberg, a wine cafe at the best of times is not a church and if anybody [who worked] in a bar was going to throw her job up because of these filthy expressions being used, you would never have a woman in a bar. A woman can be a good, moral woman and still work in a bar. She is not as you tried to suggest an immoral woman.'
'I make no such—'
'You suggested that to me.'
'I am asking you ... why you remained longer than a second after that man used that expression to you?'
'[A]s long as he did not do anything else, all the expressions in the world would not make me leave him.

Had I seen that man at one filthy thing in connection with children like that, I would have immediately left him ... I do not say I am a good woman. I am a woman of the world, understand that.' (Laughter)

'You still have not answered what I asked you—why did you remain there?'

'It was my employment and it suited me to stay there. I suppose I could have found other honest employment away from the wine shop. You can take it, I prefer to work under those conditions and surroundings.' Matthews then related the circumstances surrounding her dismissal:

> ... It was Colin Ross's brother Stan who dismissed me ... After the shooting case I went into the bar to resume duty. I did not think I had done anything [undutiful] in that day's previous proceedings in court—as you yourself acknowledge to me I did well. I went back and his brother came forward and said, 'After the evidence you gave against him like yesterday he would not have a bitch like you on the premises.' I left the premises because they told me to leave ...

Sonenberg: 'Tell me, Miss Matthews, after the Rosses expressed their intention to dismiss you, were you friendly to Colin?'

'I had nothing against him ... if I had seen Ross in the street I would [not] have passed him by ... I would have said, "Good afternoon" and probably would have shook hands. But I would not have gone back to work for him.'

[Because you felt unfairly treated?]

'After all I did for Ross, withholding statements that would have put him in gaol in connection with that shooting.'

'You lied to keep Ross out of gaol?'

'Understand I told no lie ... but I did withhold evidence that would have put Ross in. Understand I was his partner, not only his manageress. I did not lie to get Ross out of it.'

'You withheld the truth?'

'I did not withhold the truth; but there were certain things in connection with that case about which he came to me, his mother came to me, and which I said to you, Mr Ross has not told the whole truth about it. It is not because I say I helped him in the trial, I say that all the trouble that came to Ross, I as his manageress and partner took it on my shoulders and helped him as much as I could. They asked questions at the trial I declined to answer and if I had ... I do not say he might have been sent to gaol, he would.'

Further examined on her dismissal, Matthews stated: 'His older brother Ronald wrote a letter and I did not blame Colin Ross [for] my dismissal ... From the time that I left the place until this incident I never tried to see Colin Ross at the wine saloon.' Matthews said, however, that she had spoken to Stan on some occasions since her dismissal.

Sonenberg: 'Do you know a girl named Ollie [Maddox]?'

'Yes. I had seen her frequently in the saloon.'

'Have you discussed this case with her?'

'Yes ... I was coming home from [the Melbourne Hotel] to Rathdowne Street and I met this girl with two others. She comes up and says, "I think it was Colin who did that murder." I said to her, "Are you sure?"—knowing full well I knew myself. I wanted to see what she had to say. She said, "Yes, but I am afraid to go and say anything because I am a convicted woman." I said, "Well you should not allow that to stand in your light. If you saw that child in the saloon why not go and tell the police and never mind your convictions." I could not say definitely what time it was after the tragedy. It was perhaps a week.'

Sonenberg: 'From the 30th December to the 8th January did you tell the police any of the statements you are now making?'

'No.'

'When did you make a statement to the police?'

'I never told the police ... I am actually giving my statement to you at the present time ... The police did not actually know what I was going to say against Ross. That is the truth, they did not know. As to the reason I have given evidence today, one afternoon—the same day Ross was arrested ... I was in Bourke Street and two police came to me and told me I was wanted at the police office. I accompanied them to the office ... and I was asked ... did I know anything in connection with this case, as I had been in the arcade that afternoon. I said I absolutely decline to say one word for or against Colin Ross not in his presence.'

'You told Mrs Maddox to tell the detectives all she knew?'

'Yes.'

'In doing that you were acting in the interests of justice?'

'Most decidedly.'

'And yet you, to whom an alleged admission was made, remained silent until after Ross was arrested?'

'Until such time as I was brought face to face with him.'

'Supposing he had never been arrested?'

'I would probably have held my secret until such time as somebody else was arrested. No man but Colin Ross would have stood in that dock before I would have come forward and told what I knew.'

'And if no one had been brought to justice, you would never have opened your mouth?'

'It is very difficult to say ... I pledged my word to Ross that I would not give evidence against him. I advised the other girl to go to the police, that was after, on the eleventh. [Perhaps] I would not have said anything ...'

'I suggest you are seeking the greater part of the £1000 reward?'

'I think that suggestion ... is a very very wrong thing. The fact of £1000 being offered is, I think, a question you should not ask me. I am a woman, and I say I am a woman of the world. Money and those sorts of things hold no interest for me. When this man was arrested I felt I would come here and in his presence tell all I knew. I have heard talk that the barmaid is supposed to have washed the body and that sort of thing. I have no spite in the matter ... I do not suppose I will get anything and I do not want it.'

'If this man made an alleged confession to you ... why did you not rush to the first policeman?'

'... My word is my bond and if I give my word to a man or woman to stick to them I would. It is a very hard thing to say why I promised to stick to a man who had done such a diabolical murder. I asked Ross, I pleaded with him myself to admit what he did and then I wrote to him.'

'When you got no answer from him why did you not go to the authorities?'

'Because ... I knew there was more than one person in Melbourne who knew that child had been in the [wine shop]. I [decided not to say a word] until I came into the presence of this man—not behind his back ... If, as you say, I was after the £1000 I would have rushed up for my life and disclosed it.'

At 5.15pm Dr Cole adjourned the inquiry until 10.30 the next day. Ross passed several remarks to one of his escorts and then, as the court began to empty, had a short discussion with his mother, sister and two brothers. He lit up a cigarette but was soon afterward taken through a side door to the prison van. Outside, a cinematograph operator was waiting and hastily turned the handle of his camera as Ross appeared at the door.

The gates of the morgue swung open and, as the prison van was leaving, Ross called out 'Ta-ta, ta-ta' through the gauze ventilator of the vehicle to his brothers standing on the lawn. A crowd of about 100 people watched as the van was driven away and then, as they filed out of the grounds and dispersed, the old building once more resumed its neglected appearance.

That morning, Sonenberg almost certainly had no idea what evidence was to be brought against his client. Any counsel might have been disconcerted, if not staggered, by Matthews. Yet Sonenberg showed no discomposure. His manner was alert as always; there was never any trace of flurry or excitement.

12. The only remaining witness

Thursday 26 January, the second day of the inquest, started on time at 10.30am. The reporting of the first day's sensational disclosures combined with clear weather to ensure another large crowd, 200–300. A strong contingent of foot police kept order.

The initial witnesses were four police officers. The first was Portingale, his arm in a sling due to the accident in the police car. He deposed that on the day of the victim's funeral he cut a lock of hair from her head. Senior Detective Ashton was up next, telling how, on 12 January, he recovered two blankets, one brown–grey, the other grey–blue, from Ross's home in Footscray. He identified the blankets in court: they comprised Exhibit L.

Constable McGinty recognised Exhibit L as the evidence for which he was made responsible on the afternoon of 12 January. During that time, he said, the blankets resided on the end of his desk.

These witnesses were mere links in a chain. Sonenberg knew they were preparing the ground for something momentous, and largely let them pass. He sensed already

Ross was destined for trial. If he might now learn something of the Crown case, he could prepare a proper defence.

Charles Price, Government Analyst, was next. His specialist scientific opinion was that all the hairs he examined were derived from the scalp of the same person—whether they were from the sample of Alma's hair provided in an envelope, or the blankets. On the previous day, Matthews had said categorically that the brown blanket had not been in the wine saloon. As a technical witness, Price had not been excluded from the court and had thus heard Matthews's testimony. Now he added that he had found five hairs on the grey–blue blanket too. 'Those hairs were similar to those that were present on the other blanket and I would say that they were derived from the same head of hair.'

Sonenberg chose not to cross-examine. He knew better than to challenge a scientific witness unprepared.

'Call Sydney John Harding!' Witness number 26 entered. He was a stocky little man with an angular face, wearing a crumpled dark grey sack suit, a soft white collar, and black knitted tie, with a soft felt hat in his hand. After taking the oath, Harding stood looking straight across at Ross. But at other times, as the *Midnight Sun* reported, '... his eyes took on a somewhat shifty look'.

As with Matthews, certain aspects of Harding's deposition have not previously been disclosed. Because his testimony, together with that of Matthews, would form the foundation of the Crown case, a detailed account follows.

A prisoner on remand, Harding gave as his address His Majesty's Gaol, Melbourne.

> ... On the 23rd January I was in the remand yard ... There were five of us ... There was Ross, a man named

Dunstan, a man named Baker ... a man named Sinclair (charged with wife desertion) and myself. When I was in the yard our conversations was [*sic*] general for a while and after some time it veered round to Ross's case ...

I said to Ross, 'Ruby (mentioning a girl that both he and I know) told me that there was a woman held in the female division of the prison in connection with your case.' He said ... 'I wonder, was it Ivy Matthews?' I said, 'No, Ruby would know her and would tell me.' He said, 'I wonder what she said?' I said, 'I don't know. You have got nothing to be afraid of have you?' He said, 'No.' I said, 'Well, why worry?' We stopped talking ... for a few minutes and then he said, 'What do you think of my case?'

No, I'm running before my story. I said to him, 'Did you see this girl?' He said, 'Yes ... [o]pposite Madame Ghurka's.' I said, 'What is she like?' He said, 'She looked a big girl for twelve years of age ...' ... He said, 'What do you think of the case?'

I said, 'I am not qualified to give an opinion because I do not know any of the details of it.' ... Then after a while he said, 'Can a man trust you?' I said, 'Certainly he can. You have known me for some time and I have not done you any harm, have I?' He said, 'No.' I said, 'Did you see the girl? ... Were you talking to her?' ... She took no notice of him whatsoever at first and then he said to her, 'I am the owner of this place (meaning the wine cafe) and you need not be afraid and if you want to come in you can and sit down.'

I said, 'What time was this?' He said about a quarter to three or a quarter past three ...

I said, 'Did you take her in?' He said, 'Yes, into the little cubicle near the counter.' I said, 'Did not any of your customers see her?' He said, 'No, they were in the parlour. We were not very busy that day.' Then after taking her into the cubicle he offered her a drink of sweet wine.

I said, 'Who was serving your customers?' He said, 'My brother.' I said, 'Would not he see the girl?' He said, 'No, he was in the parlour with the customers.' ... 'Couldn't [your brother] see her in the cubicle?' [Ross] said no, the screen was up and when the screen was up no one dared to go into it ...

She at first refused the wine, but finally accepted it ... She sipped it and appeared to appreciate it with the result that he gave her ... in all three glasses.

Scott Murphy asked the witness to repeat in the first person only the actual words used by Ross.

Harding: 'If I use the first person some people might think it was me who done this!'

Ross leaned forward and spoke for the first time: 'You are the man they ought to have picked too, I think.'

'Quiet!' ordered the constable beside him. Ross sat back in his chair.

Harding continued, saying Ross confessed that he went to the door of the wine cafe and conversed with his girl until 6pm. He then made an appointment to meet her again at 9 o'clock that evening. Since it was 6pm, he closed the wine shop. Upon returning to the cubicle he found the girl there, asleep.

'At this stage,' said Scott Murphy, '... any lady who would like to leave the court should be given the opportunity to do so.'

Several women, including witnesses, then left the courtroom. Three chose to remain.

Harding: 'He could not resist the temptation and he had connection with her.'

... the girl woke up and started to moan and cry out. And he put his hand over her mouth. She ceased moaning then and when he committed the act he saw that the girl was bleeding and she appeared to go into a faint. After some time she started to call out again and he went back to pacify her, or rather prevent her from singing out. And he said he done his block and must have choked her.

He said he did it with his hands. He said, 'You hear them saying that a cord or wire has been used but it is not true.'

I said to him, 'Why did you stuff the little girl?' He said, 'I don't know what come over me.'

I said, 'And you have got gonorrhoea?' He said, 'Yes, but that doesn't show in the come.'

I said, 'Yes, gonorrhoea shows in the semen.' He said, 'What is semen?' I said, 'That is the germinative seed.' . . . He said, 'And if a little bit did get on the girl it would be rubbed off in the struggle and anyhow I am not the only bloke who has got gonorrhoea.'

I said, 'Suppose they open the girl's stomach and find wine in it.' He said, 'What do they want to open the stomach for when they know she died of strangulation . . . [Anyhow] I am not the only one who could give her wine.' . . . He raised his voice at that part about the wine and the other men in the yard heard ... they were commenting upon it when he was taken out to be syringed for the disease he was suffering from. He said to me after ... he had ... choked her, that he woke up to himself and lifted the girl's hand and it fell like a dead person's . . .

I said, 'You must have got terribly excited then.' He said, 'No, I got suddenly cool and started to think.'

... [H]e said he got a bucket to clean up the blood ... and some water and washed out the cubicle where the blood was and around the cubicle but seeing that the part where he had washed looked clean in comparison with the rest of the bar and might attract attention, he washed the whole bar out. I said, 'What time did this happen, seven or eight o'clock?' He said,

'About that time.' I said, 'Before you met your girl?' He said, 'Yes, I had time to clean myself and go round the town before I met her.'

I said, 'You took a risk meeting your girl ... Couldn't she see the child when she came in?' He said, 'No, she went into the parlour and I had a drink there. I would of [*sic*] taken a bigger risk had I not met her because I could not have accounted for my whereabouts. I went home with the girl about half-past ten and caught a train about 20 to 11 for Footscray. When I got to Footscray I got in the electric tram.'

[He said t]hat he made himself conspicuous by creating some ... commotion and he said he would have those people on the tram including the driver and grip man to prove an alibi of his movements. He went home then.

I said to him, 'How did you get back into town, by motorcar?' He said, 'No ... a pushbike.' I said, 'Have you a pushbike of your own?' He said, 'No, but I know of one which is owned by a person near our place.' And he had easy access to it. And he got it and went into town.

I said, 'Did you go straight into the arcade?' He said, 'Yes.' I said, 'But that iron gate is locked at night time.' He said, 'But I have a key.'

I said, 'What did you do when you went into the arcade?' He said, 'I went in and took the clothes off the girl.'

I said, 'Then did you take her straight over to the lane?' He said, 'No, I went out and walked round the block to see if there was anyone about.' And that he wrapped her in either a coat or an overcoat (I don't know which he said) and took her over to the lane.

I said, 'Was you going to put her in the sewer?' He said, 'No, I don't think so.' I [asked why not and h]e said, 'I heard someone coming ...' I said, 'Where did you go then?' He said, 'Back to the cafe.'

I said, 'What did you do with the clothes?' He said, 'I took them in a bundle on my bicycle and rode back.' When he got near the first hotel on the Footscray Road he sat on the side of the road and tore them into ... little bits, and distributed them in little strips along the road. And when he came to the first bridge crossing the river he threw one shoe and some strips into the water. Then he distributed more strips and went down Nicholson Street to the ammunition works and went to the river there and threw the other shoe and some more strips in. Then he went back and took his bicycle to the place he got it from [and] ... went home.

He said, 'What do you think of the case?' I said, 'Pretty good, have you told anyone else?' He said, 'No. Sonenberg told me to keep my mouth shut.' I said, 'Why didn't you?' He said, 'Because I trust you and you are in here anyhow.' He said, 'We are going for big compensation if we beat them and if we do not beat them I will have to get hold of some cyanide of potassium.'

Scott Murphy: 'Did he describe the appearance of the girl after the murder?'
Harding: 'He said ... "She looked in a horrible state and was bleeding badly."'
Sonenberg, cross-examining: 'Did you say to Ross, "Have you said anything to anybody about what you have told me?" and he replied, "No, not to a soul"?'
'Yes ... he just said, "No," mentioning your name. He said you told him to keep quiet.'
'I told him not to talk in the gaol.' (Sonenberg said this precisely because informers might have been planted to entrap Ross.)
'He did not mention the gaol.'
Sonenberg would later tell his friend, barrister Jack Cullity, that from this moment he knew Harding was lying. Even if Ross had been so stupid as to disregard Sonenberg's

explicit warning, then in making such a detailed confession he would surely have mentioned the lawyer's dramatic gesture in showing him the gallows. Sonenberg's next questions were to establish if Ross might have confessed prior to his warning.

'How long have you been in gaol?'

'I was arrested on the 9th of January.'

'Did you know that Ross was arrested and put in gaol on the 12th?'

'Yes.'

'[When did you talk to him?]'

'About the 12th I was in the yard talking to him for about 5 minutes. He was removed on account of [his] venereal disease ...'

'When did he first make the statement as to what you say he said to you?'

'It was Monday last, the 23rd January, when he made this statement. That was the first opportunity he got of making it.'

'How many days were you in the yard with him?'

'... Two and a half days since the 9th of January, since I was arrested ... Within half an hour of getting into the yard he opened up the whole story but it took more than half an hour to tell it. It took a couple of hours.'

In reply to further questions Harding said that the yard could be covered in about eight paces. Baker, Dunstan and Sinclair, the other three occupants of the yard at the time, were all strangers to Ross. They had heard parts of the story.

Harding went on to say he last saw Ross in September 1921; but prior to that had met him on numerous occasions in his wine cafe. 'I was a friend of his. I knew his first name and I used to call him "Colin" and he used to call me "Jack".'

'How many charges are you committed to stand trial on?'

'Two; but [Dunstan] has already pleaded guilty and made a statement on oath. He will eventually clear me of everything ...'

'What have you been in gaol for before?'

'Housebreaking.'

'Well, was that the only occasion?'

'No, I do not know ... About nine or ten or something but not all for housebreaking. For ordinary assault and that sort of thing.'

'Oh, that's a mere nothing. What else beside housebreaking and assault? Shopbreaking?'

'Yes, well that's housebreaking.'

'How many years have you served in gaol?'

'... The biggest sentence I ... ever received was 18 months. I have had about eight sentences all together, I think ...'

'So many you cannot add them up in the witness box now? What about Sydney?'

'... I have never been in any gaol except Melbourne.'

'In what period have you been in this trouble?'

'I ... had those sentences since 1909 except for four years when I was away at the war ...'

'Did Ross tell you not to squeak?'

'No, he thought I was in a position where I could not squeak.'

'Didn't he say something like this: "Look here, Jock, if I tell you the strength of things will you promise not to say anything?"?'

'He calls me Jack. No ... He told me the story simply because he was bursting to tell it to somebody ... He took it for granted that in the position I was in, and having served a sentence, I would not say anything and had it been any other crime, I would not have done so. I have a little daughter and I have an objection to that crime.'

'Don't get sentimental.'

'I am not giving sentimental evidence ... If it had been my own brother I would have told.'

'Yes, we say so, too ... Did you immediately communicate with the police?'

'In the night time I ... thought things out and then I knocked up the governor. [I said to him], "Will you send for Detective Walshe from Sydney, I know him..." Walshe [who was in Melbourne at the time] came over and I said, "I wish to make a statement in connection with this murder trial ... [It is] only what I have been told, nothing that I know myself." The governor and Detective Walshe said, "You don't expect any promise or hope of anything." I said, "No, I do not." They said, "You don't fear anything?" I said, "No, I am going to make this statement voluntarily; I do not expect or I do not think I will get anything." And I made a statement to the governor of the gaol in the presence of Detective Walshe.'

'You did not expect either monetary reward or release from your sentence?'

'No.'

'You simply spurn the money?'

'If I got it I would give it to the Children's Hospital.'

'Oh, I collapse—that finishes me!' (Laughter)

Impeccably attired, Senior Detective Piggott entered the witness stand. He wore a red rose in his buttonhole, prompting the *Herald* to remark that the Victoria Police had 'a nice aesthetic sense'.

Piggott recounted how he arrived at Gun Alley on the morning of 31 December, his visit to the Australian Wine Saloon and his subsequent interview with Ross.

Sonenberg focused on Piggott's visit to the wine saloon. December 31 was the last day of the saloon's licence, and the only opportunity Piggott had to examine the premises prior to its dismantling. After the visit he had drawn a plan of the rooms and their furnishings. His sketch was tendered as an exhibit.

Sonenberg first ascertained that Piggott's examination had gone no further than standing at the counter to have a glass of wine.

'Did you notice a couch in any of the rooms?'

'I did not ... I could not see into the little cubicle at the end of the counter because there was a curtain down.'

Sonenberg then asked Piggott how he could know the interior furnishings of the rooms, particularly the cubicle behind the bar.

Piggott: 'I did not see the interior of the small room ... I am only being guided by what I have been told by other witnesses ...'

Sonenberg had extracted a significant point. During the trial Piggott would claim he and Brophy 'had the case well in hand on the 31st'. The detectives certainly appeared to have Ross in their sights from the outset; Superintendent Bannon, to whom Brophy reported after Potter went off duty, would recollect that '[Brophy] gave me information as to Ross about 6 hours after the offence was committed'. Yet if the police suspected Ross, why did they not thoroughly search the wine saloon before it was dismantled?

Brophy was the 28th witness. At the end of his testimony, Scott Murphy prompted him to refer to White, a police witness who had failed to attend the court. White had made a statement to the detectives and on 16 January was taken over to the Melbourne Gaol by Brophy, who now recalled: 'The accused, Ross, was brought down to the front gate. White was then produced and I said, "Do you know this man?" White said, "Yes, that is the man." I then said to Ross, "This man has identified you as the person whom he saw speaking to the little girl Alma in the arcade." Ross said, "Oh." He then turned to White and said, "What time was that?" White said, 'About half past three.' Ross responded, "Yes, that is quite right."'

Brophy was stating under oath what he remembered White saying in front of him, not whether what White said was true. These statements, while incriminating Ross, were utterly flawed as evidence. They would never be sworn to subsequently by the witness himself.

Two further points regarding this evidence should be made. Ross had consistently denied that he had spoken to Alma, and it seems unlikely he would suddenly contradict himself. The second point pertains to White: he had skipped town. White was an opportunistic extortionist and liar. His real name was Robert Pommeroy, but he went to the police under the name of White as part of a scheme to extort money from the Rosses. Indeed he played both the Ross family and the police, by turns, for monetary gain and succeeded with both. At the time of the inquest, he was in Sydney flush with funds.

Since White had ignored his subpoena, Cole ordered that a warrant be issued for his arrest.

Brophy's deposition now concluded, Scott Murphy rose and remarked: 'The only remaining witness is Colin Campbell Ross.'

Dr Cole (to Sonenberg): 'What do you propose to do?'

Sonenberg: 'At the present stage I do not propose to call evidence.'

Dr Cole: 'Has Ross anything to say?'

Sonenberg: 'At this stage nothing.'

Dr Cole gave his finding, that Ross was guilty of Alma's murder, and committed him for trial on 15 February. Ross listened; the *Midnight Sun* said he showed 'a curious, slightly amused look lurking at the corners of his mouth'.

During the afternoon another big crowd of about 200 had gathered in the street outside to hear the verdict. Now they lingered to catch a glimpse of Ross or the Black Maria. After a few moments Ross was quickly escorted outside. As the car turned out of the morgue he called: 'Bye-bye, bye-bye ...'

'Goodbye Colin,' returned Mrs Ross.

13. Colin Ross

The inquest concluded, Ross was returned to the Melbourne Gaol. While awaiting trial, his treatment in prison was the same as before. He rose at 7 o'clock, put on his ordinary clothes and was placed in one of the remand yards. Here he remained until 4.15pm, when the men were put in their cells. Ross was supplied with meals from outside, a privilege for those on remand. But the food brought to the gaol was always closely examined.

But what manner of man was this, what life had he led to bring him here?

Colin Campbell Eadie Ross was born at 8 Brook Street, North Fitzroy, on 11 October 1892, making him 29 at the time of his arrest. His mother, Elizabeth Campbell Ross, nee Eadie, was 25 when she bore him. Her husband Thomas, a groom, was 32. The Rosses had recently moved from Bulla, then a small farming village 25 kilometres north of Melbourne. The couple had married in 1888 and already had two children: Thomas McKinley, aged two, and Ronald Campbell, aged four. The family would eventually comprise five children: Alexandrina, born in 1896, when the Rosses had settled in Footscray; and Stanley Gordon in 1900, the same year their father, Thomas, died. As a result of his death, the older boys left school early to take whatever work they could find, as did Colin. He was well built and strong: at the age of 11 he began work in a nearby quarry. At Veal's quarries in Brooklyn he earned a reputation for being one of the best 'jumper-men' they had ever seen, operating the heavy drill to make blasting holes in the rock. Yet after an operation for appendicitis in 1914, Colin found he was unable to perform heavy manual work. He then went to Sydney for about 15 months, working as a general labourer, before returning to Melbourne where, for the remainder of the war years, he worked as a wardsman at the Broadmeadows army hospital. Early in 1920 Mrs Ross and her sons Ronald (a veteran of the Lone Pine campaign) and Colin moved to the Donnybrook Hotel, 30 kilometres north of Melbourne. Mrs Ross was manager, Ronald licensee and Colin a partner in the business. Colin was now 27 and kept physically fit, jogging 3 kilometres each morning to the local mineral springs and back.

He had interests in Melbourne: Lily May Brown, a girl in her early 20s who worked at a city hotel. The pair had been going out for two years. Lily was quite prepared to let the relationship lapse following Colin's move to Donnybrook, but Colin was still keen, too keen.

Early on the morning of Friday 5 March 1920, Colin Ross was waiting outside the Browns' house in Brunswick. Just before 7.30 Lily was met by Colin. He told her that he had made preparations for marrying her that day. She replied that her impression was that she was going to work as usual. Ross persisted, but Lily took no notice. Colin then drew a revolver and asked if she intended to marry him. Lily replied in the negative and boarded a city-bound tram.

Colin followed her onto the tram and repeated that they would be married that day, adding that he would have her dead or alive. The other passengers knew Lily as a regular commuter and the intensity with which Colin was whispering to her was beginning to raise eyebrows. For her part Lily was becoming increasingly uncomfortable and annoyed. However, to placate Colin, she agreed to meet him again that evening at 6.15 outside Carlyon's Hotel, where she worked.

During the day she phoned the police. It was arranged that Plainclothes Constable William O'Halloran would attend their meeting. Colin was waiting and asked Lily if she had changed her mind. Replying that she had not, she inquired whether he still had the revolver. 'Yes,' Colin said boldly, 'and I will not be afraid to use it.' At this point O'Halloran arrested Colin. On arrival at the watchhouse his pockets were emptied; they included a loaded revolver and a plain gold ring.

The next morning Colin Ross was charged in the city court with using threatening words towards a young woman and carrying firearms without permission. Mr Manchester appeared for Ross, explaining that the threats were merely those of a jealous lover, and that Ross had no real intention of hurting Lily. In reply to the magistrate, Mr Notley Moore, Lily stated that she did not regard herself as being in any danger. She was, however, certainly not going to marry him.

On the charge of using threatening words, Moore sentenced Ross to 14 days' imprisonment—which was suspended on his entering into a 12-month good behaviour bond of £25. For carrying firearms without permission a penalty of £5 was imposed. Ross paid the fine.

In April 1921 the Ross family returned to Melbourne when Ronald, Colin and Stanley bought Mrs E Hoppner's wine shop in the Eastern Arcade, which specialised in the sale of bottled ports, sherries and table wines. Ronald was bookkeeper and in official terms, the manager; Colin was nominated as licensee, thus being, in practical terms, the manager, since he was responsible for the day-to-day running of the saloon; and Stanley helped out between labouring jobs. The shop came with a part-time sales assistant: Ivy Matthews. She worked two jobs, the other in a small confectionery and mixed business in Lygon Street, Carlton.

The wine shop re-opened as the Australian Wine Saloon, but Ivy Matthews lacked a barmaid's licence. She and the Rosses agreed that she be nominally considered a partner on a weekly wage. But somebody made the arrangement known to the police and Colin, as the licensee, was fined. After she left the saloon Ivy Matthews would sue Colin for wages and a share of the partnership. She claimed that she 'was a registered partner. It was in May 1921 that an agreement was drawn up ...'

Mrs Hoppner had run a quiet and dignified establishment, in contrast with the Ross brothers. They served anyone, attracting a clientele including alcoholics and others with criminal backgrounds. Matthews:

> During Colin Ross's tenancy of the wine cafe, I came into contact with all kinds of men, including thieves and fences. These men gave me their confidences, and I have never broken them. I used to have a very narrow outlook on life ... My experience in the wine bar has been a great education.

Many customers drank to excess. With the lavatories outside the premises, intoxicated patrons were continually traipsing about the arcade. Some publicly vomited or urinated; men accosted passing women with suggestive remarks. The smell of the saloon permeated the arcade, with especial rowdiness between 5 and 6pm (the six o'clock swill, when patrons got in their grog just before closing). The other shopkeepers complained to the arcade's management, who issued warnings, and to the police, whose licensing branch sent plainclothes detectives on ever more frequent visits to the saloon. Many in the arcade wanted Colin Ross's saloon gone.

While Mrs Hoppner was her employer Ivy Matthews had made every effort to get along with the tenants in the arcade. Now she tried to steer a safe course between them and the Rosses. She exerted something of a controlling influence on Colin's management of the wine saloon, at least so far as his customers were concerned. Thereby she limited the number of complaints against its licensee—and maintained her position—while simultaneously reducing the amount of urine and vomit she had to mop up. She boasted in *Smith's Weekly*:

> ... [Colin] always feared me. He would never tackle a man single-handed. When fellows got drunk in his saloon they were taken away to the lavatory, and there their cash was taken from them. Ross always regarded me as a nark. Having brothers of my own, I would never stand a man getting a rough spin. When I thought a man had had sufficient drink I would see that he left all right.

This remark looked good in print after Ross had been arrested for murder. Yet statements Matthews made in the city court on the previous 31 October, only two weeks before leaving the saloon, indicate she had more than a passive role in Ross's caper, and in fact helped set up the unwitting customers.

On Thursday 13 October 1921, two and a half months

before Alma Tirtschke's murder, John James Bayliss, 42, a travelling optician, had been drinking in Ross's saloon all afternoon. Far from ensuring 'that he left all right' when he 'had had sufficient drink', Matthews continued serving him until 5.50pm—10 minutes before closing. By then Bayliss was paralysed with drink and semi-conscious. Matthews suggested Ross should put Bayliss out. Ross 'practically dragged him' out of the saloon, across the arcade to the men's lavatory. Then Ross returned to the saloon where, during the course of the afternoon, he had struck up an acquaintance with Frank Rhodes Walsh, a fresh-faced English boy. Walsh was an unemployed pantryman; a muscular, good-looking fellow, eager to impress. Accompanying him was his 19-year-old girlfriend, Phyllis Gray. Since arriving from England, the lad had fallen in with bad company and now he had only his girl and a few bob to his name.

Walsh later told the police that Ross told him, on returning to the wine cafe, that Bayliss had 'a roll on him. See if you can get it away from him and we'll go fifty-fifty.' Handing Walsh a revolver loaded in six chambers, Ross allegedly said: 'Don't be afraid to use this if necessary.' He also instructed Walsh to wait until after 6 o'clock when there would be very few people about.

Ivy Matthews did not testify that she witnessed the exchange between Ross and Walsh, or that she saw any gun. She did, however, remember that shortly after 6 o'clock there was a knock on the door of the saloon. Ross passed the key to the arcade's lavatory through an opening in the door.

The doorknocker was Walsh. He went to the lavatory and, catching hold of Bayliss, threatened him with the revolver and demanded his money. According to Walsh, Bayliss answered: 'That cow Ross has got the money.' Walsh tried to empty out Bayliss's pockets, to strenuous resistance. During the struggle the revolver discharged, wounding Bayliss in the shoulder.

Robert Scott, who managed the spiritualistic science hall upstairs, peered down to see what the commotion was. He told detectives he saw a man with a nickel-plated revolver in his hand, and a second man bleeding from a wound in the shoulder. The man with the revolver snatched something from the injured man's pocket and ran out into Little Collins Street.

In her subsequent book, *The Murder of Alma Tirtschke*, Madame Ghurka would also claim: 'It was some few minutes after 6pm ... I was seated in my office when Ross rushed in upon me. He was very pale and greatly excited. He said, "I want to use your b[loody] phone. There's a b[loody] bastard been shot. I want an ambulance to take the bastard away." He ... sent his call through; then ... bolted out of the office and rushed out through the back entrance of the arcade into Little Collins Street ... I went, with some of the other tenants, to where there was a small crowd outside the wine shop. The victim of the shooting was on a chair opposite the wine shop door. He was bleeding freely, his shirt and other garments ... soaked in blood. I took my handkerchief and rinsed it in water, and stuffed it into ... the bullet hole to stay the flow of blood ... I looked towards the staircase which leads on to the upper floor of the arcade, and there I saw a woman in fainting condition ... Ivy Matthews.'

After the wounded Bayliss was removed, according to Ghurka, Matthews 'revived, and I gathered ... that she had some knowledge of the shooting ...' Some 20 minutes later, Detectives Holden and Sullivan called on Madame Ghurka in her office. They wanted a candle for the purposes of examining the lavatory. After their search they returned to her and asked: 'Who do you think did the shooting?' She replied: 'Arrest Colin Ross, and question Ivy Matthews, and I think you will get the one that did the shooting.'

The events following the shooting may never be fully known. However, it is possible to attempt a reconstruction, from an analysis of court records, newspaper reports and the statements of Senior Detective Edward Holden, the CIB officer assigned to the case. The statements of Ghurka, Matthews, Ross, Walsh and Gray are also taken into account, but with caution, as self-interest affects their reliability.

Bayliss was admitted to the Melbourne Hospital just after 7pm, intoxicated and unable to remember anything before he was shot. A bullet was removed from his right shoulder.

When interviewed by the detectives, Matthews deflected their inquiries or otherwise declined to answer. But it can be presumed she knew she was in trouble, thanks to Ross. He had not said anything to her about a gun or getting Walsh to do the fleecing. That was not the way it was supposed to happen. Ross did the fleecing and Matthews got a cut for potting the customer and keeping her mouth shut.

Next day it can be surmised that Matthews had it out with Ross. She asked for her share of the take. But Ross said he didn't have it: Walsh had absconded with the cash. Matthews didn't know if Ross was telling her the truth. Unknown to him, she arranged, via Phyllis Gray, to meet Walsh at a house in Preston, on the night of 17 October. Walsh told her Ross had double-crossed him—and that he would 'make him pay'.

The police continued to pester Matthews with questions. Were they watching her? She confronted Ross and told him what Walsh had said. Ross laughed and denied it. Again Matthews met with Walsh who, now desperate, said: 'It will be either Ross or I for it. He has pulled me into this and has left Phyllis and me to fight it out.'

Around this time Matthews consulted Ghurka, claiming she had no part in the shooting or even knew about the gun, but merely asked Ross to put out a drunken patron. She also told Ghurka: 'that Ross had provided himself ... with a scapegoat ... named Walsh'. That Friday, 21 October, Matthews told Ross that Walsh was still in Melbourne and had it in for him. She added that she was being badgered by the police and that it might only be a matter of time before they were all arrested. Ross gave Matthews £10, saying: 'Here. Tell them [Walsh and Gray] to go, but remember, this will come out of your wages each week.' Little did they know that at that very moment Walsh and Gray were being questioned by the police, Walsh having been arrested in a dawn raid.

Matthews went at once to take the £10 to Walsh, the plan being that he and Gray would leave Melbourne on an evening train. She found no one at the Preston house. She returned to tell Ross—but by this time he too had been arrested.

Next morning Walsh and Ross appeared in the city court charged with armed robbery. Sonenberg represented Ross, Walsh had no representation. Both men were remanded to appear on 31 October. For each bail was fixed at £300. Ross could provide the surety, but since Walsh had no money, he went to gaol.

Matthews simmered, fearing Ross might expose her part in the ploy or, worse, set her up to take more than her share of blame. She believed Walsh's version, resenting Ross for his petty selfishness and stupidity which had nearly landed all three of them in gaol. She was angry but also afraid, unsure what Ross would do next. And Ross, rather than accept responsibility for bungling the theft or admitting to double-crossing, told Matthews she was just as much to blame as he was. If he was sent down, he would take her with him.

The relationship between the pair was charged. Matthews at least had the £10 and her job. Madame Ghurka, meanwhile, was surprised to hear Ross was not in gaol. She had hoped the shooting affray would finally close the saloon—it intimidated her clientele, mainly women, who needed privacy and discretion.

At the committal hearing, with his arm in a sling, Bayliss confirmed that he had been drinking throughout the day and could remember nothing before he was shot. Phyllis Gray told the court that she overheard Ross telling Walsh to get Bayliss's roll, that she saw Ross drag Bayliss to the lavatory, and that after Ross came out, she went in and saw Walsh pointing a revolver at Bayliss's arm. She said she accidentally struck Walsh's arm and that the revolver exploded. She did not know that Bayliss had been shot. She reported that Walsh said: 'This man just asked me if I am Ross, because he has taken his money.' She told Walsh to leave, but he replied that he would return the gun to its owner.

The story could not be confirmed by Bayliss, nor would it be supported by Walsh. It was also at odds with what Robert Scott saw from upstairs.

Then it was Matthews's turn to testify. She believed she also had been double-crossed, and that, if it came to the crunch, Ross would try to make a scapegoat of her too. She told the court about the £10 given to her by Ross for the purposes of getting Walsh and Gray out of Melbourne.

Detective Holden read Walsh's statement implicating Ross, then Ross's statement: a declaration that, after 6 o'clock on the day in question, someone had called out for the lavatory key, which was a usual thing, and that he had handed it through the door.

The accused reserved their defence and were committed for trial on 15 November. Bail was fixed again, this time at £200 each. Ross put up the bail and was released; Walsh went back to prison.

Matthews's testimony was much less supportive of Ross than of Walsh. The Ross family knew that if they did not get Matthews on their side before the trial, her testimony could easily put Colin in prison.

In the meantime Madame Ghurka canvassed for the closure of the saloon and the imprisonment of its licensee:

Being satisfied Ross was the main scoundrel, I determined to try and help his intended victim. To this end, I took up a collection to get money for the lad's defence. I succeeded in collecting £7, and to this amount I added £10 out of my own pocket, and arranged with a firm of attorneys to undertake the boy's defence ...

I saw Ross standing at the door of the wine shop, and I went over to him and said, 'Mr Ross, I am making a collection to help the boy whom you have dragged into this affair. Will you contribute anything?' Ross replied and his face went livid with passion, 'Not a b[loody] ha'penny; but I'd give £1000 to put him in.' That reply shows the type of man Ross was.

During the fortnight between the committal hearing and the trial, Ivy Matthews was visited by a tearful Mrs Ross who pleaded with her not to put Colin in gaol. Other members of the family, including Colin, made a determined effort to win her favour. Matthews began referring publicly to herself as 'manageress' of the saloon, thus overstepping her share of the partnership, and drawing more money than she was entitled to from its profits. Though the Ross brothers were aware of what she was doing, they chose to tolerate it for the moment.

The case was heard before Justice Mann in the Supreme Court on 15 November. Under cross-examination by barrister George Maxwell, Matthews elaborated on several points: in the week prior to the shooting incident, Walsh had been cautioned by Ross for causing a commotion in the big parlour when Walsh revealed that he had a small revolver in his possession. Gray persuaded her beau to surrender the revolver for safekeeping; it was wrapped in a paper bag and she gave it to Matthews.

Without opening the parcel, Matthews placed it under the bar counter; it was forgotten about for a number of days. In the witness box Gray confirmed she had given the parcel to Matthews. Although the gun was never found, its cartridges were in Walsh's possession when the police raided the Preston house.

The outcome of the court case provided little satisfaction to Madame Ghurka. Ross was acquitted. Walsh got nine months' hard labour.

On 16 November, the next day, Matthews turned up for work at the saloon as usual. She was confronted by Stanley Ross who, now that his brother was acquitted, unleashed a tirade. Incensed, she left, considering herself dismissed. In the following weeks Matthews's solicitor and the Rosses corresponded. Matthews demanded a week's wages in lieu of notice. Ronald Ross wrote back on 22 November reminding her that she still owed Colin £10, that the family were aware she had been drawing more money from the business than she was entitled to, and that he knew she was drawing several pensions under false names, including one as a married woman.

The day after, Colin Ross applied before the licensing court for a renewal of his licence to continue operating the Australian Wine Saloon. The application was opposed by the Victoria Police. Constable O'Halloran told the court that in March 1920 Ross had been arrested, charged, and subsequently convicted of carrying firearms and using threatening words. 'Other police evidence was brought,' said the *Argus*, 'that Ross had been convicted in connection with charges arising from the conduct of the cafe.' Mr Lewers, who was appearing on behalf of Ross, could do little. He applied for an adjournment until 12 December. By that time, he said, Ross might decide whether he would surrender the licence and take other premises. The adjournment was granted, but the licence would never subsequently be renewed.

In previous accounts, the relationship between Matthews and Colin has not been examined sufficiently. Matthews's bitterness extended to the whole Ross family, but particularly Colin, who had double-crossed her and nearly had her arrested. His actions had put her in court, led to abuse and threats from his brothers and ultimately the loss of her job.

14. Queen of Fortune-Tellers

In the period after the Great War, many persons grieving their dead turned to mediums. And of all the purveyors of occult mysteries in the city of Melbourne, Madame Ghurka was the Queen of Fortune-Tellers. But her beginnings were humble. She was born Julia Glushkova in 1872 in Odessa. Her father Peter was a soldier and a Russian Jew, and her mother a Scotswoman, Mary Morrison. Very little can be confirmed about her early life. But she told *Smith's Weekly* that she became a revolutionary during her teenage years, which led to her being imprisoned. She escaped and returned to her parents who, '[F]earing I would be re-arrested, sent me to Warsaw ...'

By the late 1880s Julia was in England, where she met a Norwegian sailor named Christian Olsen; they married in 1890 and had two children, of whom the son, Alexander, later practised phrenology in the Eastern Arcade with his mother.

Olsen (senior) was an inveterate gambler and squandered the family's money. Julia separated from him but one night he broke into her house and stabbed her several times with a knife. Julia survived the attack, for which Olsen was sentenced to 15 years' imprisonment, but he died soon after his conviction.

In 1903 another man entered her life. Born Henry Gibson, of Bendigo, he was part Russian, a variety artist whose stage name was Zakaree Ermakov. His talents lay in stage acts involving gunpowder, pistols, swords, knives and axes. He needed a young and attractive assistant and Julia showed a flair for the theatrical. Together they embarked on a tour of Europe and married in Warsaw. To supplement their income they introduced palmistry readings, for which Julia took the pseudonym of Madame Ghurka. Zak offered head readings as a phrenologist.

Increasing anti-Semitism in Tsarist Russia led to escalating harassment of travelling performers who, even if not Jewish, were lumped together with the gypsy or wandering classes. The couple returned to England where they remained until 1916. Then, leaving their three sons at school, they visited Australia for a theatrical engagement—and because Zak had to leave England's climate on account of malaria contracted during a tour of Asia.

In 1918 the pair opened rooms in the Eastern Arcade. As fortune-telling was illegal, their business was disguised as 'character reading' or phrenology. Later that year the couple brought their sons out from England.

After arriving in Australia the relationship between the Gibsons deteriorated. Ultimately she accused him of desertion and brutality; when she rented 25–27 Rathdowne Street, Carlton, and set it up as a boardinghouse, he was not welcome.

Madame Ghurka spoke only very broken English. Her account of the Bayliss shooting was the work of an American ghostwriter named Welch, who wrote a promotional pamphlet for her, *The Murder of Alma Tirtschke: A Challenge to T.C. Brennan*. It melodramatically exploited her involvement in the Gun Alley murder.

15. Susso

While in prison Ross's gonorrhoea was treated by the government's Chief Medical Officer, Dr Clarence Godfrey. Their relationship would culminate in Godfrey performing the prisoner's last medical attention, his post-mortem. In 1922 the world was without penicillin; it would be six years before Alexander Fleming noticed the mould growing in his Petri dish and a further 13 years before the antibiotic was administered to patients. In the meantime, the bacterium *Neisseria gonorrhoeae* continued unabated, with no realistic hope of any final cure. Patients frequently had to endure treatments that were as painful as the disease itself—and the bacterium was contagious.

During the inquest Harding indicated that Ross was in quarantine for the first ten days of his remand. Significantly, Ross was released from isolation on 23 January, before Godfrey obtained a urethral smear (on the 31st) and officially had the diagnosis confirmed by Dr Rennie of the Melbourne University (on 8 February). The obvious explanation for this is that the police, with the consent of the prison authorities, prematurely intervened in Ross's isolation to see whether Harding might persuade Ross, at last among company, to speak about his case—with the other prisoners to act as witnesses.

The inquest concluded, Brophy handed pound notes out to witnesses: £2 to Maddox; £1 to Matthews. These amounts were just an advance. For being a Crown witness, Maddox would receive an allowance of £1 per day, backdated to the first day of the inquest. Matthews would receive 10 shillings per day. The allowances were paid by the Crown Law Office and were officially justified as being 'sustenance money'. Maddox would eventually receive £74 and Matthews £37—quite aside from any of the reward money.

Matthews was living at a boardinghouse owned and operated by Mrs Julia Gibson, alias Madame Ghurka. Here, together with another witness (Madame Ghurka's son, Alexander Olsen), she would reside for the duration of her time as a police witness. During this period, the house was placed under police guard: at night a uniformed constable, and during the day the plainclothes detectives Saker and Lee. The latter stated years later that he and Saker 'were instructed to be at the house practically every day until 10pm to see who called'.

On Piggott's instruction, one of Victoria's first two policewomen, Madge Connor, also paid frequent visits to the house. Her task was not so much guard duty as: 'to cheer up Ivy Matthews'. Matthews was indeed in need of comfort. On 26 January, Piggott reported to Superintendent Potter that 'Miss Matthews is ... alarmed at threats that have been placed against her.' Matthews herself would declare (*Smith's Weekly*, April 1922) that she suffered great mental distress due to the death threats she had received.

Many people came forward believing they could claim the reward.

Frank Lane Upton was an epileptic, alcoholic and itinerant labourer. He was out of work often, and forced to live by his wits. By the end of January 1922, after drinking the proceeds of a succession of jobs, Upton was stranded in the backblocks of rural Victoria. He wanted to get back to Melbourne. By 29 January, he managed to get himself as far as Donald, 240 kilometres north-west of Melbourne, but his pockets were empty.

He had last been in Melbourne a day or two before the murder and although he had been drinking in Ross's wine saloon on the afternoon of Friday 30 December—as Stan Ross confirmed in his police statement—Upton, or 'Darkie' as he was known, got so drunk that he did not realise the significance of where he had been. On 2 January, while recovering from a hangover in the Footscray Gardens, Upton found a newspaper and read about the murder. The following Wednesday, he returned by train to the Mallee district.

Upton had nothing to say about the murder of Alma Tirtschke for a month, three weeks after the offer of the £1000 reward and three days after the inquest, when the evidence against Ross had been published in all the Melbourne newspapers, including the country editions. On 29 January, without a halfpenny to his name, Upton walked into the police station at Donald and told the officer in charge that he 'was connected with Alma Tirtschke's murder'. Detective Lee was relieved for a day from his guard duty at Rathdowne Street and sent to Donald.

Upton earned a free ticket back to Melbourne under the escort of Detective Lee. Like the other witnesses, Upton was boarded under police supervision and a sustenance allowance was arranged for him. From 31 January to the conclusion of the trial, Upton was paid a total of £30/12/6.

Although he would ultimately be recognised as a charlatan, there is no evidence to show Upton was ever required to repay any of his sustenance payments.

That sustenance money was being used to reward witness cooperation is demonstrated by the payments made to both Harding and Pommeroy (alias White). On or about 30 January, Harding was temporarily moved out of Melbourne Gaol to lodgings in Williamstown. Here, as a Crown witness, he would remain under police guard until the Ross trial was over, on 25 February. Harding continued to be kept in secure custody and was then tried for housebreaking with another prisoner, Joseph Dunstan. He was sentenced on 10 April to two years' hard labour. Piggott and Brophy placed Harding on sustenance money of 10 shillings per day; from 14 February to 8 April 1922 he would earn in total £27.

On 8 February Robert Pommeroy alias Albert Ernest White walked into the Ashfield police station in Sydney and declared that he was 'the missing witness White in connection with the Ross murder [sic] in Melbourne'. He had read in the papers that due to his non-attendance at the inquest, a warrant had been issued for his arrest. It would just be a matter of time before the police picked him up. On 13 February, Constable McGinty was sent to bring him back to Melbourne, the pair returning the following day. Pommeroy, who would be compelled to attend the court daily, was quartered at Parer's Crystal Cafe in Bourke Street under the supervision of McGinty. His sustenance money would eventually total £6/4/9.

But Pommeroy would not be called as a witness. By the time of the trial, his earlier statement was recognised as untrue. Pommeroy had told the police in Sydney he had made a deal with the Ross family to disappear—his success in extorting money from the Rosses could have been valuable to the Crown, as an implied admission of Colin's guilt. However, it became increasingly obvious that Pommeroy could not be put into the witness box. It would mean exposing his use of an alias and his deception of the police. If he had monetary motives to fabricate evidence, so could the other witnesses, as the defence would in fact contend. There was a further advantage in not calling Pommeroy, in that Brophy's statements at the inquest—referring to the claim that Ross was the man Pommeroy saw speaking 'to the little girl Alma'—would be allowed to stand unchallenged. Pommeroy's presence in court ultimately was to witness, if necessary, to his dealings with the Rosses. Thus he earned his sustenance money. He received none of the reward.

The relations Pommeroy had with the Rosses are unclear. Undoubtedly he attempted to capitalise on the family's fears after Colin's arrest. Two revealing police statements still exist: one from Pommeroy, made at Ashfield police station in Sydney; the other from his brother, John. Some caution must be exercised regarding these sources, as each of the Pommeroys appears to have a hidden agenda.

Sometime between Thursday 12 January—when Ross was arrested—and Sunday 15 January, Robert Pommeroy visited Mrs Ross at her home, apparently showing great sympathy. While there, he wrote a short letter commending the bearer to his brother John for help. According to evidence given by Ronald at Colin's trial, Pommeroy had suggested his brother could donate money for Colin's defence. Following Pommeroy's visit, Mrs Ross discussed the matter with her son Ronald, who decided to investigate.

John Pommeroy recalled: 'On Sunday the 15th of January a man came to my house and said, "You are Mr Pommeroy?" I said "Yes". He said, "I am Mr Ross. Have you a brother by the name of Robert Pommeroy?" I said "Yes".' Ronald handed over his letter of introduction, which stated:

> This will introduce Mr Ross whose brother is in trouble at present and his mother a good homely person, and as a Mason I wish you would try and do something for him. I am sure his brother is innocent of the crime. Trusting you will do something I remain your fair loving brother, Robert.

John Pommeroy refused to get involved. Ronald told him: 'They have my brother set on account of that other case. The whole thing was a frame-up ...' But John Pommeroy bade Ronald good luck and closed the door in his face.

Whatever Robert Pommeroy had been expecting from John, this response was not it. He decided to proceed alone. The next day, 16 January, under the assumed name of White, Pommeroy introduced himself to Detective Brophy, who then escorted White to Melbourne Gaol where they confronted Ross. The allegation was made that White had seen Ross speaking to 'the little girl Alma'.

How did Pommeroy's scam work? It appears he represented himself to the Rosses as an unwilling witness, played on their poor view of the police and their belief Colin was being framed. In his statement Pommeroy claimed the Rosses assisted him generously—even to helping him leave the country.

Robert Pommeroy:

> I am a labourer ... I was subpoenaed in Melbourne under the name of Albert Ernest White as a witness to attend the inquest to be held on the body of Alma Tirtschke ... I had previously made a statement of what I knew concerning the above mentioned matter to

Detectives Piggott and Walshe. About four days before the inquest ... I was standing at the corner of Young and Jackson's Hotel, Flinders Street, Melbourne, when William Ross† said to me, 'Come out home mother wants to speak to you.'

I said, 'All right.' ... William Ross bought two tickets to Footscray and we went out by train ... [he] said to me, 'Don't put poor Colin's pot on as you know what it would mean to us and poor mother.'

[At Footscray] we saw Mrs Ross senior, mother of Colin Campbell Ross. Three brothers ... were also present and a sister-in-law ... William Ross said to his mother as soon as we went in, 'This is Mr White.'

But according to the letter sent by Pommeroy to his brother, and also by the conversation with Ronald that John Pommeroy describes in his police statement, the Rosses did not know Pommeroy by his alias of White. Robert Pommeroy continued:

Mrs Ross then put her arms round me, kissed me and started crying. And she said to me, 'For God [sic] sake, don't say anything about my poor boy as you know what it would mean.' I said, 'I won't.' She then said, 'Would you go to New Zealand if I got you a ticket?' I said, 'Yes.' Then ... his mother said, 'We will have to give him (meaning me) some pocket money.' The sister-in-law ... gave me £10. Mrs Ross took £6/10/–; and a general conversation ... then took place in which many of the witnesses [sic] names were mentioned, including Ivy Matthews. The eldest brother who is a returned soldier said, 'It is a pity we couldn't do away with Ivy Matthews.'

---

†Pommeroy refers to one of Mrs Ross's sons as William, though none bore that name.

> Mrs Ross senior ... said that it would not do for me to leave for New Zealand from Melbourne by the boat but that it would be better to ... [go] to Sydney.
>
> I stayed there the night ... About 4 o'clock I boarded the Sydney Express.
>
> [The family] all bade me farewell, the women folk kissing me goodbye and the men shook hands with me ...
>
> On arrival in Sydney I went to the shipping wharf ... I saw two men whom I thought were detectives and thinking they were looking for me I turned back and went to the Union company offices and stated to the sub-manager that a lady friend had purchased the passage to Auckland for me in Melbourne and that I was too ill to go. The company refunded me £6/10/– and cancelled the passage.
>
> Since then I have been lying low ...

Pommeroy had already misled the police. Now he was exaggerating, adjusting and fabricating information in order to be indemnified against prosecution, gain sustenance if not also a portion of the reward and also to get police protection against the defrauded Rosses.

Following the trial, Pommeroy was convicted in Melbourne's criminal court on a charge of larceny as a bailee. He had sold a car for £70 on behalf of an owner who had fixed the price at £200, and had omitted to account for the money. In Melbourne, while in protective custody as a Crown witness, Pommeroy would regale his police bodyguards with tales of his days as a warder in Auckland's Mt Eden Gaol. The Mt Eden part was true, but Pommeroy had a bullet wound in his back—and warders did not climb prison walls. He would later be described in *Smith's Weekly* as 'the champion liar' of the case.

16. The trial begins

Monday 20 February 1922 was a searing day and by mid-afternoon the temperature would reach 35°C. Never had a trial in Melbourne's Criminal Court created greater interest. By 7am hundreds of people had arrived in the hope of gaining admission. At 9.50am the doors opened and a wild rush ensued. The public gallery (capacity 150) filled quickly. Though the floor of the court had been reserved for relatives of the accused, members of the legal profession and the press, it was now uncomfortably crowded.

Even before George Arnot Maxwell had been briefed to appear for Ross, he was identified by legal commentators as the barrister most likely to lead the defence, with his assistant being TC Brennan. Within a day of the decision to commit Ross for trial, Maxwell started receiving hate mail, imploring him not to represent Ross.

Maxwell complained to Keith Murdoch, editor of the *Herald*. Some of his comments were published.

> These people would wish me, a barrister, to function ... as a judge ... If every barrister refused to accept briefs of this nature, there would be no such thing as justice. The whole system would break down utterly.

> ... if I am asked to appear for Ross, I shall ... Ross or any other man similarly placed must be given a fair trial.

Maxwell's words had little effect. The hate mail would continue.

Maxwell was 62 and nearly blind, but he continued to practise. He might have crossed from his chambers to the Law Courts on the arm of his daughter, but in the courts he could confidently steer his way unaided. He made a commanding impression—tall, dark and aquiline. He was not yet a King's Counsel but the honour would be conferred in 1926. By 1922 Maxwell was considered to be among the foremost advocates of the criminal Bar in Victoria. Sir Robert Menzies would term him 'the greatest criminal advocate I ever heard'.

Instructed by Sonenberg, Maxwell led the defence. However, Maxwell's disability, which prevented the noting of points outside his memory, cast much of the defence upon his junior counsel. That was why, coupled with the complexity of the prosecution argument—and its novel presentation of forensic evidence—the junior role was allocated to an exceptional barrister: Thomas Cornelius Brennan. He was 55 years old, highly literate, articulate and intelligent. A devout Roman Catholic, he had the forehead of a thinker and a look of asceticism.

The prosecutor for the King was Hugh Campbell Gemmell Macindoe, a slender, solemn man who wore pince-nez. Aged 38, he had already served as a public prosecutor in South Africa, when he was called to the English Bar in 1910. Returning to Australia that same year he was admitted to practice in Melbourne. During the war he had enlisted and had seen action at Gallipoli before being invalided home. He resumed his practice, lectured in Melbourne University's School of Law and, in 1919 won his place as Crown Prosecutor over Brennan, the decision going to the man with war service.

Now Crown Prosecutor Macindoe strode swiftly into court. The defence, Brennan and Maxwell, were already seated opposite Sonenberg. Punctually at 10.30am Mr Justice Schutt entered. He had been appointed to the Supreme Court in mid–1919, and was now 53. He would be remembered as 'a most serious and proper judge ... but direct and brief in manner'.

'Place Colin Campbell Ross at the bar,' commanded his associate.

There was a shuffling of feet on the stone steps beneath the criminal court, then Ross advanced to the rail of the dock. Standing easily with his hands behind his back, he listened as the charge against him was read.

'Colin Campbell Ross, the presentment against you is that, at Melbourne, in the State of Victoria, on or about December 31, 1921, you murdered Alma Tirtschke. How say you: are you guilty or not guilty?'

In a voice strong and clear, Ross declared: 'Not guilty.'

The empanelling of the jury followed. At the time women were not permitted to sit on juries, thus 53 men entered. Forty-one were challenged, both by the Crown and Ross. When Ross had exhausted his right of peremptory challenge—20 all told—and would henceforth have to give reasons for further challenges, the last juror, a St Kilda clerk, slipped into the box without challenge. The jury was now complete. It comprised: two tram conductors, a tanner, a plumber, a cigar maker, a wood merchant, a gas employee, a driver, a driller, a sugar worker, a 'traveller' and the clerk who, after a 5-minute consultation in the box, was elected foreman.

Macindoe began by requesting that all witnesses be ordered out of the court, with the exception of Piggott, who would remain to give assistance with the exhibits. He then presented the prosecution's case. He retraced the incidents leading up to Ross's arrest and repeated, for the benefit of the jury, the evidence presented by witnesses at the inquest. These witnesses would be called to restate their evidence, and a number of new witnesses would be called.

Macindoe concluded with a summary of Sydney John Harding's testimony in which Ross was said to have told Harding that he had torn the girl's dress into strips and scattered the pieces along Footscray Road. Macindoe paused, then said: 'Gentlemen, since Harding gave that evidence strips of the girl's dress have been found on Footscray Road—strips of blue serge.'

Dr Mollison was the Crown's first witness. He recounted his post-mortem findings as per his deposition at the inquest. Macindoe asked if bleeding would be copious.

'Yes,' Mollison answered, 'there would be a considerable amount of blood lost. It might be very copious.'

Asked whether he found any sign of alcohol in the girl's stomach, Mollison replied that he detected none.

Maxwell rose to cross-examine. 'His appearance was impressive,' says *The Australian Dictionary of Biography*. However, it adds that: 'He was a poor cross-examiner and lacking in order.'

Mollison had said that when he opened the stomach he detected no trace or smell of alcohol. But according to Harding, Ross had claimed he gave the child several glasses of wine. Therefore Harding's credibility as a prosecution witness was at stake.

Maxwell began with this convoluted query: 'Do I understand you to say that suppose a child like that has three glasses of sweet wine and within an hour or two she dies, and none has been taken in the meantime, would you expect on making a post-mortem within a few hours, such as you did, to find no odour of alcohol at all?'

'No,' said Mollison coolly, 'I do not think you would find any.'

'Have you ever tested that?'

'No I have not tested it.'

'That is a mere guess?'

'That is what I know of the observation of alcohol.'

'Have you ever had an opportunity of putting that opinion of yours to the test?'

'No.'

At that point Maxwell returned to his seat, probably believing he had satisfactorily demonstrated the difference between a fact and an opinion. At no subsequent stage would the defence call an alternative medical witness to challenge Mollison's evidence. Moreover, in 1922 it was not common practice for the defence to take counsel on post-mortem findings from a forensic medical specialist.

Mollison stood down from the witness box, and was followed by the surveyor Sherrard, swearing as to the accuracy of his plans of the crime scene. Errington was next. John Murdoch reaffirmed the identification of his niece's body. Then Mrs Murdoch was sworn and given fragments of serge.

'It is very similar to the serge she had on that day,' she said.

'All of it?' asked Macindoe.

'That has nothing to do with it, I should say,' replied the witness, discarding the largest piece. But the three other pieces, she said, were 'very similar' to the material from which she had made Alma's dress.

Questioned further, she said she recognised a row of stitching on two of the three remaining pieces. She remembered the old stitching because she had difficulty in ironing it out of the old material from which she had made the dress. It was box-pleated, and the material she had in her hand 'looks' to be box-pleated, although '... there is portion of it missing'.

The equivocations continued as Maxwell cross-examined: 'You say that the serge ... is similar to the serge [Alma] was wearing?'

Murdoch: 'I say it is similar. There are so many serges ...'

'When did you first see the serge about which you are speaking now ... who brought it to you?'

'Detective Piggott.'

'Was it shown to you as serge [from] Alma's dress?'

'No. He brought it to me to see if I could identify the colour of it ... The nearest approach to the colour she had worn on that day.'

'You knew that it was brought to you to identify as part of Alma's dress?'

'I presumed that.'

'Of course you did.'

Mrs Murdoch began to sob and was unable to continue. She was permitted to stand down.

The procession of further witnesses from the inquest continued uneventfully. Mrs Blanche Edmonds, however, offered two new details to her earlier testimony. She and her daughter, Muriel, had entered the Eastern Arcade from Bourke Street behind Alma. In cross-examination, Mrs Edmonds was able to fix the time as 2.45pm, because: 'I looked at the clock on the balcony.'

Mr and Mrs Stanley Young, who gave inquest evidence of seeing Alma leave the Eastern Arcade at about 3 o'clock, were not called by the prosecution at the trial. Did the prosecution not wish to confuse the jury with the suggestion that the schoolgirl had, in fact, passed through the arcade and was last seen (by independent and reputable witnesses) on the other side of Little Collins Street?

At 1pm the court adjourned for lunch, resuming at 2.15pm. Olsen the phrenologist testified, then Ellis the lodginghouse keeper, then the three Italians from the Cavour Club. While Rollandi was in the witness box a further point of evidence emerged. He, as caretaker of the club, possessed a key with which he had locked the back gates of the arcade (the Little Collins Street entrance) after Nicoli and Anselmi had gone: that is, Saturday, at about 1.00 or 1.05am.

Asked by Macindoe if he knew Ross by sight, Rollandi replied, 'Yes. I saw him on Friday about 3 o'clock or half past 3. He asked me for the key [of the gate] to go out ... I said: 'I can't give my key to anybody. Go to Mr Clarke, the manager of the arcade, he might give you one.'

Justice Schutt asked why Ross would want the key to go out if the gate was open during the afternoon.

Rollandi: '... he wanted to shift his things.'

This admission was unfortunate for Macindoe, for even if the jury had not understood its significance, the defence had.

Maxwell: 'Did Ross tell you he would be removing his things?'

'Yes. He told me he was going to shift.'

Maxwell: 'Next day was the last day of his wine shop ... And it was earlier in the afternoon evidently that he asked you about the key?'

Rollandi confirmed that this was so. Subsequently Ross had obtained the key from Mr Clarke, but—crucially—not until noon on Saturday. So, far from Ross wishing to borrow the key being incriminating, it seems quite the opposite, because it indicated he did not have a key of his own on the Friday, and is evidence against his having told Harding that he had a key, or having told Matthews that he returned 'between 1 and 2' when he would not have been able to get into the locked arcade.

The next witness was Francis Lane Upton. A young man, he was small though stoutly built and very swarthy of complexion, which accounted for his nickname, Darkie. He was dressed in a light grey tweed suit and brown boots. When planted on his head at a cocky angle his hat of soft grey felt conferred the look of a wily spiv. When called to give evidence, Upton began speaking confidently but became increasingly uncomfortable during cross-examination.

Upton's story was that he was an unemployed labourer in Melbourne on 30 December. After a heavy bout of drinking he fell asleep in the Flagstaff Gardens; when he came to, it was dark and he wanted another drink. He then found himself, at about 12.30–1am, at Ross's saloon. By this time he was sober but very thirsty. Seeing a light in the wine shop, he went to the second door. It was not locked; he pushed it, and it opened. He heard a woman's voice saying, 'Oh my God, darling, how are we going to get rid of it?' He then heard Ross say: 'There is somebody here.'

Ross rushed out like a lunatic. Upton said to him, 'What about a bottle?', noticing that Ross's hands were stained with something that looked like blood. The saloonkeeper rushed back and snatched a bottle from behind the bar, thrusting it into Upton's hands, and pushing him out without even waiting to take his money. Upton walked down Little Collins Street, where he discovered that there was blood on the bottle. Having taken one swig, he disposed of the bottle on the corner of William and Flinders streets, in a culvert or sewer.

Since Upton was a new witness, the defence had been given a short summary of his evidence. Brennan researched the witness exhaustively. His cross-examination concluded day one of the trial, and began proceedings on day two.

Brennan ascertained from Upton that he used the alias of Lane. 'Why did you take that name; there was nothing wrong with the name of Upton was there?'

'No.'

'Are you sure of that, now?'

[After an uncomfortable pause:] 'The only thing I was frightened of was that my wife might get hold of me.'

'May we take it then that you ran away from your wife?'

'No, I did not run away from her.'

'Keep away from her?'

'Well, from what I can see, it is an everyday occurrence for a wife to clear away from her husband and still get maintenance from him.'

'And you were determined your wife should not get maintenance from you?'

'Yes.'

'Have you any children?'

'Two.'

'Are you supporting them?'

'No.'

'Did the police know you under the name of Lane or Upton—or either name?'

'Yes.'

'Have you been in any trouble with the police before?

'Yes ... For being drunk—a couple of months ago.'

'What was the last time before that?'

'I do not know why I should answer that.'

'Well, perhaps if you don't, we will ask His Honour if you should answer it.'

'I will answer it. As far as that case goes, I was found not guilty on both charges of larceny.'

'Did you ever go to gaol?'

'Yes ... About four years back to my knowledge.'

'What was that for?'

'Larceny.'

'But that was not your first trouble four years ago, was it?'

'Yes, the first trouble—bar drunkenness ... I got fined £5 and I was also convicted once here in Victoria. The other was in New South Wales. It was for the embezzlement of 11 shillings.'

'[Had] you ever [called] into Ross's wine shop [before]?'

'I have been told I have but I do not know whether I have or not.'

'Does that mean that you may have been there in such a drunken state that you do not remember it?'

'Yes.'

Brennan: 'And before [Detective] Lee's arrival [at Donald] you knew that there was a reward of £1000?'

Upton: 'Yes.'

'When you went to the police station at Donald, did you have any money in your pocket?'

'... no, I never had any money in my pocket then.'

'Have you any reason ... as to why you did not, after Monday 2nd January, when you knew of this murder and connected the incident of the Friday night with it, then tell somebody?'

'I was too frightened. I thought they might make me connected with it.'

'Have you got a friend in the world at all?'

'No, I have not; I have not got a friend bar myself.'

'And therefore you have not got a friend whose good esteem you could lose?'

'No.'

'Now I want to take you back to this night of the 30th ... Was it near [the bar counter] that the voice came from?'

'Yes.'

'You could see the place where the voice came from?'

'Yes, you could see where he rushed out of.'

'Did he rush out of that place?'

'Yes.'

'Did you go right into the room?'

'No.'

'Where did you stand?'

'Just at the door.'

'You never went past the door?'

'No.'

'But you said you saw him rush out of that place?'

'Yes, so I did ... He rushed to the door.'

In further evidence Upton showed himself to be confused and ignorant as to the layout of the saloon, and that from where he claimed to have stood he could not possibly have seen inside the saloon.

Brennan: 'When did you first discover the blood on the bottle?'

Upton: 'I discovered it as soon as I got outside. I thought it was [port] wine until I got to the corner ...'

'Dark and red, I suppose?... If that was the first time you saw blood—on that bottle of port wine—you cannot have seen any blood on Ross's hands, is that so?... I suppose you told the police that you saw blood on Ross's hands?'

'Yes.'

Shortly after 5 o'clock, the court adjourned. Since most of the evidence had already been reported at the inquest, there was a thirst for new information—even if Brennan was busy disproving it.

STORY OF MIDNIGHT VISIT ... Blood on Bottle
(*Herald*, Late Final Extra)

TRIAL OF COLIN ROSS SENSATIONAL NEW EVIDENCE—
WHAT MAN HEARD IN CAFE
BLOOD ON WINE BOTTLE
(*Argus*)

The night was oppressive and Tuesday morning sultry and unsettled. Ominous clouds were banking up over the city as the crowds again gathered outside the Law Courts. In the courtroom, the air was thick and hot. The hearing opened with the resumption of Upton's cross-examination by Brennan.

Brennan: 'You gave evidence recently in a maintenance case at Carlton ...?'

'Yes.'

'Did you say: "I am a bad character and I want your worships to know it"?'

(Very agitated:) 'Your Honour, I want to speak on that subject; I want to have a say on that!'

Justice Schutt: 'Then tell us whether you said that or not.'

Upton: 'I did say it.'

Brennan: 'Did you say you had seen your mother and sister in bed with a man?'

'I did and I will explain it!'

'Do you think a decent woman and her daughter would get into bed with a strange man?'

'Well, my sister was there.'

'Oh! You think it makes it all right because your mother and sister were both there? Is it true?'

'It is. I was asleep in the room at the time.'

'Then why did you give evidence against your mother?'

'I went to my mother and sister and all of them and said that if they chucked Billings out ... [eight words illegible] ... court, otherwise I would go into the court.'

'You would get into the witness box and give evidence against your own mother?'

'Yes, I did it to save my own sister.'

'Is that the way you save your sister, by swearing that you saw her in bed, when you were not a party to the case?'

'I was a party. Both my father and myself were affected.'

'You were not either the plaintiff or the defendant?'

'No.'

'And you gave that evidence on behalf of the defendant?'

'Yes.'

'Was the defendant being sued by his wife for maintenance?'

'Yes.'

Brennan: 'Are you sure that this is not the result of your imagination?'

'It was no imagination at all.'
'No more than the bottle business?'

Brennan continued: 'Do you know a pawnbroker named Diamond?'

Upton: 'Yes.'

'Do you remember trying to pawn some [of your children's] clothes there?'

'Yes, and I will give you the reason.'

'Have you contributed to the support of your two children?'

'No! Neither has my wife. I suppose she is in the court now waiting to get a crack at me ... I have been in about ten hospitals with a bad leg. My wife left me with the two children to look after. I had to wash the five-months-old baby before I went to work in the morning and I had to get up in the night to give the children drinks. I tell you I had a time of it. I broke down on it and lost my work.'

Macindoe: 'It is said you pawned your children's clothes?'

'Yes. To get food for the children.'

'What about Billings?'

'He was staying with us at West Melbourne as a boarder—a star boarder he was—and he got my father and myself kicked out of our own home. He was passing my child off in Burnley as his own.'

'He was sued for maintenance by his wife?'

'Yes, he was; and it was more luck than anything else that he got out of it.'

Justice Schutt: 'Who did you give evidence for?'

Upton (in disgust): 'For Billings.'

Brennan had exposed Upton as a disreputable opportunist. Yet his achievement would be overshadowed by the sensational evidence of the following witnesses. Thus, while some newspapers did report on Brennan's second session with Upton, there would be no undoing the damage of the earlier headlines.

17. Unsettled weather

A massive low pressure system was sweeping in from the Southern Ocean, tipping the scales on barometric gauges across the city. In the packed courtroom, collar, tie and jacket were de rigueur. Sweat shone on the faces of prosecution and defence alike.

Olive Maddox was next. She wore a navy frock of jersey silk. Her hat, worn well over her face, was of navy silk too, with ostrich feathers in the same shade drooping over the brim. Her gloves were grey and she had a plain gold bangle on each wrist.

Although Maddox's evidence did not diverge from the inquest, it is worth reviewing one or two points. While her description of the girl she said she saw in the beaded room partly tallied with newspaper descriptions of Alma Tirtschke, there were curious discrepancies. One, on which Maddox insisted, was the girl's age: 14 or 15 years. Further, Maddox said some of the girl's hair was 'hanging over one of her shoulders in front', while 'some of her hair was pinned up at the back'. But Alma was not known to have worn her hair up. As at the inquest, Maddox was handed a photograph of Alma and again she hedged, saying that on the one hand 'the photograph has a strong likeness', while on the other, 'the girl I saw was different because she looked older'. She finally concluded: '... you could swear that the girl and the girl in the photograph were one and the same'.

Cross-examined by Maxwell, Maddox admitted that, before going to the police, she had learned Alma's description secondhand from newspapers: 'I am not too educated and cannot read big words so I do not get interested in the papers. I had heard the case discussed among my friends and I knew that it was a little college girl who had been murdered.' She said she had discussed it with Ivy Matthews on 10 January, the day the increased reward of £1000 was announced in the press. Asked how many people were in the saloon when she was there, she gave an estimate of seven or eight persons who were in as good a position as Maddox to have seen Alma. Yet none of these people had come forward to corroborate Maddox's story. Had the child been in the saloon at all?

'Call Ivy Matthews,' ordered the Crown Prosecutor.

She entered, and many in the court were struck by her fashionable attire: a cream-coloured two-piece of light gabardine. Her hat was of gold tissue with curled white feathers projecting over the brim.

As Matthews stepped into the witness box the first heavy raindrops pelted the court's roof. Between peals of thunder, Macindoe asked, 'What are you by occupation?'

'... Just at present I am not doing anything. I was a barmaid. I was employed by the accused at his wine cafe ... until November of last year.'

Shown a plan of the wine shop, Matthews described its interior in detail.

'Was there anything on the couch in the cubicle?'

'Yes, a pair of blankets.'

The two blankets taken from Ross's residence were handed up. 'This is one,' Matthews said of the grey–blue blanket. 'In my time it was kept on the couch in the cubicle and was one of a pair kept there. This other one, the darkest one'—and here Matthews indicated the reddish-brown blanket—'was not there in my time.'

During a temporary lull in the storm, Macindoe asked the witness if she remembered 30 December. Yes, she said, she remembered it well.

Macindoe: 'Were you in the saloon that afternoon?'

Matthews: 'I was at the door at about 3 o'clock ... talking to Stan ... brother of Colin Ross.'

'Where did you see Colin Ross?'

'He came out into the bar, from the cubicle, when I was standing at the door. As he passed through the curtains I looked across Stanley Ross's shoulder and saw a little child sitting on a chair in the cubicle. You must part the curtains to come through—'

A sudden explosion of thunder erupted. Judge Schutt queried whether the jurors could hear; he asked the witness to speak more loudly.

'She was a child ...'

Two more thunderclaps. The rain was now coming down in torrents and Macindoe repeatedly asked Matthews to speak up. 'The jury must hear you,' he said. 'What was the child like?'

After some moments, the storm eased just enough for Matthews to finish her sentence: 'She was a child with a pretty shade of auburn-coloured hair. I did not get a very good glimpse of her the first time ... Ross walked along the bar and poured out one glass of drink—I could not see what kind it was—and he walked back into the cubicle. It was then that the child parted the curtains and looked out. She had on a little mushroom-shaped hat, white, with a maroon band, like the one produced. She had it pushed back from the face. She was wearing what looked like a white linen blouse. Her hair was a sort of auburn shade, not particularly ginger. She struck me as being 12 or 13 years of age.'

'Did you see anything else?'

All that could be heard of the reply was: 'Ross did not speak to me nor I to him that day.'

Schutt spoke to Macindoe. 'I can't hear you either, Your Honour,' replied the prosecutor.

Outside, the storm roared. To make matters worse, the roof leaked rainwater onto several of the spectators and press representatives. Proceedings were suspended for 10 minutes. Maxwell stood and suggested that the court might adjourn until the storm had subsided. The response was two loud peals of thunder.

Maxwell (jumping): 'That is a more direct answer than I have succeeded in getting from the witnesses.' (Laughter)

Justice Schutt: 'Yes, it seems like an answer. This witness has not a very carrying voice, and I think we will adjourn.'

The court was adjourned at 11.45am. Between 11.00 and noon that day the Melbourne Meteorological Bureau registered a record-breaking 141 points of rain. So heavy was the downpour that houses and footpaths were flooded. In the same hour, the temperature plunged from 31°C to 20°C. The storm was among the most powerful to strike Melbourne since meteorological records commenced in 1855.

Yet throughout Ross sat quietly in the dock.

After lunch the court was lit, owing to the gloom of the unsettled weather. Ivy Matthews again entered the witness box. She continued giving her evidence in reply to Macindoe's questions. As she proceeded, her testimony acquired new details not previously given at the inquest.

Matthews told the court that, at 3 o'clock on Saturday 31 December, she was at the Melbourne Hotel, where she read a news report of the murder of the schoolgirl. She then proceeded straight to Ross's wine saloon.

> He was busy serving behind the bar and I walked past the wine cafe door twice. I mean that I walked past and I came back again. The second time he saw me and he came to the door ... I said, 'I see about this murder; why did you do it?' He said, 'What are you getting at ...?' I said, 'You know very well what you did. That child was in your wine cafe yesterday afternoon, for I saw her.' He said, 'Not me.' And with that he said, 'People are looking at us; walk out into Little Collins Street, Ivy, and I will follow you.'

Macindoe: 'When he came into Little Collins Street, what did he say?'
Matthews: 'First of all he tried to make out that I had not seen the little girl.'
Justice Schutt: 'Well, what did he say?'
Matthews: 'He said it was not the child. He simply said: "You know I did not have that child in there." I said, "Gracious me, I looked at the child myself, and I know it was the same child by the descriptions given," and for a long while he hung out that this was not the child ... at last he told me that ... the child came to him while he was at the door, on the Friday afternoon. He said there was no business; there was no one there and he was standing at his door, and when the child came up and asked him for a drink he said, "I took her in and gave her a lemonade." I said, "When the child came and asked you for a drink, why didn't you take her to the bar? Why did you take her to that little room?" I said, "I know you too well. I know what you are with little children." He said, "On my life, Ivy, I did not take her in there with any evil intention, but

when I got her there I found that she knew absolutely what I was going to do with her if I wanted her."'

This comment would be the cause of much pain to all who knew and loved Alma. The myth that victims of sexual assault are in some way responsible persists still today. None would it affect more deeply and more lastingly than Alma's sister, Viola.

Matthews: '... She stayed there until about four. He said a girl named Gladys came to see him and he told the child to go through to the little room with curtains ... he kept her in there until Gladys Linderman left, and he then brought her back into the little room.'

Macindoe: 'What did he say then?'

Matthews: 'After that he said he stayed with her during the rest of the afternoon, with the full intention at six o'clock of letting her go; but when six o'clock came she remained on. He said that after six o'clock, when Stanley went, he left us in there together ... he said that between six and eight o'clock he had outraged her.'

Macindoe: '... Well, I suppose he didn't say, "I outraged the child"?'

'No, that is the hardest part of it. I cannot say it ... the language he used is too foul ...'

'Will you write it down?'

'I will try to the best of my ability to say it ... He said, first of all, "After Stan went, I got fooling about with her, and you know the disease I am suffering from, and when in the company of young children I feel I cannot control myself. It was all over in a minute ..."'

Justice Schutt: 'Is that the substance of what he said?'

'Yes, that is the substance, and he said: "After it was all over I could have taken a knife and slashed her up, and myself too, because she led me on to it." He tried to point out to me that, so he believed, she went there for an immoral purpose. That is what he said to me. That is what he tried to imply to my mind.'

'Can you remember his words?'

'I can remember them, but I do not know that I should say them here.'

'You must either say it or write it down.'

Macindoe handed Matthews a paper and pencil. Concealing her features with a gloved hand, Matthews then wrote some words on the paper and handed it to Macindoe. After perusing the paper, he said: 'But you have left blank the one word that we want.'

Matthews, after writing in the word asked for, broke down and wept silently. The words on the paper were not read out to the court. Never previously disclosed, they were: *He said you know what a kid means to me Ivy. I had fucked her before I knew what I had done. She played about with me through the afternoon and that she had been well fucked before I got to her.*

Matthews continued: 'After it had happened ... [h]e took the body of the little girl and put it into the beaded room, and left it wrapped up in a blanket, and at 9 o'clock, or half-past nine, he brought a girl named Gladys Linderman there. She stayed until 10 o'clock. He took her home ... and came back between ten and half past ... and removed the body from the beaded room into the small room off the bar ... He then went to Footscray by train, but came back again between 1 and 2am. He looked for a place to put the body ... He said, "I did the very best thing. I put it in the street."'

Macindoe: 'Did he tell you at any time how the girl had died?'

Matthews: '... He said he strangled her in his passion. He said he heard or saw ... they were saying a cord had been round the child's neck. He said that was not so, [that] she was dead before he knew where he was. That was just his words to me.'

The defence's cross-examination of Matthews was intended to test her credibility, and proved to be tempestuous.

Brennan: 'You have not told us where you are living, Mrs Matthews?'

Matthews (appealing to the judge): 'Is it necessary for me to say where I live?'

Justice Schutt: 'I don't see why you should not.'

Matthews: 'I should say that I prefer to be called Miss Matthews. And I am living at 25 Rathdowne Street, Carlton.'

Brennan: 'Why the hesitation? What harm was there in saying where you live?'

'No harm at all. But I hardly think it necessary to bring in where I live in this court.'

'Who else lives with you in the same house?'

'About 25 different people.'

'It's a boardinghouse then?'

'It is both a boardinghouse and an apartment house—about half and half.'

'Amongst the people there, is there a woman named Julia Gibson?'

'She is the proprietress.'

'Is the name Julia Gibson another name—the right one—of a person who goes by the name of Madame Ghurka?'

'I don't feel called upon to answer for the names Mrs Gibson assumes. That has nothing to do with me.'

'That is not for you to say. You are not the judge of what is or what is not necessary in this court.'

'I know her only as the proprietress of my boardinghouse.'

Pressed further, Matthews admitted that she knew Mrs Gibson and Madame Ghurka were identical and that she had spoken to her a few times at the arcade.

Brennan: 'You have given today an account of your conversation with Colin Ross?'

'Yes.'

'And you gave an account at the inquest?'

'Yes.'

'Are you conscious of anything important you said today that you did not say at the inquest?'

'Perhaps I had not been asked.'

'You will remember that you were not asked today. Did you mention the name of Gladys Wain?'

'I know her as Linderman. I don't know that I mentioned her.'

'You know of course the evidence that Olive Maddox gave at the inquest.'

'Yes, through the papers.'

'You know that Olive Maddox said she saw a girl answering to that description in that cafe?'

'She said that to me. I don't know what she said at the inquest.'

'Do you know that at the inquest Olive Maddox did say that she saw the little girl in that place?'

'She told me that.'

'Did you say at the inquest one word about Colin saying that after Stanley left these things happened?'

'No.'

'Did you say one word about Colin having said he shifted the body from the cubicle into a little room, left it there, and then took it back again?'

'No.'

'Did you intentionally omit that?'

'No. I answered Mr Sonenberg's questions. I think you will find I said more then than here.'

'During the time [you were employed by Ross], were you in any way friendly with Madame Ghurka?'

'I would not say friendly. I would pass the time of day with her.'

'Did you go to reside in the same house with her?'

'Yes, about a week after I left Ross.'

'Your relations with the accused, as far as you were concerned, were on a purely business basis and quite respectful toward one another?'

'That is so.'

'He hardly treated you with respect when he used the words you have written down.'

'He gave me every respect a man could give a woman.'

'You parted in bitterness when you left the wine shop?'

'Not with him but with the family.'

'You had litigation pending against accused?'

'Does that require bitterness?'

'You can examine me on that when you get an opportunity. Did you instruct your solicitors to write to accused claiming one week's wages and a share in the business?'

Matthews admitted this, adding that a protracted correspondence then ensued between her solicitor and Ross over these matters. Although Matthews said that she and Ross had never spoken from the day she left his employ until the day she spoke to him about the tragedy, she still denied that there was any ill-feeling between them.

Brennan: 'Is your name Ivy Florence Matthews?'

'To the best of my belief it is.'

'Is that your baptismal name?'

'I will not have my parents' name dragged in.'

'Is your married or single name Matthews?'

'Absolutely I decline to tell you.'

'Before I appeal to His Honour I will tell you this to show we are fighting fair. I put it to you that you are not married and that you have received money from persons you alleged to have been your husband, and that both in this and other proceedings you have declined to give your name because you are not a married woman. Were you ever married?'

'I am a married woman.'

'Where were you married?'

'I decline to tell you.'

'Were you married in this or another State?'

'I decline to tell you.'

'Do you decline to tell me your husband's name?'

'I do. My husband is an invalid and I will not divulge his name. (With great emotion:) Do you think it is fair to stand there and catechise me—'

The judge intervened to restrain the witness who had risen indignantly from her seat in the witness box and was speaking in excited tones.

Brennan: 'Did you ever go under the name of Ivy Sutton?'

'I may have.'

'Are you not sure?'

'I may have.'

'Have you ever gone under the name of Ivy Dolan?'

'I may have.'

'Did you ever work at Cameron's tobacco factory under the name of Ivy Marshall?'

'Not under that name.'

'Did you ever work at Cameron's tobacco factory at all?'

'I may have.'

Asked whether there was any reason for not replying, Matthews said, 'It may be necessary to find employment and I don't think it's a fair thing. In the last court I said I worked for five years at Charles M Read's and Love and Lewis's and I have had letters from some firms that have asked me not to say where I worked. I have given my word.'

Brennan: 'But you had said at the lower court that you had given Colin Ross your word—'

Matthews (rising from her chair and speaking excitedly): 'Would you expect me to keep my word in such a case as that?'

Brennan: 'Are you drawing pensions on account of any persons who were at the war?'

'I may be doing so.'

Justice Schutt: 'You must answer the questions.'

Matthews: 'I have five brothers. I have drawn pensions for them at different times.'

Brennan: 'Have you drawn any for your own benefit?'

'I absolutely decline to say anything about the pensions I have drawn.'

Brennan: 'You are married?'

(Weeping) 'You think that I am not but I am.'

'Why did you take all those different names?'

'Well, for the next ten years I will be taking different names on account of this case. Did I acknowledge I had taken all those names?'

'What did you say then?'

'I said I may or may not have taken them.'

Brennan took the witness over the list of names again and to each she answered: 'I cannot tell you.'

Brennan: 'Your Honour, you see what type of witness she is.'

Justice Schutt: 'What I may or may not see is another matter.' (To witness:) 'You must answer the questions.'

Matthews: 'I'll have to say that I don't remember. I decline to say what my name is, or my husband's name, particularly.'

Brennan: 'Do you remember being questioned by the police when you were going under the name of Marshall?'

'I cannot answer.'

'I am only asking because it will be put to the jury that you are untruthful.'

'I don't think so.'

'Do you still decline to answer those questions I put to you?'

'Yes, I absolutely decline to answer any questions. I leave it to the jury.'

Matthews's credibility should now have been seriously in question. Yet Brennan was becoming gradually aware that instead she was attracting sympathy. Her appearance and tearful demonstrations were diverting attention from the lack of substance in her testimony. The sudden appearance of new detail in her account of Ross's alleged confession was particularly suspicious, as it consisted of information which had been reported in the newspapers between inquest and trial.

The location at which Ross was supposed to have confessed to Matthews had also altered. At the inquest, Matthews said their conversation began in Little Collins Street—at the end of the arcade—and was resumed a short distance from the end of the arcade, but still in the street. At the trial Matthews claimed it began at the door of the saloon, then resumed, when Ross suggested people were looking, out in Little Collins Street.

In his subsequent book on the case Brennan noted: 'The significance of this change will not be realised unless it is disclosed that just prior to the trial, notice was served on the defence that it was proposed to call as a witness on the trial Julia Gibson, otherwise Madame Ghurka, to prove that she saw Ross talking to Matthews on the Saturday afternoon.' As it happened Madame Ghurka's evidence would not be needed and she was not called as a witness.

Nevertheless, a copy of the notice to the defence, dated 17/2/22, still exists:

> Ross v. the King. Take notice that it is intended if necessary to examine the undermentioned person as a witness at your trial besides those already produced at the Police Court. Viz—Julia Gibson, to prove that she saw Ivy Matthews with you on the afternoon of the 31st of December last *in the Eastern Arcade*.†

Brennan would comment: '[Ghurka] could not, from her door, have seen them in conversation in Little Collins Street.'

---

†Author's italics

18. A tangible memento

Wearing a returned serviceman's badge on his jacket lapel, Sydney John Harding entered the court on crutches. In a world without antibiotics an infected leg meant a long sentence of pain and trouble. He repeated the evidence he gave at the inquest, projecting his voice in a practised manner. It was a strong and confident speech, one to which most of the court, and particularly the jury, would incline sympathetically, given his war service and the crutches. But to anyone with a cynical ear, he presented his evidence like a spruiker. Maxwell chortled, which to some seemed disrespectful.

Maxwell: 'Have you done any public speaking?'

'Yes, a good deal: recruiting.' (During the war Harding was a speaker at recruitment meetings. He claimed he was 'a lecturer on the war' and toured Queensland 'giving [fundraising] entertainments'.)

'Did [Ross] not tell you that he had told [Ivy Matthews about the tragedy]?'

'No; each time he mentioned Ivy Matthews it was with some execration.'

'And he told you he had told the story to no one but you?'

'Yes.'

'And that was in spite of what he had been told by his solicitor?'

'Yes; he was simply bursting to tell someone. The other men in the yard couldn't help hearing something.'

Born in Hamilton, Victoria, in 1883, Sydney John Harding considered a religious vocation but decided on medicine. He began the course at Melbourne University but after two years his father died and funds came to an end. He needed a job, and found one with a firm of sawyers in South Melbourne.

Embezzlement was the start of it, he would later tell *Smith's Weekly*: he was collecting money for a firm and put it into his pocket. But Harding's prison record began in October 1902 with a charge of insolent language—for which he was offered the choice of a fine or 14 days' imprisonment. He was then nineteen. His convictions in Victoria alone under multiple aliases and including additional offences committed while in prison numbered 27 by 1922, including several for assault, 'false representations' and 'making false verbal statements'.

In 1915 he got a one-week sentence for 'making a false verbal statement about a [prison] officer', and his military record shows that in 1917 he spent 28 days in army lock-ups for insubordination evolving from false statements. Comments attached to his military file by senior officers state 'he is a worthless person to have in the service'. His discharge was processed while he was in an army lock-up.

Asked about his prison record on oath, Harding made a number of statements—almost universally false. He gave his age as 30 (he was 39); he admitted to being convicted 'about nine or ten times, it might be eleven', but in fact he had lost count. He listed some of his offences without reference to false statements and concluded: 'Previous to

1909 I had not been in trouble. I was a schoolboy then.' However, he had convictions in 1902, 1904 and 1905. By 1922 Harding had deserted his wife and daughter and was living in a de facto relationship with Ruby 'Harding'. His non-military convictions alone fill two extensive entries in the Victorian Register of Male Prisoners and prove that he was a confirmed and hardened criminal.

Calamitously the defence had not subpoenaed Harding's record. Nevertheless, they were apparently confident they had enough evidence to discredit him.

The prosecution then called Joseph Dunstan, a 24-year-old prisoner, to corroborate Harding. Wearing a grubby white collar and dirty rag tie under a sack suit jacket, Dunstan's black hair was matted; his eyes were a shrewd blue and his left ear stuck out slightly more than his right, giving him a perpetually cocked look. He had four previous convictions for receiving, assault, larceny and obscene language.

Dunstan had been awaiting trial with Harding for housebreaking. At the police court he had pleaded guilty and exonerated Harding. But when the two men were tried on 10 April that year, the jury did not believe him. Harding would be found guilty of receiving.

Dunstan was one of four prisoners in the remand yard with Ross on 23 January. He was reading a book while Ross and Harding walked back and forth in conversation. Dunstan claimed that he heard eight answers made by Ross, but only one question put by Harding. The answers were 'I was talking to the girl'; 'If they do find any wine inside her, that ain't to say I gave it to her'; 'My brother was serving'; 'I left my girl at half-past ten'; 'I ain't the only man that's got gonorrhoea'; 'No, a bike'; 'I will ask the old bastard what he was doing there at half-past one'; and 'ammunition works'. The one question he heard Harding ask was: 'How was she dressed?'

Dunstan had not been called at the inquest. He explained that this was because he did not tell the governor what he had heard until afterwards. Dunstan admitted he had had opportunities for talks with Harding between the conclusion of the inquest and making his statement, but he denied there had been any conversations about the evidence.

Had Dunstan been influenced by newspaper reportage of the case? He was shown a copy of the *Herald* of 26 January, with Harding's photograph in it. On being asked if he had seen that before, Dunstan answered: 'I do believe I did.' He could not say when, but it was while he was in gaol. He said that he never read a paper in gaol, but that didn't mean he had never seen one. He said it was only a passing glance he had of the *Herald*.

Harding, who had been out of court, was now recalled and further cross-examined by Maxwell. He admitted that on the day following the inquest, he and Dunstan were reading a paper, either the *Age* or the *Herald*—he was reading it aloud, and Dunstan was looking over his shoulder. Harding said he often had papers lent to him, and on those occasions Dunstan got the benefit of them.

At 5.25pm the court adjourned.

Proceedings resumed at 10.30am on Wednesday 22 February. The first witness was Mrs Violet May Sullivan of Kensington. With a tanned face and small, slight build, she wore brown with a red knitted shawl and a black hat. She spoke quietly but clearly. On 26 January, on the left-hand side of Footscray Road going to Kensington, she saw some fragments of blue serge on the footpath.

Maxwell: 'Perfectly visible to everyone?'

'Yes. You could not miss it.'

'You handled it and threw it away?'

'Yes, I never saw it again.'

'When did you next see serge?'

'The next day; in the gutter on the other side of the road.'

'By that time you had read that a prisoner named Harding had said, at the inquest, that Ross had told him he had torn up the clothing and distributed the pieces along the road?'

'Yes, I had read it in the *Age* that morning [27 January].'

'And on the very day you read about it in the *Age* you saw this second bundle of serge that you handed to the police?'

'Yes.'

The serge was produced in court. None of the four fragments looked like they had been in the dust of a busy road for four weeks.

Brennan would later write:

On January 23 [when Harding made his statement] the police knew that Ross was supposed to have said that he scattered the fragments of the girl's dress along the Footscray Road. If this could have been verified it would have clinched the case against Ross, for it would have established ... the fact of some confession ... [T]he detectives should have got half a dozen men to take the road ... to discover the serge ... The local police did not find it, the detective's agents did not find it, but a casual wayfarer stumbles across it twice, because 'you could not miss it ...'

Next, Henry William Kroger, sergeant of police at Kensington, deposed that on 27 January Mrs Sullivan brought him the pieces of serge. His constables had not seen the serge, nor had they made a search along this busy road.

The court now stilled as Detective Portingale took into his hand a tangible memento of Alma: an envelope from which protruded a lock of auburn hair. He identified the hair as that which he had cut over the ear and 'about six inches from' the dead girl's head. Senior Detective Ashton then told how he recovered the blankets from Ross's home. Charles Price, Government Analyst, recounted his inquest testimony. It was an historic moment: the first move towards authoritative scientific evidence in Australian courts of law. Price duly adopted the mantle of scientific authority.

'They were not identical in colour with the hairs in the envelope,' said Price of the 22 hairs from the reddish-brown blanket; 'they were of a light auburn colour ... They were not cut-off hairs; they had fallen out, or had been taken from the scalp somehow or other. They did not appear to have been forcibly removed ...'

Charles Taylor, who was assistant government analyst in 1922, would tell writer Alan Dower decades later that: '... I knew ... Ross's defence would be caught off-balance by novel evidence of this kind ... [Because we were o]n the Crown side, we believed that all the hairs found on the blanket were those of Alma Tirtschke. But ... [we anticipated the defence] would deny our conviction that these were Alma's hairs. And it might counter with the proposition that the hairs fell from the head of one of the many other women known to have been willingly in Ross's little parlour nest while the blanket was there.

'If the defence could not produce a female witness with hair of identical colouring, it might try to confuse the jury by insisting that hairs which came from another part of a head could sometimes be darker than those found at the back.

'So Price and I resorted to strange tactics for responsible, allegedly respectable Crown scientists. We snooped on women in the city streets. Each lunch hour for several days we separately went down into the heart of Melbourne seeking women with crowning glories similar to Alma's ... Some days I did not strike one copperhead. At other times I would find two.

'Price and I received some very bleak and haughty stares from red-haired women who ... found us peering closely at the napes of their necks. Some tried to call the police. It was embarrassing at times. But the embarrassment was worthwhile. Finally we had the shining answer. In the case of a copperhead there can be a slight, but scarcely noticeable, lightness in colour up near the bulb end of hairs at the nape.'

Taylor did not mention how the women wore their hair. If the hair was pinned up, it might have exposed the nape hair, which would lighten from exposure to the sun. But Alma always wore her hair down so her nape hairs ought to have been dark.

Taylor continued: 'We had found that slight lightness of colour at the ends of Alma's hair—and of hairs on the blanket. In short, the hairs on the blanket had come from the nape of a female copperhead.'

Such was the basis on which Price proposed the similarity between the hairs on the blanket and the hairs from Alma's head! However, in his trial evidence, Price stated the exact opposite: '... the conclusion I formed, as regards the hairs I found on the blanket, was that they did not come from the frontal portion; that they had not been exposed much to the light; that they came from the back portion of the head, and that that is the reason why their colour was not as deep as those on the front portion.'

But the new point that Portingale had made in his evidence, as to where the lock of hair had been cut from Alma's hair, in fact contradicted Price. The sample did not include any nape hair.

Price had been nervous about producing his evidence in court, and so Taylor coached him behind their locked office door, rehearsing a credible and convincing delivery. Taylor played the part of a 'character-assassinating barrister'. Yet the methodology of these two scientists was so flawed, even disreputable, as to warrant such assassination. In addition, the inexpert handling of the evidence by the police allowed many opportunities for contamination.

The two sets of hair, Price continued, were 'very similar'. Microscopically, they agreed, because there was a kind of coarseness about them, and when treated with caustic soda it tended to bring out the pith portion of the hair, 'and that pith was identical with the hairs on the blanket'.

Under cross-examination, Price made no pretence at being an expert on the matter of hair; he knew nothing about the subject beforehand, and his experiments and reading were principally done after the event. For all he knew, the pith of all hairs may be identical.

Maxwell: 'When did you last examine the hairs from a woman's head?'

Price: 'Several years ago—about three years ago.'

'Can you give me any idea how often altogether you have made such examination of women's hair?'

'I have made very few.'

'Do you say that the hair on the brown blanket and the hair on the grey blanket are, in your opinion, from the same head?'

'Yes.'

'And they differ in colour and in diameter from the hair taken from Alma Tirtschke?'

'Yes.'

'So I suppose it is possible that the hair on the blankets might have come from another head?'

'It is possible—yes.'

'Don't you think it probable?'

'No.'

'Why not?'

'Because of the general similarity.'

'Can you say that when you have not examined many heads?'

'Since I received the hair I have examined many heads of the same colour.'
'Did you find great variations?'
'Yes.'
'Were any of the hairs like those of Alma Tirtschke?'
'They were somewhat similar.'
'Did you not find some quite as like hers as those taken from the blankets?'
'I did.'

This admission should have destroyed absolutely the probative force of Price's evidence, for, as Brennan would later point out, it exposed his proof as being no more than that which may be expressed in a basic syllogism:

> This hair is like Alma's.
> All hair like Alma's is not Alma's.
> Therefore, this hair may (or may not) be Alma's.

In other words, although Price found hairs that were 'as like Alma Tirtschke's hairs as the hairs on the blanket, and while this does not prove that they were not Alma's hairs, it prevents, by an elementary rule in scientific investigations, any deduction that they were.'

An examination of the facts suggests that the hairs on the blankets were not those of Alma Tirtschke. First, the hair was not of the same average length, that from Alma's head being, on average, 15 centimetres longer; secondly, the hair from the blanket was of a light auburn colour, while that from Alma's head was an auburn tending to red or deep red; thirdly, the diameters differed between the two sets of hair; fourthly, Price's tests suggested that where the hair was exposed it lightens in colour, and yet in this case the hairs (which the Crown claims came from the back of Alma's head when the blanket was allegedly dragged out from under her in the lane) were actually lighter than those in the sample, which was taken from nearer the front.

Furthermore, would 27 hairs remain on the blankets after a fortnight, during which time they had been aired on a line and frequently used at the Ross's home?

Maxwell: 'Did the detectives ask you to make an examination of the blankets to find if there were any trace of blood?'

Price: 'I looked for that, but did not find any.'

'Were you told that the man supposed to be responsible for the stain was suffering from a disease?'

'I don't think so. I did not take any notice of it as a matter of fact. Afterwards I was told that probably he was.'

'Did you look for any trace of it?'

'I did not get any normal appearance from the portions I removed that would make me look for it.' This was evasion: Price had not bothered to test for gonorrhoea because no one had thought it important enough to suggest he should.

Under re-examination, Macindoe returned Price to the hair: 'And so in your opinion the hair found on the blanket is similar to that of Alma Tirtschke's?'

'Yes,' replied Price.

The witness withdrew and the jurymen shifted restlessly in their seats. Lunch was still more than an hour off. If nothing else, though, most of the 12 at least got the gist of that last question—and the 'expert's' reply.

Despite Price's nervousness, neither of the defence's two barristers had assassinated his character. Indeed, it is apparent that both men respected his authority. Had an independent analysis of the hair samples been performed, matters might have progressed differently. But when Sonenberg had requested such a test on 30 January it had been refused by the Crown solicitor, because it was of 'the first importance' that such exhibits be preserved 'in the same condition precisely' as when the witness gave evidence about them.

19. All in the same sugar bag

'Swear Colin Campbell Ross,' said Maxwell. Amid audible whispers, Ross walked to the witness box from the dock. As he did, Ivy Matthews left the court.

After six weeks in gaol, Ross was physically worn down and in poor mental and emotional condition. Lifting the Bible he repeated in firm, clear tones: 'I swear by Almighty God that the evidence I will give in this case will be the truth, the whole truth and nothing but the truth.'

Maxwell: 'I want you to come right up to December 30. When did you go into the wine cafe on that day?'

Ross: 'About 2 o'clock in the afternoon.'

'Who was in charge of the cafe that afternoon?'

'A brother of mine, Stanley.'

'Was he in the cafe when you arrived there?'

'Yes.'

'Where had you come from?'

'Home. I was living in Ballarat Road, Footscray.'

'What were you doing at the cafe during the afternoon?'

'Just talking among the customers.'

'Were you serving?'

'No.'

'Do you remember any of the customers?'

'Yes. One or two of them. One was a chap named Allen and another chap was named Lewis.'

'During the afternoon did you speak to Ivy Matthews?'

'No.'

'When was the last time you had spoken to her?'

'About two days before my last trial in the robbery under arms case—about two months before December 30. Since that case I had not seen her, let alone speak [*sic*] to her.'

'Did you see or speak to her on December 31?'

'No, I never left the cafe that afternoon.'

'You had sued her and there was bad feeling between you?'

'Yes, bitter feeling.'

'On the afternoon of December 30 did you at any time see a little girl answering the description of Alma Tirtschke?'

'Yes.'

'Did you speak to her?'

'Never, at any time.'

'As far as you know was she ever in your wine saloon?'

'No.'

'What was she doing when you saw her?'

'The first glance I had of her was when she was walking towards Bourke Street, and the next she was looking in Valentine's fancy dress window, and the next time she was walking toward Little Collins Street.'

'... When did you leave the saloon that afternoon?'

'Ten past six. I went home ...'

Ross had arrived home at 7 o'clock, had tea, then left with his brother Tom, taking the tram to Footscray and the train to the city.

Maxwell: 'Did you see anybody on the tram going toward the Footscray station?'

'Yes. Mrs Kee and a chap named Dawsey ... I said "Good evening" to Mrs Kee and had a conversation with Dawsey about the Hanging Rock races.'

'What time was it when you saw them?'

'Somewhere about eight or a little after.'

'What time did you arrive at the Eastern Arcade?'

'About a quarter to nine. I had an appointment at that time with Gladys Linderman ...'

'Were the gates of the arcade in Little Collins Street closed at that time?'

'No. They were wide open ... I met my friend a little after nine and went into the cafe.'

'How long were you there?'

'About an hour and a half or an hour and three-quarters.'

'Had you any business to transact with her?'

'She came to look at some linoleum. My lease of the cafe was up on the following day ...'

'About what time did you leave the cafe that night?'

'Between 10.30pm and 10.45pm with Gladys Linderman.'

'By what exit did you leave?'

'Little Collins Street. We went along Russell Street and along Lonsdale Street until we came to King Street. We spoke there for a few minutes, and I left her about ten past eleven. She lives in King Street. I went to Spencer Street railway station, and from there I went home to Footscray.'

'Was anyone on the train with you?'

'No.'

'What time did you get to Footscray?'

'Fourteen minutes to 12. Then I got on the tram, which takes me right to my home. There was a chap named Herb Studd on the tram and I had a conversation with him.'

'About what time was it when you reached your home?'

'About 12; it might have been a few minutes afterwards.'

'Was there anyone up?'

'Yes; my mother ... My brother Ronald was in bed. I went into the bedroom where he was; there was a light in the room and we were talking.'

'... Did you leave your home between the time you arrived at about midnight and the time you got up in the morning for breakfast?'

'No, I did not.'

It was now one o'clock and the court adjourned for luncheon. Proceedings resumed at 2.17pm.

Maxwell: 'You said before that you saw the detectives that morning at the arcade ... You heard Detective Piggott give an account of the interview he had with you? Is that substantially correct?'

Ross (after a moment's hesitation): 'Yes.'

'On the Saturday you were preparing for removal on the Monday, I understand?'

'Yes.'

'And on the Monday you did remove?'

'Yes.'

'Where were the things sent?'

'To Footscray.'

'As far as the saloon is concerned what blankets or rugs had you?'

'Two grey blankets. [Looking at the exhibit] This blanket was there.'

Another blanket of a reddish-brown colour was handed to Ross and he said it had never been in his saloon.

Maxwell: 'Do you know that blanket?'

'Yes.'

'Where has it been?'

'The last time I saw it was at Donnybrook.'

'That blanket was never at the saloon?'

'No.'

'The grey blankets were removed to your mother's house in Footscray?'

'Yes, on the Monday.'

'Will you look at this blanket?' Sonenberg produced a grey blanket.

'Yes; that is one which was in the cafe. It is the mate of the one exhibited.'

'How were they sent to Footscray?'

'Rolled around some pictures.'

'Did you subsequently see those two grey blankets at Footscray?'

'Yes; I saw them on the clothesline and on the veranda at home.'

'Did you see them anywhere else in the house?'

'Yes, under the pillow on the couch.'

Answering further questions by Maxwell, Ross described his movements after he was interviewed by the detectives on the evening of 5 January.

Maxwell: 'At any time that night did you see the woman Maddox?'

Ross: 'No, I did not.'

'You remember the interview with Brophy and the man White? What is your version of that?'

'I was called to the front gate of the gaol and the governor said, "You are here for identification."

'I said, "Right oh!" A man was brought into the front office and put in front of me.

'Brophy said, "Is that the man?"

'White replied, "Yes."

'I said, "Well, what about it?"

'Brophy said, "This man says he saw you talking to a girl in the arcade at 3.30pm on 30 December and I said, "That is correct."'

'Was the name of any girl mentioned?' Maxwell questioned.

'No.'

'You heard what the witness Upton said about his visit to the saloon on 30 December ... Is there a scintilla of truth in his statements?'

'No, none.' Here Ross smiled.

'You have heard Harding swear ... Is there any truth in that?'

'No, not one word.'

'Was the case mentioned while you were in the remand yard?'

'I remember a few words.'

'... You say that the statement by Harding that you told him that you murdered this girl, tore up her clothes and scattered them along the Footscray Road, is not true?'

'Not one word.'

'Now, is there any truth in the suggestion that you had anything to do directly or indirectly with the death of this child?'

'None whatever.'

Macindoe first questioned Ross as to the wine cafe itself and its appointments: 'You could get water round the corner from the first room off the bar?' he asked.

'Yes; there is a tap and a gully trap there.'

'You could empty dirty water there as well?'

'Yes.'

'Did you see a little girl in the arcade on the afternoon of 30th December whose description corresponded with that of Alma Tirtschke?'

'Yes.'

'Did you speak to her?'

'No.'

'Did you notice her carefully?'

'Not carefully, just casually.'

'Did you give a description of her to Piggott?'

'Yes.'

'Did you see Olive Maddox in the saloon that afternoon?'

'Yes.'

'Where was she?'

'At the bar counter. I said, "How do you do, Ollie?" She said, "All right, Col." That was all that was said.'

'She didn't say to you, "That's a young bit of a kid to be drinking there"?'

'No.'

'Then that must be pure invention?'

'Absolutely.'

'Can you suggest why Olive Maddox should invent that?'

'For £1000.'

'Do you suggest that she gave that evidence so she could get £1000?'

'Yes; a prostitute will come at anything.'

'All her story then is invention?'

'Absolutely.'

'What time did you get in [to the city that evening]?'

'Twenty-five to nine.'

'You went to the arcade and met [Gladys] Linderman?'

'Yes …'

'Is that her right name?'

'No, it is Mrs Wain.'

'Are you fond of her?'

'Oh, no.'

'Just as a friend—quite platonic?'

'That is so.'

'What did she go to the wine shop for?'

'To look at some linoleum and a picture.'

'Did it take her an hour and three-quarters to do that?'

'No. We were talking together in the saloon.'

'She was a married woman, wasn't she?'

'Yes.'

'And you say there was nothing immoral in your relations with her?'

'Nothing whatever.'

'You know that she has a disease?'

'No.'

'You have?'

'I had. At that time.'

Macindoe: 'Did you have any commotion on the tram?'
'No.'
'Did you ever tell your brothers that you did?'
'No.'
'Did you ever tell your brothers to go to the Footscray electric tram people and to ascertain what took place that night?'
'No, and I do not know that they actually went.'

Macindoe: 'You say the brownish-grey blanket was never in the cafe?'
Ross: 'Yes.'
'Where was it?'
'In the Donnybrook Hotel nine months ago.'
'Where has it been since then?'
'I don't know. I never noticed it about anywhere.'
'How did it get to your home?'
'Shifted there in the belongings from the hotel, I suppose.'
'Then any hairs on that blanket must be nine months old?'
'I could not tell you how old they are.'
'Can you suggest how the hairs got there?'
'No. My idea is that they have been put there by the police.'
'With what object?'
'To fit me, to get me hung.'
'How else have they tried to fit you?'
'In several other ways. I have forgotten a lot. It is six weeks ago and I have been locked up, and my memory is in a bit of a mist today.'
'Can you tell us why any member of the police force should try dishonestly to fit you?'
'Because I beat them in the last case. That's the reason.'

'Do you suggest that either Piggott or Brophy was in the last case?'

'Not in that, but they are all in the same sugar bag up there.'

'You don't suggest that because a jury found you not guilty of one offence the police force as a whole would try to get you hanged?'

'Exactly. That's my idea.'

Macindoe: 'According to you White said, "That's the man." He said he'd seen you speaking to a girl at 3.30pm?'

Ross: 'Yes. I said, "That's right," a girl, at 3.30 or somewhere about that time.'

'Did you think that White was saying that you had been speaking to Alma Tirtschke?'

'No.'

'What! Whom then did you think he was talking about?'

'Mrs Wain.'

'And you didn't think he meant to convey he saw you talking to the murdered girl?'

'No; because I wasn't talking to her.'

'You and Miss Ivy Matthews had been, we are told, in business together?'

'No, she was my barmaid, not my manageress. She was paid 30 shillings a week, and was not to get a share of the profits.'

'You knew her pretty well?'

'Yes, I was very friendly with her up to some time ago.'

'Confidential?'

'No.'

'She tells us that you told her that, at 9 o'clock on the 30th, you brought a girl named Wain to the cafe. How did she know that?'

(The answer is plain: the information must have come from either Ross or the police.)

Ross: 'I couldn't tell you.'

'Do you suggest that the detectives told Ivy Matthews?'

'Yes. They would come at anything.'

'Ivy Matthews says that you told her that [the little girl] had not been strangled with a cord. Is that true?'

'No. She made that up ...'

'Why?'

'Well, revenge is sweet, isn't it?'

'Is that the reason?'

'Yes, to get even with me.'

'What? The only reason? What about the £1000?'

'She might be in for a cut of that. She might be like the other one—give it to the Children's Hospital.' (Ross here alludes to Harding's statement at the inquest that he would donate any funds to the hospital.)

'Why does she want to get revenge?'

'One thing, for sacking her.'

'For sacking her from a position worth 30 shillings a week? She wants to hang you for that?'

'Yes.' [Laughter.]

'What is the other reason?'

'Because she could not get even with me. The solicitor's letters she sent me were to get a share out of the business.'

'You want these 12 men solemnly to believe you?'

'Yes, she framed that up on me because I gave her the sack.'

'And worse still, she used her influence with the police to frame up a case against you?'

'Yes. She is a copper herself.'

'Has nothing else occurred to you?'

'I might think of something later on. I might frame a few up. I might invent a few reasons.'

'Invent a few? Tell lies?'

'I might. You never know.'

Ross had not the faculties to resort to anything now more sophisticated than a child's bitter irony. From henceforth, he could be relied on to condemn himself.

Macindoe: 'Had you known Harding before?'

Ross: 'I met him on a couple of occasions. I was warned against him for being a dog.'

'A dog?'

'Yes, dog. D-O-G. It means a shelf among prisoners in gaol.'

'What is a shelf?'

'A prisoner who lags on other prisoners. A man to be kept away from.'

'Does he tell the truth?'

'With a bit added. He hears one thing and builds on it.'

'You were in the yard with him, weren't you? ... What was the talk about?'

'... I remember Harding said, "What do you think of your case?" and I said I didn't think much about it as they had nothing on me. I said I was only there to keep the public's mouth shut.'

'A scapegoat for the police force?'

'Yes. I was the only one they could lag. If there had been a snail behind me he would have been taken.'

'Did you tell [Harding] you had a disease?'

'No.'

'Did he know?'

'Yes, he could not help but know.'

'You heard the analyst say there was a stain on the blanket which was in the wine saloon?'

'Yes.'

'Can you account for it being there?'

'No.'

'Was the blanket used at home?'

'It may have been. I saw blankets on the lawn and the veranda, with men and women lying on them at night time.'

Ellen Tirtschke with her two children, Viola (on rocking horse) and Alma, in southern Rhodesia, 1913. The family's African servant stands in the background.

ABOVE: Alma and Viola Tirtschke, c 1916.

RIGHT: Alma Tirtschke's father, Harry Tirtschke, and stepmother, Emily Kate (née Rennell).

The Eastern Arcade, Bourke Street, January 1922.

Eastern Arcade interior, looking towards Little Collins Street. A white-helmeted policeman indicates the location of the rooms of the Australian Wine Saloon.

The Australian Wine Saloon: rooms 34 and 32 of the Eastern Arcade.

Little Collins Street looking east. In the distance a white-helmeted policeman stands at the entrance to Gun Alley. In the foreground, to the right, is Alfred Place and George Ellis's ramshackle Hopetoun House (formerly the Adam Eve Hotel). It was at this spot Alma Tirtschke was last seen by May and Stanley Young.

Gun Alley. The policeman stands where the easement runs off the lane.

The easement off Gun Alley. The cross marks the place where Alma Tirtschke's body was found.

WHO SAW THIS CHILD?

Page one of the *Herald*, 4 January 1922—a photograph taken c 1916. Pictured from left are: Alma; her grandmother, Mrs Elizabeth Tirtschke; and her sister, Viola.

CLOCKWISE FROM TOP LEFT: Senior detectives Frederick John Piggott and John O'Connell Brophy at Melbourne's Supreme Court on the fourth day of the Ross trial—Thursday, 23 February 1922; TC Brennan, c 1930; Madame Ghurka; Olive Maddox; Sydney John Harding as he appeared at the Tirtschke inquest; Ivy Matthews.

Moments after being sentenced to death, Colin Ross, manacled and firmly held, is escorted from the Supreme Court to the waiting prison van for his return to Melbourne Gaol.

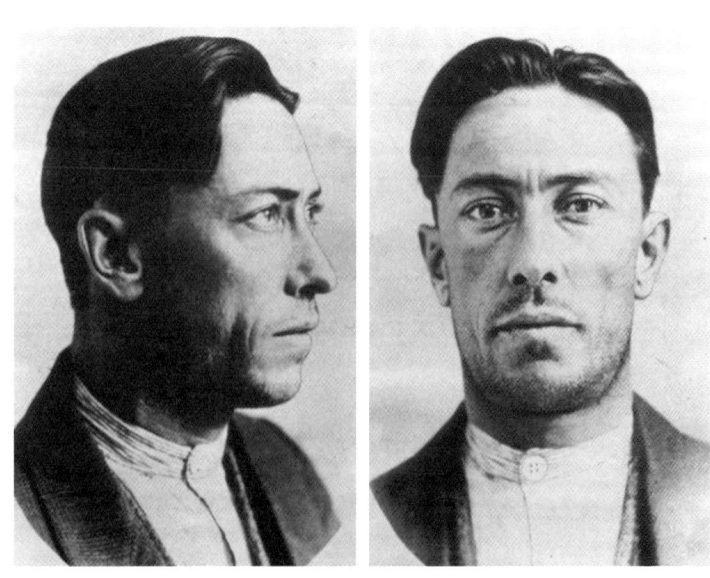

The last photographs of Colin Campbell Ross—taken in Melbourne Gaol in January 1922.

Hair from the head of the deceased, Alma Tirtschke (top); hair from the brown-grey blanket (middle); hair from Mrs Wain (above).

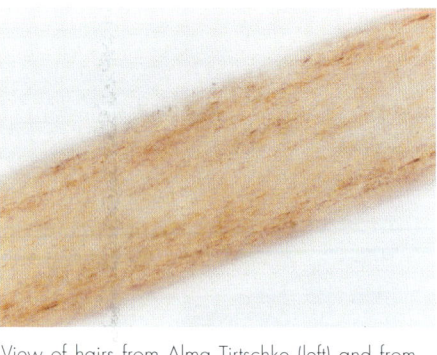

View of hairs from Alma Tirtschke (left) and from the grey blanket (above) at x40 magnification.

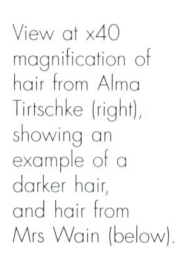

View at x40 magnification of hair from Alma Tirtschke (right), showing an example of a darker hair, and hair from Mrs Wain (below).

'Do you suggest the stain got there in those circumstances?'

'It may have. I don't suggest that it might.'

Maxwell: 'In the cubicle did any immoral activity take place?'

Ross: 'Yes, on several occasions.'

'Did Alberts ask you for the loan of a pencil on the evening of 31 December?'

'No.'

Macindoe: 'Have you got gold-filled teeth at front?'

Ross: 'I have gold crowns. [Ross displays his teeth.] Want to have another look at them?'

'Yes,' said Macindoe.

Ross displayed his teeth again and said, 'I've a mouth full of 'em.'

To His Honour, Ross said that Mrs Wain was just a friend.

Colin's brother Stanley, in response to Brennan, offered a number of points not recorded by the police when they took his statement: he had not seen Ivy Matthews on the afternoon of 30 December and Alma Tirtschke could not have been in the saloon without him seeing her.

A little after 4 o'clock he had noticed Colin talking to Gladys Wain, and at about 5pm Gladys came into the 'cubicle' (though Stan had not heard it referred to by that name before). Stanley remained in the bar until a little after 6 o'clock, when he locked up, went and had tea and returned around 7.30pm. He visited the lavatory and returned the key shortly after. There was nobody in the saloon. He returned there the following morning, swept and scrubbed it out. He saw no signs of it having been cleaned the previous night.

During the morning Stanley was seen by Piggott who gave him, he says, (though this is denied by Piggott) a description of the dress worn by Alma Tirtschke. Stanley said he passed the description on to Colin when he arrived for work later that morning.

The prosecution had noted two points on which Stanley's evidence varied. Asked if he knew the witness Upton, Stanley replied he did not. Upton was then directed to stand and Stanley denied seeing this man at the cafe on 30 December. Reminded that he had said he saw a man known as Darkie in the saloon on that day, Stanley replied he now believed that this man was named Allen. He had not recalled the man's real name when referring to him previously. Upton, by his own admission, was so drunk that Saturday that he did not know where he was.

Regarding the evening of 5 January (when Maddox claimed Colin confessed to her) Stanley said he went to Ballantyne's in West Melbourne, where the family of Mrs Tom Ross lived, at about 9.30. There he encountered Colin and various other people; then, at about 10.30pm, he, Colin and two others left for Footscray. He went with his brother Ron to see a tramway conductor named Kinsella after Colin was arrested. They wanted to know if Kinsella could remember Colin on his tram on the night of 30 December.

Macindoe: 'Did you know where Ivy Matthews lived?'

Stanley: 'No ... I know she lived in Rathdowne Street, but I could not take you to the place.'

'Did you and your brother Ronald go to Madame Ghurka's or Mrs Gibson's house on the night of February 3?'

'No.'

'... [D]id you say to Ivy Matthews: "If you give evidence, you will have your lights put out."?'

'No.'

Ronald and Mrs Ross were also asked about this alleged harassment of Ivy Matthews (for which Matthews must have been the source), and denied it.

Mrs Ross stated that Colin left home after midday on Friday 30 December and came home at about 7 o'clock. She served him his tea and he left the house afterwards with her married son Tom. She did some shopping in Footscray, it being late shopping night. She returned at about 10pm; her eldest son Ronald arrived shortly after—'He had a paper and went to bed. About midnight I was lying down reading. I heard Colin come ... He went into the room where he and Ronald slept ... I saw him ... talking to Ronald. I passed later, and the light was out, but they were still talking. I locked up and went to bed.'

Mrs Ross said that arrangements had been made prior to the closure of the wine saloon 'for Colin's effects to be removed to my place on the Monday morning 2 January. Among them were two blankets.' Examining the two blankets, Mrs Ross confirmed Colin's account of them. Mrs Ross said she had not noticed any hairs on the blankets. She had not washed them since they came from the saloon. Some of the auburn hairs on the brown blanket may have been Miss Alice Ballantyne's, a relative who had stayed at her house. They were also like that of her daughter-in-law.

Macindoe knew it wouldn't take much to push the Rosses into losing their tempers in the witness box, speaking and acting in ways that portrayed them unfavourably to the court. Asked about the alleged harassment of Ivy Matthews, Mrs Ross indignantly replied: 'Ivy Matthews is a woman I would not demean myself to talk to ... (In rising tones:) I had one conversation with her [at the time of the shooting affair] and that was enough for me ...'

To Maxwell: 'I have reason to be fond of Colin. He has been a good son ... I have talked about the case with visitors who came to sympathise with me, but not discussed the evidence. Sometimes the spare blankets were used by visitors or on the veranda when we were sitting out. Lemonade may have been spilt on them.'

As a witness, Mrs Ross had been excluded from the court when Price testified the stains were semen. Suggesting they were lemonade caused sniggers.

The fourth day of the trial, Thursday 23 February, was one of those cloudy days so typical of Melbourne after a cool change. The forecast was for intermittent showers and cold southerlies.

Thomas McKinley Ross corroborated his brother's evidence on the following points: that Colin had tea at his mother's home shortly after 7pm on 30 December; that he and Colin met friends (Mrs Kee and Oscar Dawsey) in the tram on the way to town later; and that Colin was in bed when Thomas visited the house again at 6.45 the next morning (after spending the night at the house of his mother-in-law, where his wife resided).

Macindoe: '... Had you seen Mrs Kee on the tram before?'

Thomas: 'Yes, several times.'

'How then do you fix the night of seeing Mrs Kee?'

'Well, for one thing, it was the night before New Year's Eve.'

Thomas affirmed that he saw Colin at Mrs Linderman's at 8pm on 5 January. About an hour later, Colin came over to the Ballantynes', remaining there until 10.30. From there, Stanley, Thomas and Colin went home together.

Macindoe: 'Can you tell me anything of the conversation that took place at Mrs Linderman's on the night of 5 January?'

'No; there were others in the room. They were just laughing and chatting.'

'What! Laughing? Do you say they were laughing at this matter?'

'Well, in a way; they thought it a hard thing that my brother should have been detained. I thought too that my brother would have been the last man in the world to be detained.'

'And so you laughed!'

The last Ross brother to testify, Ronald Campbell Ross, stated that on 30 December he arrived home at about 10.30pm and Colin about midnight. Ronald suffered from malaria, contracted during wartime service in Palestine, and was a light sleeper. He did not think it would be possible for Colin to have left the room without disturbing him.

Macindoe: 'You realise that your brother is charged with a—er—nasty offence?'

'He is charged with a nasty offence.'

'And his defence interests you deeply?'

'Certainly it does.'

'Have you been interviewing witnesses on his behalf?'

'I have been getting witnesses.'

'Did you interview a Mr Patterson?'

'He came to me first.'

'Did he tell you he was on the tram and was introduced to your brother?'

'Yes. He said it was something after 11 o'clock.'

[Macindoe is now referring to the tram by which Colin journeyed home late on 30 December:] 'Did he say there was a disturbance on that tram?'

'No.'

'... Did you interview the conductor, Kinsella, of the tramways?'

'I might have ... To see if he could remember seeing my brother going home that night.'

'Did you tell the conductor or the driver that ... there was a disturbance?'

'No ...'

The Crown was mistaken here: no disturbance took place on the tram. After the trial, this misinformation would be traced to the police at Footscray. It occurred when the witness Patterson, hearing of Ross's arrest, identified himself voluntarily to Ronald Ross and the Footscray police, declaring he had travelled home with Ross. Patterson said that he remembered the date because there had been a disturbance in the Footscray fish shop where he had supper, before taking the tram on which he saw Ross. The local police reported the disturbance to Russell Street as having occurred on the tram.

Harding had claimed the disturbance on the tram was initiated by Ross to establish an alibi. How curious that he should have the same misapprehension as the police.

Macindoe: 'What did you go to St Kilda for?'

Ronald: 'I was sent by a man, Robert Pommeroy, who came to the house.'

'What did he tell you?'

'He said that if we wanted any help or money his brother would do what he could for us ...'

'Did you believe him?'

'No; I didn't. I jumped straight away to the conclusion he was a pimp. He kissed my mother and sister-in-law before he left, after having a jolly good meal. That's the sort of man he is.' [Laughter.]

Macindoe then asked about the alleged harassment of Matthews, which Ronald also denied.

'Call Gladys Wain,' ordered Brennan. Wain was youthful and pretty, with auburn-coloured hair. Dressed in a navy-blue crepe de Chine frock, she wore a transparent hat trimmed with flowers and carried a black fur. She began by stating she was married and her address—her mother's house.

Brennan: 'You are living in the same house as your husband, but are not living with him otherwise?'

'That is so ...'

'The question was put [yesterday] to a witness: "Do you know that Gladys Wain has a certain disease?"'

'It is an absolute lie.

'Did you see Colin Ross [on December 30]?'

'Yes. He was speaking to a woman at the front of the saloon. He asked [her] to excuse him and he came to speak to me. That would be about a quarter to four.'

'What time did you leave Colin Ross that afternoon?'

'It would be 20 minutes or half-past five ... I [had] asked Mr Ross if he could give me a drink, and I walked through to the recess, the small room at the end of the bar.'

'How long did you remain in that cubicle?'

'About ten minutes.'

'And when you went in with Ross were there other people in the bar?'

'There were several men in the bar at the time.'

'Where did you go after you came out?'

'... Colin Ross walked out to the Little Collins Street entrance with me, and I left him and went to George's. That would be somewhere about 5.30pm.'

'Now, I am sorry, Mrs Wain, but I really think we had better have your hat off. [Gladys removed her hat, revealing a head of curly, light auburn hair.] During the time you were about the saloon, in the saloon, and after you came out, did you see a little girl about 12 or 14 years of age with auburn hair?'

'I did not notice any child about.'

'Before you left Ross did you make any arrangements as to the evening?'

'Yes, we arranged to meet about 9 o'clock. I had arranged to go shopping with Mrs Kennedy.'

'What was the reason of your appointment with him in the evening?'

'According to the arrangement, my mother was to have come with me and have a look at the furniture before the place was closed, but my mother could not come.'

'And subsequently to shopping you entered the arcade?'

'Yes. Mrs Kennedy did not come all the way. I met Mr Ross somewhere about the saloon.'

'Did you see Ross before you parted from Mrs Kennedy?'

'Yes, and Mrs Kennedy saw him.'

'And where did you go?'

'Into the saloon.'

'What time did you leave?'

'It would be about 20 minutes past 10 when I left—with Colin Ross.'

'Where did you go then?'

'Home. I carried with me a picture from the saloon ... I left him at the corner of Lonsdale and King streets between 11.00 and 11.15pm.'

Macindoe: 'Are you fond of Colin Ross?'

(Laughing) 'Oh, no.'

'... Were you his girl?'

'Oh, certainly not.'

(It was Harding who had been making free use of the expression 'his girl'.)

'Did you go into the beaded room [on 30 December]?'

'No.'

'So you cannot say whether a little girl was sitting there or not?'

'No.'

'Was anything said about the linoleum?'

'Yes. That's when we made arrangements to come back at night ... I told him the shops closed at 9 o'clock, and he said, "What about making it then?" ...'

'So you went in there at night by yourself?'
'Yes, and stayed from 9 o'clock to 10.20.'
'What were you doing all that time?'
'Looking at the prices of every article in the place.'
'Have you ever lain down on the couch?'
'Never. I sat down on it that Friday afternoon.'
Justice Schutt: 'Was that the only time?'
'Yes.'
Macindoe: 'Did you take your hat off?'
'No.'
'Your hair is what is called "bobbed" ... When was it last cut?"
'About six or eight months ago. It ought to be cut now. It is caught up at the back.'
'Have you any hair fifteen inches in length now?'
'I could not say as to that.'
At the request of Macindoe Gladys again removed her hat. She unpinned the longest strands of her hair, holding them out from her head to show their length.

Macindoe: 'Did you give anyone a sample of your hair? For examination?'
'I gave it.'
'Is it naturally curly?'
'Yes.'
'Can you account for any hair of yours getting on the blankets in that cafe?'
'No.'

Agnes Kennedy, widow, testified that she remembered going shopping with Gladys on the night of 30 December. Going through the arcade, she saw Colin Ross standing at the Little Collins Street entrance. She next saw Gladys at 11pm at the corner of Lonsdale and King streets, talking to Ross.

Tram passenger Mrs Mary Kee stated that she knew Colin Ross just to nod to and had never had a conversation with him. On 30 December at 7.50pm she boarded a tram heading towards Footscray railway station and saw Ross with his brother Tom in the smoking compartment. He raised his hat and she nodded. 'He was speaking to a Mr Dawsey whom I knew.'

To Macindoe: 'I first remembered that I saw Colin Ross on that night after he was arrested. I went and saw Mrs Ross. I met her in 1914 when she and I had boys in camp together. My son was killed in the war and she was one who came to me in my trouble. I thought it was my duty to go to her. This was before the inquest ... I had never seen Colin Ross since the end of the war until 30 December. I had often seen his brothers. His brother Tommy was sitting with him on the tram.'

'You couldn't be mistaken as to the night?'

'No. It was the late shopping night ...'

'Have you any reason for remembering the time as 10 to 8?'

'Yes. I had left my grandchild with my husband, and I said I would be back at half-past 8 or a quarter to 9. When I came out I said, "It is just a quarter to 8 now..." I got home again at 20 to 9.'

Tram driver Oscar Dawsey also saw Colin and Tom Ross on the Footscray tram at 7.50pm, 30 December. He went to Ronald Ross when he heard of Colin's arrest. 'I thought it was important Ronald Ross should know I had seen Colin that night.'

That Ross was seen at 7.50pm heading back towards the city on a Footscray tram patently contradicted the claim of comedian David Alberts that he was asked by Ross for a pencil some 15 minutes earlier in the Eastern Arcade. Unfortunately, however, Alberts had been given permission, after his evidence had been taken, to leave the court as he had to travel interstate. He could not now be brought back for further examination.

Herbert Studd, driver, corroborated Ross in respect to the return journey later that night: 'On December 30, I saw Colin

Ross on the tram. I was with a chap named James Patterson. I introduced Patterson and the three of us spoke. This was about half-past eleven.' [Though Patterson admitted the time 'could be half an hour either way'.]

Macindoe: 'Why were you talking to Ronald Ross just now? What did you say to him?'

Brennan glared at the witness; Sonenberg put his hand to his brow.

'Um,' said Studd, 'there was no particular business.'

Macindoe: 'Come now, what did he say to you?'

Justice Schutt: 'If you remember, say it.'

Studd: 'I don't remember.'

Macindoe: '[Ronald Ross] went out of the court and talked with you just now?'

'It was early this morning.'

'I mean after he gave his evidence a few minutes ago?'

'No; I don't think he did.'

'Will you swear he didn't?'

'I won't swear it.'

'Are you nervous?'

'Not more than you are.' (Laughter.)

Studd was directed to hold up the Bible. He complied.

Macindoe: 'Now swear you did not speak to Ronald Ross within half an hour ago?'

Justice Schutt: 'I think he said he could not say either way.' [To Studd:] 'You don't remember him speaking to you just before you entered the box?'

Studd: 'I was standing in the corridor speaking to a couple of chaps.'

Yet the damage was done, the implication being that Ronald Ross colluded with or influenced Studd.

James Patterson, labourer, said he was introduced to the accused by Studd while on the tram on the night of 30 December. But he, like Studd, could not say precisely what the time was, only that it was between 11 and 12pm.

William Henry Clarke, manager of the Eastern Arcade, said the door of Ross's cafe nearest to Bourke Street had two locks on it. There was no key in the lower lock and it was possible to open the door from outside without a key.

Clarke: 'I was in the arcade, backwards and forwards, on Friday afternoon December 30. I know Ivy Matthews. At no time did I see her ...'

Macindoe [to Brennan]: 'Are you going to bring all Melbourne to prove they did not see her?'

The first witness after the court resumed that afternoon was George Frederick Bradley, ropemaker. On 30 December he had caught a train from Flinders Street at 11.17pm, arriving at Footscray at about 11.30 from whence he caught a tram. Here he saw Ross, at 11.45. The pair alighted and walked as far as Ross's house, where Bradley farewelled him at around midnight.

Macindoe responded by generating confusion over train times, claiming something must be wrong if Ross swore his train left Flinders Street at 11.32. The mistake appeared to the court to be Bradley's. In fact it originated in Piggott's verbal evidence, his recollection of when Ross had said he caught the train. Ross had actually said in his statement to police that after parting from Gladys in King Street, he then caught the train, not from Flinders, but Spencer Street. The Footscray train departing Flinders Street at 11.17 would arrive at Spencer Street at 11.22. This same train would reach Footscray at 11.32.

Caroline Ross, wife of Thomas and sister-in-law of Colin, said she visited Colin's saloon on 28 December with her sister Alice Ballantyne. That afternoon they were in the room at the end of the bar sitting on a couch, and before they left both she and her sister each let her hair down, combed it and tidied it up. On 5 January Caroline saw Colin at Mrs Linderman's; she and her husband left there at about eight o'clock. An hour later she again saw Colin, at her mother's place in West Melbourne, at 9 o'clock. He stayed there until about 10.30. There were about ten persons present in the house.

Macindoe: 'Would you call your hair auburn?'

Caroline took off her hat and displayed her hair.

'Do you know the colour of your hair?'

Caroline: 'I don't know what you would call it.'

'What would you call it?'

'Fair. I should think it would be a light auburn.'

'On the afternoon of your visit to the wine saloon, you did your hair?'

'Took it down and combed it.'

'While you were sitting on the couch?'

'No, standing in front of the mirror. The couch was under the mirror.'

'Do you suggest that some of your hair might have fallen on the couch?'

'It may have.'

'Or your sister's?'

'It may have.'

Agnes Linderman, widow, said about a fortnight prior to the murder she spoke with Colin Ross about purchasing some of the saloon furniture. She remembered her daughter Gladys talking about going to see it on 30 December. Gladys and Mrs Kennedy went out shopping that night, but she was unable to go because she was ill. Gladys came in at about 11 o'clock that night. Colin Ross came to her house on 5 January, a little after 7pm.

Macindoe: 'As a matter of fact you are an invalid, aren't you? And your memory is not at all clear as to what happened on 5th January.'

Mrs Linderman: 'My mind is perfectly clear. Colin Ross came to my house after 7pm and left at something to 9.'

Alice Ballantyne, sister of Caroline Ross, was a pretty girl in her mid-teens. She testified that she was in the saloon for about two hours, arriving at about 12 o'clock and leaving at about 2pm.

Macindoe: 'During that time where did you sit?'

'In the little room off the bar, on the couch.'

When Alice was asked to remove her hat, she revealed auburn hair of the colour closest to Alma Tirtschke's of any witness. She said that in the saloon, she too let her hair down and combed it while standing before the mirror near the couch. On 5 January, she confirmed that Colin had been at her home between about 9 and 10.30.

Brennan: 'You have been pretty closely connected with the Ross family since your sister married Tom. Have you ever stopped out at their house ...?'

'Yes.'

'Slept there at times?'

'Yes; at weekends, but not too often.'

'Have you, at any time when you have been there, either used or seen other members of the family using the rugs or blankets in or about the house?'

'I noticed a brown one over the couch in the vestibule.'

'Have you ever lain on that couch or slept on it?'

'I have been sitting there.'

'Have you ever used them as rugs in the garden?'

'Yes.'

Macindoe: 'How old are you?'

'About 17.'

'How long have you had your hair up?'

'About two years.'

'When you comb your hair does it fall out all over the place?'

'Yes, it does fall out.'

'On the occasion when you slept at Ross's house ... [d]id you ever use that brown blanket?'

'Yes ... When I have been sick I have sat on it on the couch.'

'Did you do your hair over the blanket?'

'I can't remember.'

Stanley Young was now called for the defence. He stated again that the last he saw of Alma she was standing near the Adam and Eve Hotel, on the corner of Alfred Place and Little Collins Street. In answer to Macindoe, Young said that the girl looked back towards the arcade: 'She appeared to be waiting for somebody or lost.'

Maxwell now announced that this concluded the evidence for the defence.

Unexpectedly, Macindoe asked permission to recall two witnesses. Maxwell immediately objected: the Crown's case had officially closed the day before. Macindoe argued that Olive Maddox had not been asked by defence counsel when she saw Ross on 5 January. Brennan declined the responsibility for what was, for both sides, an oversight.

Macindoe also asked permission to recall the Government Analyst, Mr Price, in connection with Mrs Wain's hair.

Maxwell's response: 'But there were dozens of people in that cubicle with all kinds of hair!'

Justice Schutt allowed both witnesses to be recalled.

In answer to Macindoe, Price stated that a sample of the hair of Gladys Wain had been handed to him by Detective Piggott. It had no similarity to the hair on the blankets. Cross-examined, Price admitted he had not seen a sample of Miss Ballantyne's hair, nor that of her sister.

Macindoe then recalled Olive Maddox. The Crown case having officially closed the previous day, Maddox had been permitted to be in court and thus heard the evidence for the defence, including the times Ross was said to be at the Ballantynes' in West Melbourne.

Macindoe: 'What time was it?'

Maddox: 'It may have been—it was—any time after 10 to half-past 10, when I first seen [*sic*] him.'

Macindoe: 'From 10 to half-past 10!'

'From nine to half past nine—any time from then.'

Maxwell: 'Have you spoken about the case to anyone since you were here?'

'No, I have been too frightened to say anything ...'

Maxwell: 'And you are certain the time was from nine to half-past nine?'

'I am positive that was the time.'

Maxwell turned to His Honour and announced that this was the end of his case.

20. Judgment

At 4am, when the city was still asleep and the artificial lighting in the neighbourhood of Gun Alley resembled that on the night of the tragedy, the jury visited the scene of the crime. Returning at a quarter to six, the jurors breakfasted and prepared themselves for the addresses of counsel and the summing-up of the judge. It was a weary-looking body of men that shuffled into the jury box at 10.05am on the trial's fifth day.

The day was muggy, the courtroom hot and oppressive. Maxwell rose to begin his address to the jury. The *Age* said it seemed 'a stupendous task for a man afflicted with blindness and unable to read his brief, to array, dissect and riddle, if he could, the mass of ... evidence produced against the prisoner'.

Maxwell confronted the jury:

> I feel that no man has ever stood in that dock more heavily handicapped than the man you are now trying—Colin Campbell Ross. Before he was put on trial ... his case had been judged by the community. Sentence had been pronounced before a single word of evidence in this trial had been given. I know of no case ... where the public mind has been so inflamed and public passion so aroused

... [E]very scrap of information in the press ... was eagerly seized on by the community, and discussed and rediscussed and conclusions drawn. Before that man was put in the dock the community of Victoria—yes, of Australia—had firmly made up its mind that Colin Campbell Ross was guilty of the murder and ought to be hanged.

Maxwell lifted his hand—

But, gentlemen, thank God that ... verdicts are not obtained by popular acclamation, and a man is not condemned by an irresponsible community.
... in all human probability there is no man sitting in this jury box this morning who ... had not read everything ... in this case; who had not practically made up his mind ... [But e]ach of you has taken a solemn oath that in this matter you will find a verdict according to the evidence ...

During the previous four days of the trial the court had never been so quiet.

Maxwell referred to the witnesses as the reputable and the disreputable. That the whole of the Crown case relied on a 'quintet of disreputables'—the two women, Maddox and Matthews, whose stories obligingly stretched according to the evidence required, and the three men, 'the gaolbirds Harding and Dunstan and that solitary derelict Upton'.

Maxwell spent an hour comparing the similarity in outline, but inconsistency in detail in the alleged confessions made by Ross to Matthews and Harding. He then considered the other evidence. The Crown would have the jury believe Alma was last seen in the arcade by Mrs Edmonds at 2.45pm—

There the Crown would have [the schoolgirl] disappear, but there is a witness named [Stanley] Young ... whom the Crown has not called at this trial, who carries the movements further ... One of the Italians had said that there was a light in the cafe at a quarter to 1 o'clock in the morning ... [they] might have mistaken the reflection of a light there.

The *Midnight Sun* noted the prisoner's composure. '[Ross] sat in the dock and listened. Even the people outside, who had condemned him ... would have admitted that he was bearing the ordeal remarkably well ...'

Maxwell suggested the pieces of serge were scattered along the Footscray Road by hoaxers after the publication of Harding's inquest deposition.

Would not the police have seen the serge if it had been lying on the road since December 31? The only inference to be drawn was that it was not there when the police looked for it.

Aware, however, that there was indeed another inference—police malfeasance, as Ross had openly suggested—Maxwell attempted to dignify his address by renouncing a claim which he himself found unacceptable. It was a miscalculation—

I absolutely dissociate myself from Ross's statement that the police are trying to prove that he did this dastardly thing on framed-up evidence. From my knowledge of the officers involved, they are incapable of such a thing and I say that the case, so far as the police are directly concerned, has been most fairly conducted, and that they gave their evidence as fairly as possible.

Forever afterwards, Piggott would consider Maxwell's remark a gratifying vindication of police conduct in the Ross investigation.

The *Midnight Sun*: 'While Mr Maxwell was speaking, the faces of the jurors were a study. Every one of them listened intently; but they were tired, and you could not help thinking, from the expressions of some of them, that a number had already made up their minds ... Two or three of the younger men, seemed to be revolving deeply a mental problem. But these were the minority. The majority had rather a set look.'

Maxwell concluded:

> It is not the evidence in this case that I am afraid of, it is the preconceived opinion and judgment ... If a verdict were asked today from the public outside, a verdict of guilty would be given without hesitation. You are representing that community. [But y]ou have been set apart, and have taken an oath to find a verdict only according to the evidence ...

Maxwell finished at 12.40pm. The court adjourned until 2 o'clock.

In his address after lunch, Macindoe said the Crown had proven beyond all reasonable doubt that Ross was guilty. 'It has been suggested to the jury by Mr Maxwell that the Crown has suppressed the evidence of Young ...'

The defence were now to begin paying for Maxwell's praise for the police.

> ... [But] Young's evidence is quite immaterial in view of the evidence of a reputable witness that Ross admitted to a man named White ... that he was talking to the girl at 3.30pm on the 30th. That witness is Detective Brophy and the defence do not deny that [he] is an honest man. The only denial came from the prisoner.

Maxwell had questioned the credibility of the 'five disreputables', but Macindoe denied it:

> Olive Maddox might be all that Ross says she is, but ... is it conceivable that she or any woman would attempt to hang a man for the sake of £1000 ... Ivy Matthews, a fool she might be, but do you think, having seen her and heard her, that she is a woman who would stoop so low ...?

As to Harding (and, by implication, Dunstan too): 'He is only a shopbreaker, and such a criminal is preferable to an attacker of innocent little girls, who is a cur at heart, while the shopbreaker, after all, is a bit of a sport.'

Macindoe was either deliberately misleading the jury as to the gravity and extent of Harding's past convictions or he was genuinely not aware of Harding's criminal record. It seems most likely that Macindoe knew that Harding was more than a shopbreaker.

'There is one feature of the case,' Macindoe continued, 'that my learned friend has never dealt with. Did you hear him explain how it was that Ivy Matthews or Harding ever knew that the girl Linderman was in the saloon that night? Did he ever suggest that, gentlemen? Did he?'

As a matter of fact he had. Maxwell had noted that Matthews had made additions to her original testimony in order to accommodate the evidence of the other witnesses, including Harding, whose evidence (including the reference to Linderman) was published in all three Melbourne dailies after the inquest. But Macindoe was persuading the jury to forget this: he knew the defence had no right of reply now.

'But Harding, how did he know about Linderman? And how is [my friend] to get over that?' asked Macindoe:

> Matthews deposed to certain things that Harding also deposed to. It is not suggested that they saw one another

before the trial. Accused says the coppers told them, but my friend, quite rightly, refrained from saying anything against the members of the police force. How comes it that these people know these things if the prisoner has not told them?

Upton had proven an embarrassment.

Gentlemen ... I tell you quite candidly that I would not ask you to swing a cat on the evidence given by Upton.

Turning his attention to the defence witnesses, Macindoe asked:

Can you not see Mrs Kee, a sympathetic soul, going along to sympathise with Mrs Ross when her son was arrested? Can you not see these two old women talking things over and looking about for loopholes, hear Mrs Kee saying, 'I remember seeing him on the tram one night,' but, not remembering the particular night, she fits in the night of December 30. Mr Dawsey is not telling the truth; he has given no satisfactory explanation as to how he fixed that particular night or why he should regard what he saw as important ... Is it not clear that Bradley is making a mistake and thinking of some other night? Patterson said he could not tell within an hour what time it was he saw Ross. Studd is a little more definite, but statements as to time have always to be taken with great caution.

Of the alibi disproving that Ross spoke to Olive Maddox on 5 January, Macindoe stated:

The real crux is where Ross was between 9 and 10 o'clock. It is suggested that he went to the house of Mrs Ballantyne. The house was full yet not one stranger is brought here ... No; we have Tom Ross's wife and her sister Alice—that little girl who combs her hair all over the place and drops it all about.

As Brennan would later explain, other people at the Ballantyne house on Thursday 5 January were not called as witnesses because the evidence already seemed overwhelming that Ross was there soon after 9pm on that date. 'They would have been called,' Brennan said, 'had it been known that Olive Maddox was going to say that it was about half-past nine that she saw Colin at Jolimont. But that was not said until after the case for the defence was closed.'

'But the best witness for the Crown in this case is the prisoner himself,' continued Macindoe:

> Did he not strike you as a desperate man ...? An innocent man faced with a charge like this does not make charges of corruption and conspiracy against police officers. Do you believe one solitary word of that? His counsel would not have it ... Who are the other witnesses? The brothers and the poor old mother. If the mother were called here to complete an alibi, do you think she would hesitate?... What about the brothers Ronald and Stanley? Do you believe anything they said?... What would one expect them to do if their brother was charged with murder?... And Tom and Tom's wife, and the little girl of 17 with auburn hair. Did not the little girl strike you as a witness who would say anything? A girl of 17, brought here with her hair up to make her seem like an adult.

Brennan [interjecting]: 'She swore she had worn her hair up for two years!'

Macindoe: 'She sat "on the couch" at Footscray, and her hair "might have fallen out". Unfortunately that was some months ago. That woman Gladys had her hair compared with the hairs found and with Alma Tirtschke's hair and the analyst said it was nothing like. Why did not the defence take a sample of Alice Ballantyne's hair to the analyst and ask him to compare it with Alma Tirtschke's and that on the blankets? It might have been as easily distinguished from the dead girl's as Gladys Linderman's was.'

[The defence had tried to get tests of its own done on the hairs, but the Crown had denied the request.]

Having spoken for an hour and 20 minutes, Macindoe concluded:

> The Crown case is built up on a foundation of circumstances ... and on to that is grafted the various admissions made by the accused to these different witnesses. If any one of those witnesses alone had to be considered you might be justified in saying 'we will not convict', but ... [h]aving regard to all the circumstances and the accumulated effect of all the different statements, I put it to you beyond all reasonable doubt that the prisoner should be found guilty of wilful murder.

At 3.22pm, Justice Schutt embarked on a two-hour address to the already-tired jury. He emphasised that a jury cannot convict the prisoner unless they are satisfied of his guilt beyond all reasonable doubt. They were told: 'You must entirely free your minds from any opinions you might have formed of the case before you heard the evidence ... your verdict must be grounded on that evidence and on nothing else.' Schutt never indicated any weaknesses or inconsistencies in the Crown evidence. He merely restated it.

As Brennan would later observe, 'Once Ross was put upon his trial nothing was, or indeed could be, said which did not appear to point to his guilt.' At one point Justice Schutt reminded the jury that Ross denied the words of Brophy, Matthews, Maddox, Harding, Dunstan and Upton. But His Honour never noted the implausibility of

White/Pommeroy's admission to Brophy; the conflicts between the Matthews and Harding confessions; that Dunstan had read Harding's inquest evidence in the newspaper and then confirmed it; that Maddox's evidence that the girl was awake in the beaded room at 5 o'clock conflicted with Harding having her asleep in the cubicle at that time.

The jury was not directed to consider why Ross should have confessed at all. Nor were they told that they should approach an alleged confession quite differently from evidence dealing with substantive facts.

It was 5.20pm. Schutt invited the jury to retire and consider their verdict.

Brennan would later hypothesise about the jury's deliberations:

> It is extremely likely that, in dealing with Matthews's and Harding's evidence, [the jury] would reason that 'Harding says this,' and 'Matthews says this,' and then draw inferences unfavourable to Ross from the supposed cumulative effects of the two sets of evidence; and extremely unlikely that they would reason that 'Harding says that Ross said this,' and 'Matthews says that Ross said that,' and then go on to draw inferences favourable to Ross from the fact that they make him say totally inconsistent things. Yet this is what they should have done.

He also suggested that, on the basis of Justice Schutt's summing-up, it was impossible the jury could have realised:

> ... that they were dealing with a case absolutely without parallel in the annals of British criminal jurisprudence, in which they were invited to hang a man on contradictory confessions, which he is alleged, by thoroughly

disreputable witnesses, to have made, which on his oath he denied having made, for the making of which no reason could be assigned, and which were so seriously in conflict as to suggest that they were never made.

All that day crowds had thronged the streets adjacent to the Law Courts. At 9.18pm the command was given to place the prisoner at the bar. The *Age* said Ross was '... obviously suffering under great strain'. His lips twitched involuntarily, and he gazed earnestly at the jurymen as they trooped in.

But the jury, after four hours' deliberation, had failed to reach a verdict. Justice Schutt, himself looking very tired, suggested that the court and the jury should rest for the night.

Saturday. Leaden skies and the occasional moist breeze. At 10.30am Justice Schutt took his seat. Though looking worn, Ross appeared more composed. The jury stood in two lines in front of the jury box.

'We have not been able to reach agreement,' said the foreman.

Schutt: 'Do you think it will be any use considering the matter further?'

The foreman: 'Perhaps within the next hour we may have something to say.'

The atmosphere again became tense as the jury withdrew. Outside, those waiting remained on tenterhooks. The crowd was growing every minute. Across the road, personnel from the Navy Office had come out onto the footpath. Even as far down the street as 'Central', the telephone exchange, girls perched precariously on the window balconies.

The *Midnight Sun*:

> The callousness of those waiting hundreds was remarkable ... and rather ugly. The words 'guilty' and 'hang' were uttered in quite cheerful tones. You could have said that crowd in Lonsdale Street was enjoying itself ... they had eager looks on their faces. They were there for the thrill of it ...

At 11.26 the 12 men emerged. Ross was brought back into the dock.

The judge's associate: 'Gentlemen of the jury, have you agreed upon your verdict?'

The foreman: 'We have.'

'Is the prisoner at the bar guilty or not guilty of murder?

The foreman: 'Guilty.'

Ross started slightly, moistened his lips with his tongue, and stared ahead.

The associate [turning to Ross]: 'Prisoner at the bar, you have been found guilty of murder. Have you now anything to say why sentence of death should not be pronounced upon you according to law?'

Ross: 'Yes, sir. I still maintain that I am an innocent man, and that my evidence is correct. If I am hanged, I will be hanged an innocent man. My life has been sworn away by desperate people.'

Schutt: 'Prisoner at the bar, you have been found guilty of the crime of wilful murder and it only remains for me to pronounce the dread sentence of the law.'

The associate solemnly carried a folded square of black silk up to the judge and placed it upon his wig. Justice Schutt had never before passed a sentence of death. 'Prisoner at the bar, the sentence of the court is that you be taken from the place where you now stand to the place whence you came, and that you be taken thence at such time and place as His Excellency the Governor shall direct, and that you then and there be hanged by the neck until you be dead.'

Ross: 'I am innocent, Your Honour.'

Justice Schutt: 'And may God have mercy on your soul.'

Ross: 'I am innocent!'

The warders hurried Ross out of view.

Outside the verdict was greeted with cheers and applause. The crowd began to surge forward, forcing themselves into the courtyard from all directions. A dozen police formed a cordon to guard the van. With his hands manacled before him, Ross was brought to the waiting van. Only now did the prisoner betray signs of collapse. All around, the crowd shouted and jeered. They were forced back, leaving just sufficient space for the Black Maria. Amid cries of 'Scoundrel!' 'Serves you right, you cur!' 'Hangin's too good for you!' the vehicle swept up Lonsdale Street towards the gaol. Hundreds lingered, cheering for Harding and, later, for Olive Maddox and Ivy Matthews.

At Russell Street the mood was like Christmas. Superintendent Potter provided a doorstop press meeting. He stated that while many police had contributed to the work of the prosecution, the chief credit was due to senior detectives Piggott and Brophy. Potter welcomed Maxwell's dissociating himself from the prisoner's comments. He added: 'Regarding the allegations of framing up—and other things—whatever there might have been in the past there is nothing of that nature now. There are too many checks and counterchecks on the detectives for that sort of thing to happen these days.'

While most of the press fully supported the verdict, the *Midnight Sun* commented:

Ross had been tried by public opinion before the jury went into the box. Mr Maxwell had significantly said: 'It is not the evidence here I fear; it is the preconceived opinion.' ... [T]he extraordinary publicity given to the charges made it impossible for any average collection of men to clear their minds of convictions on one side or the other.

A further flaw in Ross's trial was revealed the day he was condemned. Victorian Attorney-General Arthur Robinson was informed that both the *Herald* and the *Argus* had published the names, addresses and occupations of the jurors, leaving them open to interference. The Victorian Legislature had not yet acknowledged that newspapers could be thus in contempt of court: there was no law to prevent it. But, as a result, a clause was inserted in the Juries Bill—one of several historic firsts wrought by Ross's trial.

But what of the victim, the child who had been obscured, even maligned, during the trial?

21. Alma

Nell Alma Tirtschke was born on 14 March 1909, on a mining station in the arid heart of Western Australia. Her mother was Ellen (Nell) Emily Eliza Alger, born in 1878 at Bendigo, Victoria, the daughter of Henry Charles Alger, a clerk, and his wife, Emily Louisa Alma Holder. Alma's father, Charles Henry Tirtschke, Harry to all who knew him, was born at St Arnaud, Victoria, in 1876. He was the eldest child of a Prussian immigrant, Heinrich Charles August Tirtschke, a builder, and Elizabeth Le Maitre.

Harry and Nell married in May 1908 at St Augustine's Church of England, Leonora. A town 220 kilometres north of Kalgoorlie, it was surrounded by harsh and desolate country. Harry worked as a carpenter for Northern Mines, in a township called Lawlers. It had the nickname 'Lawless' and was a further 120 kilometres north, up a dirt road that, when drought broke, was impassable. In 1903 a travelling writer observed: 'Lawlers is a WA Siberia ... Everyone must carry water and take more than usual risks. Were it not for the fortnightly visits of Faiz and Tagh Mahomet with their camel team, Lawlers would be as isolated as the mutineers of the Bounty on Pitcairn Island.'

Harry and Nell made the journey from Leonora to Lawlers, where they set up a modest home in company-provided accommodation: a shack without amenities. Here, Nell gave birth to the couple's first child. They named her Nell after her mother, and Alma for her maternal grandmother.

In 1911, Harry Tirtschke earned a coveted position in Southern Rhodesia (now Zimbabwe), with paid assistance for the family's relocation. There, at the mining centre known as Kimberley Reefs, Nell gave birth to her second child, Viola, in January 1912, after a difficult pregnancy marked by fever and oedema (an excess of fluid in the body tissues). The birth was registered in Salisbury and gave the father's occupation as a mining contractor.

After three years in Africa, Nell became pregnant again. She wanted to return to Australia for the birth, where she could have a proper attendant present, perhaps even a qualified doctor. Nell and the children took a separate steamer passage home to Australia, probably because Harry had to finalise his work commitments in Rhodesia. She secured two berths on the SS *Runic*. Nell would stay with her parents in Melbourne until Harry arrived.

But Nell had been suffering for some time from what would later be described by her family as Bright's disease—a disorder of the kidneys associated with oedema and loss of protein in the urine. While these symptoms are indicative of Bright's disease, in pregnancy they can signal a far more dangerous condition. It appears that neither Harry nor Nell knew this fact. On Boxing Day 1914, between the ports of Albany and Adelaide, Nell toppled from her berth and suffered a series of seizures. Finally she lay dead. The process of miscarriage being incomplete, the ship's doctor finished the job, taking from her a foetus which, though dead, was recognisably male.

In the *Runic*'s log, James Kearney, Ship's Master, wrote:

At 8.40am on the 26 Dec 1914 in lat 35.18 S long 125.48 E Mrs Ellen Tirtschke died of Puerperal

Eclampsia at the age of 35. She being a native of Victoria Australia leaving on board 2 children aged 5 and 3 years.

The next day Nell was buried at sea.

Did Alma remember her mother's death? Although only three at the time, Viola did recall the ship, and an occasion when she lay beside her sister, and, looking upward, observed the underside of the berth in which her mother lay.

The *Runic* steamed into Port Phillip Bay. Before she docked, Alma and Viola were sent ashore to the quarantine station at Portarlington. Two weeks later they were brought to Port Melbourne. Viola recalls: 'I can remember Grandpa Alger and Grandma Tirtschke, they came to ... Port Melbourne [to meet us] ... we got on the cable tram and came to Hawthorn ... then it was [decided], even on the tram ... they made up their minds as to who would take the children. And my grandmother won—if you'd like to say that ...'

The tram rattled out to the Bridge Road terminus, where the party alighted. Here in suburban Hawthorn the children would live with their father's parents, Henry and Elizabeth Tirtschke, in the house known as 'Thelma' at 6 Connell Street. The grandparents could rely for help on their five married daughters: Elizabeth Stuart, Maie Murdoch, Ellen Cooper, Ivy Park and Alice Scott. Harry Tirtschke returned to Melbourne in 1915, but did not stay long; nor did he take his children with him. He returned to the Western Australian goldfields alone. His parents understood he must pursue the work for which he was qualified, and agreed to take care of the children for the time being.

At 'Thelma' Alma and Viola settled into a disciplined routine. They shared a room of their own with a window looking out on to a passionfruit vine that sprawled over the property's side fence. It was a simply furnished room with a dresser, a two-door wardrobe near the window and, occupying the main space, a double bedstead. For the next seven years—until 1921—both children would sleep in this bed, Alma on the side nearest the door and Viola on the side closest to the window.

Their 68-year-old grandmother was vigilant to a fault. Both girls were usually consigned to bed no later than 7 o'clock and sometimes even earlier. Discipline was strict. As the eldest, Alma was expected to know better than let her younger sister do something naughty. Alma knew her limits, but Viola tested them. Being held accountable meant the older girl was the more prudent child, reticent in behaviour and speech.

The children's aunts sometimes looked after them for a few hours or a day, providing a welcome break for their grandparents. After the war, the annual Anzac Day parade of returned soldiers through Melbourne's city streets became a regular feature of life for Alma and Viola. Auntie Lizzie and Uncle Jim (Mr and Mrs Stuart) or their daughter Jessie usually collected the girls from Connell Street on Anzac Day morning and took them into the city by tram.

Both girls wore ribbons in their hair and were dressed in their best frocks for the outing. Grandma had even bought Viola a brand new pair of black patent leather lace-up shoes. They arrived in the city at about half-past ten, and stood at the edge of the footpath, the children at the front, cousin Jessie, Aunt Lizzie and Uncle Jim standing behind them. Some children waved miniature Union Jacks on sticks, others Australian flags. Drums were beating, a band played; and then at last the soldiers came marching past.

It seemed a long time, the soldiers passing. Perhaps Jessie's fiancé, George Murphy, would not be well enough to keep pace this year. He had to watch his breathing. And then, finally ... there he was! Uncle Jim gave a cheer, Jessie and Aunt Lizzie clapped. And the girls looked on, weary from standing at the kerb all morning but doing their best to applaud their cousin's future husband. They knew that if they could just hold on a bit longer there'd be ice-cream.

Restless Viola was releasing some of her pent-up energy in a little jig on the bluestone flags of the gutter. Nevertheless, when George came by, she applauded and it seemed he gave her a wink. Or was it Jessie he winked at? Viola couldn't tell.

Afterwards, there was a cold buffet at the Murdochs' flat at Masonic Chambers. On the way to the tramstop in the afternoon, Aunt Lizzie bought ice-creams for her two nieces. Then the girls boarded the tram for Hawthorn with their cousin. Free of Aunt Lizzie's authority, Viola persuaded 22-year-old Jessie to sit them at the front of the tram, in the dummy. It was a breezy ride back to Hawthorn.

The girls arrived at the terminus windblown but happy. 'Thelma', in Connell Street, was just over the bridge and a block down. In Burwood Road the basalt pitchers of the gutters had all been pulled up and left in a line along the edge of the footpath.

Viola was keen for a run, but Jessie disagreed: 'You'll never learn to be a lady if you go running and jumping all over the footpath like that.'

Viola hopped up onto the line of assembled bluestone pitchers and trotted off along the top of them. 'Come back here!' Jessie called.

'But I'm not running!' replied Viola.

Occasionally she missed her step and once she fell, grazing a knee. Her feet slipped more and more on the wobbly and uneven stones. 'Viola!' Jessie cried, afraid the little girl might sprain an ankle. Alma, who looked suspiciously like she was enjoying the chase, was told to stifle her merriment and keep up with her older cousin. Once past the park, Viola dashed down Barton Street to the corner of Connell, where she waited, panting and dishevelled, for Alma and Jessie to catch up. When they did, both girls were hot and out of breath.

Neither Jessie nor Alma could say a word before Grandma smacked Viola all the way down the hall and into her bedroom. It was Viola's new shoes that gave her away. They were scratched and scuffed and utterly ruined.

Alma was six when, on 12 May 1915, she was recorded in the Pupils' Register of State School number 293, Hawthorn West. She skipped grade two, being promoted to grade three at the end of 1916.

Her grade six year in 1920 was an important one. In 1918 the Hawthorn West State School had become a Central School, which meant that the courses for the first two years of secondary education, or high school, were now taught in place of the elementary grades seven and eight. Children in grade six had to face their 'quallies'—exams for the qualifying certificate—which determined eligibility for secondary schooling. The inspector's report for that year stated:

> Grade six is very well taught ... and the quality of the work is very creditable. Very intelligent answers were given on the thought of the reading lessons and the teaching of arithmetic, grammar, drawing and history ... was much above the average ... Work books and home

exercises are very good. It was a pleasure to observe the work and to test the knowledge of this grade ...

Of the 55 students in Alma's grade six who presented for the qualifying certificate, 38 obtained it, including Alma. Her school reports survive, with the teacher's comment for the first term of 1921—'Good ability, but talkative'.

School ended for the day at 4 o'clock. Alma and Viola would walk home, not dallying, for Grandma expected them. Viola: 'If we were late home from school she'd be halfway up the street looking for us.'

In July 1921 the girls' grandfather became seriously ill with bronchial pneumonia. He struggled to breathe lying in his bed, so he was moved to the front parlour and sat up in his armchair by the fire where Grandma nursed him. When it became clear the end was in sight, each of his five daughters visited to pay their respects. He was able to say little between the rasping breaths of his fluid-filled lungs, yet at some point on his deathbed he expressed concern for Alma and Viola. It might have been an innocuous remark, suggesting it would be a pity or a shame if the children were separated. Years later Grandpa's words would be relayed to Viola portentously. She was told he'd said: 'Do not part those children or there will be tragedy.'

On 29 September 1919 Harry Tirtschke had remarried in Western Australia, to an English girl named Emily Kate Rennell. He had since returned to Victoria, where he was now working as a carpenter at Maffra, a country town 180 kilometres east of Melbourne. He had bought a block of land there and was building a house on it so that eventually he, Emily Kate and the children could start a new life together.

In the first week of August, at the age of 86, Grandpa died. On the morning of Friday 5 August 1921 a private service was conducted in the front parlour of 'Thelma'. The two little girls wore black frocks and stood on either side of their father. Their stepmother was not present, having remained in Maffra.

Grandpa's casket lay open for viewing. Alma laid a posy of jonquils on her grandfather's breast, and Viola a bunch of violets:

> And we said goodbye to Grandpa that way ... then the hearse came along, a horse-drawn hearse ... And that was it. Then the blinds were drawn for about ... three months ... Grandma went into deep mourning.

It was a five-hour train trip back to Maffra and time off work meant time without pay; besides which, Harry had his wife to return to. He wanted to begin the process of reuniting his family and in view of Alma's comparative maturity and obedience and the fact that her studies were progressing well, it was decided she would be the better company and greater help to Grandma over the ensuing months. She remained in Melbourne, while Viola left with her father.

> I left straight away with Dad, he had no time to wait. I can't remember really any loving arms or anything like that. I don't know where Alma was. See, Alma would have been at school most probably when I went ... It was all in a hurry.

School records for the second term of 1921 show that despite Grandpa's death Alma attained third place in her class of 33 and was dux of the F form's 16 girls.

May Hepburn was in the F form in 1921. She described Alma as being quiet but full of fun and life.

> Being in the same class, I knew her very well. She was always friendly with others in the class, and though she made a special friend of Mary Brown, she was always agreeable, and spoke and chatted with her other school mates.
> But once outside the school ground she was very reserved and spoke to nobody.

May went on to say that she thought Alma very clever, that she was a beautiful writer, and that her maps and drawings were the best in the class.

As a student in the E form in 1921, Aggie Reid, then fifteen, would see Alma Tirtschke from day to day in the Central School.

> [Alma] was very clever at her lessons, but in every other way was different from the other girls. The only friend she seemed to have was Mary Brown. Alma was very quiet and seldom spoke to the girls and never to the boys at the school.

Many years later Aggie would elaborate:

> I can see her now, a little slim red-headed girl. Very neat ... The teachers were showing her as an example of how she did her work ... She used to do her schoolwork in one exercise book and then she had another one at home that she would rewrite it in and it was beautifully done. I remember the teacher talking about it.

The exercise book in which Alma did her best work was covered in brown paper and on the front bore the announcement, in neat lettering, that it was begun on 1 June and finished on 10 November 1921. It contained essays, conjugations of French verbs, maps and notes on history. Towards the back of the book appeared the one imposition, 'I must not smile in school', written 20 times in her small, uniformly neat hand. In due course, Grandma would proudly send this exercise book to Sydney and extracts from it, including Alma's last school essay, 'Duty First', would be reproduced in *Smith's Weekly*.

Grandma had taught the girl obedience. Alma knew not to ask impertinent questions. She was no prodigy but she was hardly permitted to be anything else. In the end she was everything her family, her education and her social world allowed her to be, the model of their expectations. For some, including many who knew her—and many who did not—Alma Tirtschke would become a paragon of innocence and virtue. But was this perhaps just a trick of the light?

Alma's docility with her elders, her attentive obedience to their instructions, her good conduct and her application to schoolwork gave her, in Grandma's words, a 'popularity with her masters'. At school Alma was the headmaster's right hand. Sometimes she would help him with the work of the office.

In 1922, Uncle John Murdoch said of her:

Though of a bright disposition, she was somewhat reserved, and did not make friends readily like some girls. She lacked the vivacious manner that encourages chance acquaintance.

Alma's reserved nature is confirmed not only by her schoolmates Aggie Reid and May Hepburn, but by her sister too, who remembers Alma as 'soft in speech and soft in manner'.

Some time towards the end of November 1921, Alma went to school as usual and delivered some news about herself to her classmates apparently out of character, and yet disturbingly prescient.

On 4 January 1922 Mrs Sharp, a neighbour of the Tirtschkes, spoke to a *Herald* reporter. Mrs Sharp's daughter, Doris, had been friendly with Alma.

> ... I knew the grandmother and Alma as well as anybody. My little girl was one of the pall-bearers at [Alma's] funeral yesterday.
>
> They were people who were in very comfortable circumstances, and when Mrs Tirtschke sold her house six or seven weeks ago she obtained more than £1000 for it. Soon after the sale, Alma came to me one day and told me about a visit to a spiritualist.
>
> 'What do you think, Mrs Sharp,' she said, 'my grandmother has been to a spiritualist who told her that she would very soon have terrible trouble.'
>
> Alma gave me no other details. As Mrs Tirtschke had lost her husband only in August ... I thought it was possible she did go to a spiritualist. Later on, however, one of Alma's schoolmates, Mrs Pooley's little girl, told me that Alma had informed her friends at school that she herself had been to a spiritualist and had been told that she would not live three months ...
>
> I have thought a good deal ... about Alma's version of the visit to the spiritualist, and I think now it is possible she was keeping something back. She was always a sad-faced child, but when she spoke about trouble for her grandmother she was undoubtedly very concerned about something. She wasn't the kind of girl who would imagine the incident.

The reporter needed confirmation that Alma had attended a spiritualist and had then made fateful remarks about herself to her classmates. The Pooley family would not cooperate with him, but he'd obtained another name, possibly from Mrs Sharp.

The reporter bowled along up Burwood Road to number 29, the home of a schoolgirl who knew Alma. He had a word with her father and after a while the man agreed to fetch his daughter. She came reluctantly into the front room. So traumatic had recent events been, that initially the reporter had difficulty extracting any information from her. Finally she agreed to speak on condition that her name would not appear in the newspaper. That Wednesday night, 4 January, the *Herald* carried the story on its front page under the heading 'Tragedy Foretold'. The reporter described his young source: 'One of the [school]girls, fifteen years of age, of a high order of intelligence, has just left the school where Alma had been attending.'

When her father showed her the *Herald* that night, the girl laughed. It was the first good laugh she'd had since the shocking events of the New Year. Because of the description of 'a high order of intelligence', the girl knew her anonymity was secure: everyone knew she'd repeated the seventh grade! Seventy-five years would pass before Aggie Reid would be prepared to confirm that what she had told the reporter that day was true.

In her interview Aggie says:

> Some weeks ago Alma told us at school that she had been to a spiritualist and that she had been told she would not live for many months. I don't remember now if Alma said three or six months, but at the time I told my mother and when we heard of Alma's death, mother said that I had said three months. Of course, we girls took no notice of it at the time, and regarded it as fun ...

The *Herald* of 5 January carried not only a further corroboration of the spiritualist story from May Hepburn, but more complete details from Grandma herself. 'After reading the *Herald* last night, the old lady ... did not permit a moment's hesitation to influence her in her desire to do justice to the memory of her little relative ...'

> Sometime after I had sold my property in Hawthorn, while I was living in Jolimont, I was contemplating buying some house property. At that time Mrs Plum was recommended to me as having excellent powers as a spiritualistic medium ... I thought, therefore, that no harm could be done by my calling on her for advice regarding the buying of this property, about which I had to decide, at the latest, the following day.
>
> With the view of getting one of my daughters to accompany me I called at Masonic Chambers, but unfortunately all the adults of the company then present were engaged. One of my daughters then suggested I should take little Alma for company, and I agreed to do so.
>
> We went down to the place where the seance was to be held—in Mrs Plum's rooms, at Furlong's studios, over the Royal Arcade ...
>
> Upstairs in the room there were several people present in addition to Mrs Plum. I had with me papers relating to the property about which I wanted to get advice. They were in an envelope, which I handed to Mrs Plum. She put this to her forehead and closed her eyes. After thinking a little while, she told me I was not to decide to buy the property the next day.

The reporter then asked if any reference was made to her granddaughter. Through her tears, Grandma said:

> I had known for some time that little Alma's father had intended to take her up to Maffra to live with him and Violet [*sic*], her younger sister. Alma had been a

companion, friend and grandchild to me for many years, and I was contemplating her probable absence with great unhappiness. I asked Mrs Plum whether she could tell me if my son intended to take Alma away only for a little while or for good.

Mrs Plum again closed her eyes, said 'No' and shook her head ... We then left. There was no reference made to any probable trouble by death for anyone.

If Alma made those statements to Mrs Sharp and her schoolmates, we can only conclude she did so in some childish desire for a little notice, and exaggerated what she thought she had overheard.

Had some element of the seance troubled or disturbed Alma? Had she misheard or exaggerated what the medium, Mrs Plum, said? Had something of Grandpa's cautionary words about her separation from Viola been relayed to her and was this preying on her mind? What was it that compelled this normally reserved child to forecast her own imminent death?

Perhaps neither the seance nor Mrs Plum were the root of the problem. Only Mrs Sharp notes that when Alma spoke about the spiritualist, the girl was 'undoubtedly very concerned about something'. It can only be assumed that something very troubling was going on in Alma's mind, and that it was something she could not comfortably discuss nor openly bring to the attention of her aunts or her then 74-year-old grandmother. Perhaps Alma did not know how to discuss her problem because no one had taught her that it was possible to discuss it. As Grandma explained to *Smith's Weekly* journalist HC Maddison: 'No subject that a child should not hear was discussed in her presence.'

Alma was on the brink of puberty. Changes to her body were only just beginning, of which she knew nothing. As Viola explains, 'I was never taught anything. Anything like that was a sin and the devil would get me. And that's all—

how I was brought up.' These were times when children were kept in the dark about all matters sexual. And Alma could expect no enlightenment from her school. Like Alma, most young girls at the Hawthorn West Central School, even as they entered puberty and began menstruating, would still face years of blind ignorance about what was happening to them. The girls were taught nothing of the male physiology, either. Aggie Reid recalls:

> We weren't told anything. We were stupid, not like today. When you think of today ... No, no, it was never discussed. Our parents never told [us] ... No, we were absolutely stupid.

Viola:

> Alma would have been quite innocent ... She had no mention of men or anything like that. She was an innocent. A very innocent person.

In February 1922, after only six months in Maffra with her father and stepmother, Viola returned, aged ten, to her grandmother, then 75. Grandma would live to the age of 92 and would continue caring for Viola until 1933. For those next 11 years, until Viola's 21st year, Grandma would exert an unremittingly strict and oppressive vigilance over her granddaughter. Having lost Alma, Grandma would not under any circumstances allow Viola from her sight. In her late teens, Viola was finally, and on a few rare occasions, permitted to go out with friends. She recalls:

> Grandma said to me, 'Don't you dare come home with a baby otherwise you'll be kicked out,' and that's the story I got if I went out ... That was as much as I learnt about that.

Asked if Grandma ever told her anything about where a baby might come from, Viola answered: 'No, never, never, not a thing. I knew nothing. I was absolutely ignorant.'

For Viola, the transformation from young girl to young woman did not occur until her mid-teens; at that time, she recalls, she had left school to take up office work as a junior secretary:

> ... it was late, I was round about 16 ... I came home from work one day and my grandma said to me, 'Into the bathroom you go, Vi.' Right, I went into the bathroom ... and she gave me all these squares [of towelling] that she had made. I never inquired about it, I just accepted it for granted ... She'd made [the squares] for me. You know, this was, er, ah—menstruation ... She said ... 'You've got to wear these every month,' and that's how I started ... I never asked what it was about. I was never told ... I didn't know a jolly thing. I had no parents. I had no one. And neither did my sister.

22. In the midst of life ...

Alma last saw her schoolmates on 28 December 1921, when the Hawthorn West Central School had its annual end-of-year celebration. The children in the senior classes were invited and their teachers organised the evening. Tables were set up in the Christ Church hall and laid with fairy bread, cupcakes, slices of date loaf, apple slices and vanilla blancmange. To drink, there was lemonade, ginger ale or raspberry cordial. The social ran from 7.30–10.30pm.

That day Alma was at Grandma's new flat in Jolimont Road. Since the young girl would be moving to Maffra early in January, the social would be her last opportunity to farewell her teachers and friends. Alma wanted very much to attend the evening, but Grandma was concerned about the girl catching the tram home alone and in the dark. Finally, it was agreed that Alma could attend the social briefly, and then come straight home. It was no small victory for Alma. As Grandma said, within a week of Alma's death:

She just put in an appearance at the party and then tore herself away—with a consideration worthy of an understanding adult—to come back to allay my possible distress. She gave up her enjoyment on the great annual night of her school year in order to bring peace to my mind, and on that night, in view of her ability at her lessons, and popularity with her masters and schoolmates, a great fuss would have naturally been made over her.

One of the games played that night was called 'Assassin', otherwise known as 'Murder Wink'. Players form a circle in which one of them has secretly been designated the assassin. The players take it in turn to guess who they think is the killer. Meanwhile, the murderer may kill any of the circle by giving them a surreptitious wink. Murdered players must sit out of the game. The players remaining can only stop the killing by correctly guessing the murderer's identity. Aggie Reid remembers the student teacher, Mr Atkins, slaying her with a wink. She blushed to be winked at by such a young and good-looking returned soldier.

Did Alma have the opportunity to join in, before rattling sadly home on the cable tram?

Throughout 24–30 January 1922, the week before the school summer holidays ended, Gun Alley was, as the *Herald* noted, 'one of the most popular holiday resorts'. It had been one month since Alma was killed and the police guard was no longer thought necessary. Early on Monday 30 January, the Foundation Day holiday, a wreath of white lilies was laid where the body was found. Throughout the day family parties made their way to the alley. As the day progressed, further tributes of flowers, some in jam tins, were brought to the spot.

Around five thousand people visited—at times there was a queue nearly 100 metres long. As the afternoon faded the crowd dispersed. Some people bought 'finals' from newsboys under the clocks at Flinders Street station. And were confronted with the news that the body of Harry Tirtschke, father of Alma and Viola, had been discovered that morning in a field near Maffra. He had been out rabbit shooting and had a bullet wound in the back of his neck.

The Murdoch family had been under considerable strain during the inquest into Alma's death and had decided to send their 14-year-old-son Gordon to Maffra, to stay with Uncle Harry's family. Though 'short for his age', the boy was also a 'bright lad, handsome, and intelligent looking'. Gordon, however, resented his parents' wish to have him out of the way. According to Viola, 'he made a heck of a fuss', throwing a tantrum and sulking.

Finally, Gordon said he would go on condition he was given his own rifle and allowed to go rabbit hunting with Harry. And he would later state, 'My father bought the pea rifle for me the day before I left Melbourne.'

Harry had not attended the inquest. He was in partnership with another carpenter named Harry White and they were completing a construction contract. He was also finishing the house he was building for himself and his family.

Frustratingly for Gordon, Uncle Harry postponed the rabbit shoot. The boy pestered Harry about it, since he would be returning to Melbourne soon to resume his schooling. At last Harry agreed to go shooting on the Sunday of the long weekend: 29 January.

Viola:

On the Saturday Dad was working in the dining room and ... this hammer fell—he must have had it on a ledge up top—and it fell and hit him on the head and he wasn't well at all. [The next day] he said to Gordon, 'I don't think I feel like going [out to shoot rabbits].' And Gordon howled and made such a fuss that Dad said 'Oh rightio, we'll go.' So we went ... and he [and Gordon] left Mum and I and the dog at blackberry bushes and we were ... picking blackberries, when the dog started to howl. And it howled and howled ...

Gordon:

At about midday on the 29th January 1922, my uncle and I went two miles past Newry. We were riding bicycles. I had [my] rifle and my uncle had his gun ... We left our bicycles beside a tree on the side of the lane ... I fired 20 shots there and shot 2 rabbits, my uncle fired his shotgun several times and killed 6 rabbits ... We retraced our tracks ... My uncle said, 'You go down and see if you can get a shot in the gully while I go along by the fence on top of the hill. But keep behind me.' I saw my uncle go on ahead of me ... I fired two or three shots at some rabbits. I did not hit any of these rabbits. I did not see my uncle then. I walked along the gully a little way and then I went up along the road and walked along inside the fence till I came to where the bicycles were. I had 4 or 5 cartridges left then. I ... fired about two shots and hit one rabbit. I then went back towards the bikes ... I called out, 'Uncle!' ... and came back again to the bikes. I was calling out several times. It was getting dark then so I sat on a log. I had a letter from my mother in my pocket. I wrote on the back of it with a piece of charcoal: 'Gone home.' I pushed the piece of

paper into the hole in my uncle's bicycle. After that I
called out again. I got on my bicycle and rode towards
Newry ...

It was 8 o'clock and dark by the time Gordon pedalled down the main street of Newry. He asked directions to Maffra from James McCole, a grazier. On being asked what he was doing out so late, Gordon replied that he had lost his uncle in the bush while shooting. Seeing the boy's distress, McCole suggested the lad stop the night at his house. He telephoned Clem Woodhouse, the Maffra ironmonger, who in turn notified Emily Kate.

Viola and her stepmother had returned home, having finished their blackberry-picking hours before. As the darkness fell, Emily Kate became increasingly anxious, waiting with Viola at the front gate. They knew now that Gordon was safe, but there was no word about Harry. 'Mum and I walked up and down Church Street all night,' Viola recalls, 'with the dog crying all the time [too].'

McCole telephoned the police at Maffra, but the search was postponed until daylight. Meanwhile, Clem Woodhouse had fetched Arthur Waugh, who had access to a motor car. The pair drove to McCole's home and collected him and Gordon. It was 10.30pm when they arrived at the site of the rabbit shoot and even with the vehicle's headlights, the search proved fruitless.

McCole went out again at 4am to join a search party; Gordon, exhausted, slept. He was up and breakfasting when McCole returned. 'Did you find my uncle?' Gordon asked.

'Yes,' McCole said, 'we found him dead.' The boy did not say anything, but McCole noticed tears in his eyes.

At the coroner's inquest on 31 January, the doctor testified:

I discovered a punctured wound ... like a bullet wound and there were no marks of burnt powder about it ... I found the spine just below the head shattered and the spinal cord injured. Lying in the nervous substance I found the bullet ... Death would have been instantaneous.

Clement Woodhouse deposed about selling ammunition to Gordon:

I have had a pretty large experience in the use of firearms. The rifle produced is a 1902 model Winchester .22 calibre. In my opinion a point-blank shot could kill at 150 yards. In my opinion the bullet produced is a .22 calibre and it appears to be similar to those I sold the lad Murdoch. It is the same calibre as the rifle produced.

The coroner, Patrick Elliget of Bairnsdale, found that death was an accidental shooting by Gordon Murdoch. The boy had stated, during interrogation by Detective Bell from Melbourne. 'My uncle and I have always been on good terms ...'

After a short funeral service at Maffra, Harry's coffin was placed on the night train for Melbourne. Family members who had travelled to Maffra returned to Melbourne. In a brief graveside ceremony at the Brighton Cemetery, Harry's body was laid to rest in grave ZA 2178 that Wednesday. His grave was ten paces from that of Alma.

Following Harry's death Emily Kate stayed at Masonic Chambers. She was an Englishwoman, with no family in Australia. The *Herald*: '... she has expressed a desire to return to England'. In the weeks following Harry's death, it appears relations between Emily Kate and her husband's family became tense. She was suffering from depression and during this time, Grandma began taking charge of Viola more and more frequently. On 21 April, at the age of 31 years, Emily Kate made a will, nominating her mother Emily Kate Rennell of Plymouth, sole executrix, and bequeathing to her 'the whole of my real and personal estate' with the exception of some jewellery which she bequeathed to her sisters, and her signet ring which she left to Viola's most sympathetic aunt, Alice May Scott.

There was also the problem of Viola's custody, which Grandma wrested from the grieving widow. Two weeks afterwards, Emily Kate boarded the SS *Berrima*, a P&O branch line steamer bound for England by way of Durban and Cape Town. Emily Kate never again saw England; she died at sea on 9 June, a week out of Cape Town, near Dakar in Senegal. The following day her body was committed to the ocean.

'My two mums lie buried in the ocean,' says Viola. 'And I sometimes wonder if they ever met.'

Viola is insistent that her stepmother 'died of a broken heart'. Indeed, as recorded in the marine register, the cause of Emily Kate's death was 'morbis cordis syncope'. Accurate technically, the term might be legitimately, if loosely, translated, as the stoppage of a broken heart.

Viola was now a ward of the State and committed to the charge and keeping of her grandmother until the age of 21. Eleven years later, in 1933, Viola—finally of her majority and entitled to move out of home—discovered a letter addressed to her but still sealed, among her Grandma's possessions. It bore the postmark of a ship at sea—the SS *Berrima*.

My dear Viola,
  I'm wondering how you are & where you are. I regret I didn't bring you with me. I know you would have enjoyed the voyage, the children on the boat have such a splendid time, plenty of fun & games, & lots of room to run about. Our first port of call is Durban & then Cape

Town, somewhere near where you lived. We only call at the two ports. From Cape Town we go direct to England, reaching there on the 21st June. 'England's longest day.'

I haven't been seasick yet & we had a few rough days; the weather is perfect and very mild. We have been eleven days at sea & all looking forward to stretching our legs at Durban where we stay two days. Only one ship passed us & we've only seen a few 'flying fish', but I dare say we shall see something exciting at Durban.

Dear Viola I trust you are being a good girl & not doing those few naughty things I use[d] to get so angry over.

I want you to write to me every month regularly & tell me about yourself. With love & good wishes I remain—

EK Tirtschke your sincere mother.

Three weeks later Emily Kate died. The letter had been kept from Viola, perhaps because it arrived only days after the wired news of her stepmother's death. In due course, Emily Kate's will was executed. One instruction was that the body of Alma Tirtschke be disinterred and laid to rest with her father's remains. And it is there that Alma lies today.

23. Brennan appeals

Following Ross's trial, two jurors spoke anonymously to the *Herald*. They will be referred to here as Juror X, published on 3 March 1922, and Juror Y, published on 24 April 1922. Juror Y admitted that the jury 'discounted the veracity of the evidence for the defence from the first ... For the first three or four days of the trial, I think that every juror wished to hide from his fellow man what he thought ... During our evening leisure the subject was never seriously discussed, even after evidence for the Crown, which seemed incontrovertible, had been given.

'... it seemed to me as if some of the jurymen were afraid to say openly what they thought of Ross's evidence in case the jury should eventually fail to agree, and the hand of public scorn might point them out forever. The foreman later announced that he had thought all along that the best manner by which to ascertain the verdict of each juror should be by secret ballot, and after that pronouncement everyone seemed relieved.

'While Ross was giving his evidence ... he would glance at the jurors, and every time I caught his eyes he would drop his gaze. He could not bear my direct look for more than a fraction of a second ... I had no faith in him after that. I think that I am right in saying that at the close of the fourth day there were altogether nine of us who believed Ross to be guilty ...

'... We realised that in fairness to the prisoner and to the prosecution, a great deal of the evidence on both sides would have to be reconstructed [during our visit to the murder site].

'The first thing we did ... was to check the evidence of the man Upton. It will be remembered that this witness said he stood on the threshold of the door of the cafe, nearest Bourke Street, and from there, without having entered the cafe itself, he could see the end of the bar in the room nearest Little Collins Street. By investigation we ... found he could have seen the end of the bar only by going at least 3 feet into the room. After this we wouldn't have any of Upton's evidence ...'

He added that the jurors experimented to see if the mysterious noise Ellis heard at 1am came from Ross slamming the cafe door. The conclusion was that— whatever the noise was—it did not come from this source.

Juror Y: 'I think I am correct in saying that our lengthy visit, and the careful investigations we carried on, convinced us that the case for the Crown, except for the evidence of Upton, was a complete one.

'The real work of deliberating and estimating ... began ... after the judge had summed up ... All of us to a man relied on the evidence of Mrs Murdoch when she identified the serge produced in court ... We next examined the hair taken from the girl and the hairs found on the blankets. We concluded that they tallied, and ... we almost all decided that the hairs found on the blankets were different in colour to the hair of the two witnesses ... who said they had combed their hair in the cafe ...'

However, no samples of Alice or Carol Ballantyne's hair were provided as exhibits. It appears that the jury based their decision upon memory of the witnesses' hair in the witness box.

'After this we analysed the evidence for the Crown ... ten of us at once declared we believed [Ivy Matthews] ... the majority regarded her evidence as the most important for the prosecution. Harding's evidence then came under consideration. Six of us, including the foreman and myself, believed it. Four others wavered, and the two who could not bring themselves to believe ... Ivy Matthews, also supported the contention of the defence regarding Harding.

'I think I can say that none of us believed the prisoner ... we could not understand how any man could have given so minute a description ... of a girl whom he had seen passing by on the previous day, unless he knew more about her ...'

'When we were ready for the first ballot the foreman handed us slips of paper ... Some of the writers had actually printed the words in capital letters rather than risk their handwriting being subsequently recognised.'

At the first vote ten jurors recorded votes of guilty and two of not guilty.

'The foreman later addressed us. I think he suspected who were the two dissenting jurors. He pointed out that we were all agreed that Ross was responsible for the outrage and the death of his victim, and that the question of manslaughter or murder did not come into it. Ross's own counsel had not even suggested that it might be a case of manslaughter. The theory of insanity—even of temporary sexual insanity—had not been put forward, and we had to decide simply ... whether the prisoner was guilty or not guilty of murder.

'The two doubting jurors immediately recognised that if Ross had outraged and killed the girl, as they themselves believed, there could be no other verdict than that of guilty of murder.'

Less than an hour after the first ballot, a second ballot was taken: unanimously guilty.

'After the case had ended and we had drawn our fees, I

chatted with one or two of the other jurors. Our topic of conversation was that it seemed remarkable we should have been so long arriving [at our verdict] ... [They] ... said that from the first they had been struck by the fair way in which the Crown case had been presented, and we agreed that had it not been for the two dissenting jurors we would have arrived at a verdict of guilty within a few minutes. Even as it was we discounted the veracity of the evidence for the defence from the first, and our verdict confirmed the view.'

Juror X: 'Two of the jury had broken down and were sobbing like stricken men. One of them—an elderly man—had taken it to heart very poignantly when Mrs Ross had given her evidence. We had also felt heartily sorry for the woman ... When they became more composed we filed into court for the last time, and sent Ross to his doom.'

The *Herald* journalist: 'And you?'

'I confess that when I reached home ... I also broke down, but was able to get a little rest. I never want to serve on another jury charged with having to decide on a man's fate again.'

One further note on the jury. Piggott's grandson, Eric Beissel, recalls a warm friendship between the detective and the jury foreman, George Annand, who would visit the former detective at his home for a friendly talk or game of chess. If Annand had not been a friend of Piggott's prior to the trial, he certainly became one afterwards.

Following the pronouncement of his death sentence, Ross was returned to the Melbourne Gaol. Strict rules applied for men under sentence of death. While on remand he had been permitted to wear his own clothes; now he would wear the garb of a convicted man: white moleskin trousers, a blue and white shirt of Scotch twill, a tweed coat and vest, grey woollen socks and a pair of prison slippers. Before dressing, Ross was searched physically. He was also examined by Dr Godfrey who noted he was suffering from want of sleep and nervous strain, neither of which Godfrey thought serious.

Henceforth Ross was to be isolated from the other prisoners and would exercise alone in one of the exercise yards. His food would be cut up for him, and his only cutlery would be a spoon. Ross remained in the exercise yard from 7.15am to 4pm each day when, before being returned to the condemned cell for the evening, he was searched closely by his warders. Since Harding had claimed Ross would, if the worst came to the worst, poison himself with cyanide, the authorities gave him no chance.

Each day, going to and from the exercise yard, Ross passed the gallows: a platform of iron and wood built into the landing of the corridor's middle tier of cells. The condemned cell was on the ground floor—Cell 10—and measured 2.7 × 1.5 metres, about as narrow as a grave. Twenty years previously, Albert McNamara had attempted suicide on the morning of his execution by striking his head on its bars. Since then, the bars had been padded.

No matting of any kind was permitted on the floor of the cell and the walls were painted a spotless white. High up in the rear wall was a heavily barred window, 60 centimetres square. It was glazed with a glass block 2 centimetres thick. Furnishing consisted of a small wooden stool and bedding. Other prisoners were allowed a wide plank for a bed, but a plank might be used as a weapon, and so the condemned man slept on the floor, with a little mattress, sheets, pillows, and blankets.

On the Saturday night of Ross's conviction, the Ross family and their remaining friends rallied at 'Glenross'. Sonenberg had explained to them that an appeal to the State Full Court was possible. The family had no hesitation, but after the costs of the trial practically no funds were available. It was decided that a mortgage would be taken out on their home.

That night a small hope arrived at the house. She was a respectable girl, a tailoress, who had not wished to be publicly associated with the case. But since Colin Ross had been condemned, she felt compelled to come forward. When Olive Maddox had recalled her visit to the wine saloon, she had said that when she entered at 5.05pm there were two girls whom she knew in the parlour and one whom she did not know: the Ross's visitor, Florence Rudkin.

First thing on Monday, Rudkin made a statement in Sonenberg's office. She used to go to the saloon, she said, because it was in a quiet spot. As she was on holidays on 30 December, she remained for over an hour, arriving before 5pm, going into the big room (the parlour) and staying until shortly before 6pm. She stated she saw Maddox come into the room and leave, the worse for drink and talking excitedly. Maddox had claimed to have left the saloon for three-quarters of an hour, returning just before 6pm. Rudkin said her stay had in fact been unbroken. Why would Maddox lie about this detail? Brennan later surmised it would reduce the chance of Maddox's evidence being dismissed as drink-affected, and to 'save her having to explain how the murdered girl got out of the room and where she went to'.

Rudkin also revealed that she had not seen a young girl answering to the description of Alma Tirtschke in the saloon. In fact, when departing, Rudkin passed the entrance to the beaded room and saw no one there.

Rudkin added that on 31 December she again went to the saloon, arriving there shortly after 3.30pm. She said she had occasion to leave there for a few minutes, but then returned to the big room where she remained until 5.30pm. During that time Colin Ross served behind the counter. Only once did he leave it for a few minutes—despite Ivy Matthews claiming that she had met Ross and walked out to Little Collins Street with him.

Sonenberg had suggested Brennan should take chief responsibility for the appeal: Brennan had a more open mind than Maxwell, in particular regarding the possibility of police tampering with the evidence. Nine days after the conviction the appeal was lodged.

The Court of Criminal Appeal consisted of three judges, which could include the trial judge, thus creating a potential conflict of interest. Before an appeal could be admitted to the court for consideration, it had to be based on several specific grounds: the inadmissibility of evidence; that the judge erred in directing the jury; that the verdict was against the weight of evidence; or that fresh evidence could be called. In the latter case, the rules were strictest: it had to be clearly demonstrated that (1) the new evidence could not have been obtained at the original trial; and (2) that if it had been presented it was likely to have affected the verdict.

The time for the hearing had first to be set, and the Crown applied for an early date. On 7 March Macindoe appeared before the Full Court (the Chief Justice, Sir William Irvine, and justices Mann and Schutt). He sought an order that the Crown be provided with full particulars of the grounds of the appeal.

Brennan, opposing Macindoe's application, contended that this case was such that it should not be hurried. The whole story had not yet been told. The fresh evidence that was coming to hand had to be sifted and investigated and it would be utterly impossible to have the case properly prepared in less than a fortnight or three weeks—especially with regard to the fresh evidence.

Brennan: 'Since the time of the trial other witnesses have come forward, one of whom tells an extraordinary story—so extraordinary indeed that it has to be closely inquired into ... We are not yet prepared to state the particulars of this evidence upon affidavit, as we are now checking it.'

Justice Mann: 'But you cannot hold the court up while you are investigating this additional evidence.'

The Chief Justice: 'The court may find that justice may be done without allowing further time ...'

Brennan: 'Surely in a case of life and death time should be given to prepare the appeal?'

The Chief Justice: 'The duty of this court is to see that the case is brought on as promptly as possible.'

When the court reconvened the following day—Wednesday 8 March—the Chief Justice referred to the strict provisions of the *Crimes Act* by which the court was bound. In appeals against the death sentence: 'We have no discretion in the matter ... *the appeal should be heard with as much expedition as practicable* ... We therefore fix the application for leave to appeal—and for the appeal itself—to come on next Wednesday ...'

Brennan had one week. The court further directed that Brennan should file, no later than Saturday, an affidavit setting out the facts on which Ross's appeal relied as to fresh evidence, and that Brennan should submit also the particulars of the objections—from a legal point of view—on which the appeal was based. He had his work cut out for him.

The appeal was a four-day hearing over 15 to 20 March. Ross attended, dressed in his own clothes. The *Herald*:

... He has given no trouble whatever to the warders, and all his talk has been principally about his appeal. Under the strain he has grown a little careworn, and he showed some anxiety this morning. Upon arrival he expressed surprise at seeing such a loud crowd about the courts, and told the warders that he hoped in the end he would not be going back in the van.

At 10.30am the appeal began, with Chief Justice Sir William Irvine and justices Schutt and Cussen presiding. First, Justice Schutt's report of the trial was read. In it he noted that the defence had not objected to his summing-up, nor made any application for further evidence.

In opening the case, Brennan dealt first with the summing-up. It was awkward, since Schutt was sitting on the appeal hearing. 'The task is not an altogether pleasant one,' Brennan said. 'It is rather like stabbing His Honour in the back.' Brennan did not suggest Schutt had been unfair, and admitted that, 'If I had known as much before as to the [limited] value of confessional evidence, I possibly would have called attention to it at the time.' He submitted that Schutt had failed in his summing-up to deal adequately with the defence, the weakness of the Crown case, and the need for corroboration.

Brennan did not yet know that a police officer had visited Harding in the gaol on 22 January, although he had suspicions. He did note the information in the Harding and Matthews testimonies that had been previously published in newspapers. Brennan contended also that the judge had failed to direct attention to the conflicting evidence of Matthews and Harding:†

---

†This is Brennan's comparison of the two confessions. For consistency of reference, the rooms indicated are described in the terms applied to them throughout the trial rather than the terms used in the confessions.

MATTHEWS	HARDING
1. The child came up and asked him for a drink. He gave her a glass of lemonade and took her into the cubicle.	When the child got opposite his place he spoke to her, and she took no notice of him at first. He said, 'You have nothing to be afraid of; I own this place, and if you are tired you can come in and sit down.' She went in and he took her into the cubicle and induced her to take three glasses of sweet wine.
2. She stayed there until about 4 o'clock. Stanley could see her too. A girl named Gladys Wain came to see him, and he told the child to go through to the beaded room, and he 'kept her in there' [how?] until Gladys left, and then brought her back into the cubicle.	About this time a woman whom he knew came to the door of the cafe, and he spoke to her for about three-quarters of an hour, and when he went back to the cubicle the girl was asleep. A little later 'his own girl' came to the door of the cafe, and he spoke to her until nearly 6 o'clock. Stanley couldn't see [the little girl] when he was serving because the screen was down, and when the screen was down no one dared go into the cubicle.

MATTHEWS	HARDING
3. After 6 o'clock, when Stanley left, he got 'fooling about with her' (she being quite alert and knowing what was meant), and it was all over in a minute. 'I strangled her in my passion.' After it was all over, 'I could have taken a knife and slashed her up and myself too, because she led me on to it.'	At 6 o'clock the girl was still asleep in the cubicle, and 'I could not resist the temptation.' She moaned a little and seemed to faint. 'I left the room and after a little time she commenced to call out again, and I went in to stop her, and in endeavouring to stop her I must have choked her. I got suddenly cool and began to think.'
4. He had to meet a girl friend, so he took the body from the cubicle and put it in the beaded room off the big room, and brought Gladys Wain into the cubicle, and when Gladys was gone he brought the body back into the cubicle.	'Could Gladys not see the girl when you went into the cafe?' No, as the body was in the cubicle, we had our drink in the big room.
5. I asked him how he got back, and he said he came back by motor car.	I said: 'Did you go back by car?' He said: 'No.' He had a bike. I said: A motor bike?' He said 'No, a push bike.'

Brennan noted that Harding made Ross speak throughout of the little compartment at the end of the bar as 'the cubicle'. Yet the Rosses 'had never even heard the word, and prior to the trial did not know what it meant'.

Since the trial, *Smith's Weekly* had been profiling Crown witnesses and others associated with the case. In the issue of 4 March 1922 Harding had appeared, including his boast that he had served as a medical assistant 'on No 2 AHS'.

Brennan: 'I submit [Harding] was employed on a hospital ship, and [cubicle] is the expression used in hospitals to denote a little room with a couch in it ...'

Continuing, Brennan said the Crown case was that between 12.45am (when the two Italians left the arcade) and 1.05am, the body was removed, which conflicted with the statement that Ross returned between 1 and 2am.

Brennan: '... it was proved by overwhelming independent evidence that Ross did catch a train at Spencer Street at about 11.30, and caught a tram which left him ... not far from his home shortly before midnight.'

Here, said Brennan, the Crown case became not only 'absolutely incoherent, but absolutely inconsistent'. The evidence of the Italians, the caretaker, Ellis, Harding's claim that Ross heard the old man coming—all this was intended to prove that after the two Italians had left and Ellis had retired, and before the caretaker had closed the gate, Ross chose to carry the body to Gun Alley. However, the Matthews and Harding confessions claimed that Ross came back, and with a key of his own, unlocked the gates and disposed of the body. The Matthews confession has this occur 'between 1 and 2', while Harding makes Ross say, in effect, that the gates were locked when he got back.

Brennan: 'The stories fail hopelessly to fit in the one with the other ... If the Ellis evidence is true, the Harding and Matthews evidence on this point cannot be true.'

In dealing with the improbabilities of the Crown witnesses, about which the judge had said nothing, Brennan noted the extreme unlikelihood of the chance meeting between Ross and Maddox at Jolimont on the night of 5 January. Maddox did not give the time of this encounter at first, but later amended her evidence, fixing it at 9.30pm, which would least conflict with the defence's overwhelming evidence as to Ross's movements on that day.

Referring to the evidence of those termed the disreputable witnesses, Brennan contended that their object was a reward. Maddox had said nothing until after the rewards totalled £1250 and she had spoken to Matthews. Maddox and Matthews were old and close acquaintances and Brennan proposed that what happened was as follows:

Matthews said she saw a drink being brought into the cubicle to the child at 3 o'clock. Maddox was to say that she saw the child in that room at 5 o'clock, with an empty glass before her; but Maddox, who was by her own admission 'not too educated', blundered and put the child in the wrong room. The rooms at the time had no distinguishing names: not until the trial were they termed 'cubicle' and 'beaded room'. At the trial Matthews tried to repair the blunder 'by telling how Ross got the girl to go into the beaded room, and kept her there by some form of mesmerism for over an hour, while he entertained Gladys Wain in the cubicle.'

Brennan: 'At the trial, Matthews ... had obviously amplified it to make it fit in with the prisoner's statement ... at the inquest.'

Schutt: '... I should have told the jury that she had obviously amplified the statements she made at the inquest?'

Brennan: 'I merely put it that it is now quite clear that that is what she did.'

Proceeding, Brennan respectfully submitted it was the duty of the trial judge to indicate to the jury the points of conflict, inconsistency and improbability in the Crown's evidence, especially in this case where it was impossible to get a consistent story of what took place on the day of the murder.

Brennan quoted from the summing-up in which the judge had referred to the severe criticism of several of the Crown witnesses by the defence: '"... you will have to consider very carefully whether you are prepared to accept the evidence of those people." That is the nearest His Honour comes to anything in the nature of a warning ...' Brennan contended Schutt should have told the jury that they must scrutinise that sort of evidence carefully, because English courts had always held it to be of the weakest kind.

After lunch, the judges closed ranks. The Chief Justice declared that the material presented did not show that the extra witnesses could not have been called at the trial. Brennan reminded the court of the short time he had been permitted to prepare, and said he would be able to file an affidavit the next morning.

Regarding the fifth ground of appeal, non-direction as to manslaughter, it should be said that both Maxwell and Brennan had been confident as to Ross's innocence on both charges. Manslaughter was now introduced as a strategy, although it might seem an admission of guilt. If accepted, it might at least extract the prisoner from the inexorable expedition of a death sentence appeal, allowing counsel the time for a proper appeal brief.

In relation to ground five, and Harding's evidence, Brennan said Schutt should have directed the jury that it was open to them to find a verdict of manslaughter. On this point Brennan proposed to refer to the inquest depositions. He intended to quote both from Harding and Matthews, to indicate, as Matthews said, 'He did not intend to kill her'—a point Matthews omitted to make during the trial. The move was disallowed. Brennan was forced to show a case for manslaughter from the trial transcript of Harding's evidence only. According to Harding's statement, the killing was accidental. Killing during a felony was murder, but accidental killing afterwards might be manslaughter.

If, in the present case, said Brennan, there was any evidence to support manslaughter, His Honour was bound to put it to the jury, even if the defence had not called attention to it ...

The Chief Justice: '... Now you say there has been a miscarriage of justice because the jurors had not before them the issues which you, as Ross's counsel, deliberately refrained from placing before them.'

Referring to the first ground of the appeal, Brennan acknowledged that the appeal court felt loath to interfere with the findings of juries. 'I submit that this court ... has only to take the stories of the two witnesses Harding and Matthews, and compare them ... in order that their falsity could be exposed.'

The Chief Justice: 'Do you contend our function is to form an independent judgment on the evidence?'

Brennan: '... Their Honours now had in writing what those people had said.'

The admission of Price, the government analyst, that he had found the hair of other people to be as similar to that of Alma Tirtschke as that found on the blanket, Brennan submitted, disposed of the evidence regarding the hairs for all time. Other evidence that might have come out involved whether Stanley Ross had received a description of the little girl in the arcade, and had in turn conveyed to Colin that description.

The Chief Justice: 'How would that have been relevant?'

Brennan: 'As refuting the contention of the police that Ross had noted the girl very carefully ...'

Brennan stressed that strong public feeling had influenced the jury. He and Maxwell had received anonymous letters: 'Where is the stopping place between such views and lynch law?... It was impossible for the jurors to rid their minds of the prejudices gathered outside.' Brennan submitted the jury were 'unconsciously swayed' by the media, a notion far ahead of its time. Some months after the trial and the two subsequent appeals, leading Melbourne lawyer AJ Buchanan would agree:

> No trial in Australian history has created such a public sensation as did the trial in Melbourne of Colin Campbell Ross ... anything in the nature of a dispassionate review was impossible. Public opinion was inflamed as it has not been inflamed within the memory of this generation. Ross was tried for his life in an atmosphere charged and overcharged with suspicion.

Brennan himself would write:

> Never in the history of serious crimes in Victoria, or indeed, in the British Empire ... has a man been convicted on such a jumbled mass of contradictions ... The only explanation is that ... the jury quite unconsciously formed opinions before they went into the box, and, with their judgments clouded by their natural indignation, they were unable to view the matter dispassionately.

Referring to the new evidence, Brennan presented a number of affidavits pertaining to new witnesses. Sonenberg had certified that none of the defence counsel had knowledge of this evidence during the trial. It was an important point over which the *Crimes Act* was very strict. However, the defence had also to prove to the court's satisfaction that they could not 'with reasonable diligence' have uncovered the evidence before the trial.

Argument then followed as to whether the new witnesses' evidence should be admitted. What of Florence Rudkin?

Schutt: 'The prisoner Ross must have seen her [in his saloon].'

Brennan: '[The Ross family] only knew her as Florrie and searched for her without success ...'

But there were others in the wine saloon, Brennan noted, equally confident that Alma was not present. One was a man called Allen, who was unable to be located before the trial. He would testify that as many as 15–20 people were in the saloon, including a man named Harold Jordon.

The Chief Justice said that if diligent inquiries had been made through the police, Allen could have been located.

Brennan said Jordon had gone to the police. He would depose that on Friday 30 December 1921, he was at Ross's saloon from about 3.15 to 4.00pm. He saw Albert Allen and Herbert Edwards there, but no schoolgirl. Jordon had gone to the detective office on 6 January and told Piggott and Brophy what he knew. When Piggott was in the witness box, he had been asked about this interview but the question was disallowed and Jordon was not called as a witness for the defence.

Brennan said the fact that Piggott did not apparently act on Jordon's information showed that he wanted nothing except that which would tend to a conviction.

Herbert William Victor Edwards and Victor McLoughlin would each depose to the same effect as Jordon. Brennan stated these men came at different times and 'between them they covered the whole afternoon'. All knew Matthews but none saw her that afternoon, nor did they see Ross leaving the saloon. 'Two of them sat on the form, with their backs to the flimsy cubicle for some time, and they are confident that, even if the little girl had been asleep in that room, they would have heard her breathing or moving.'

In another affidavit a man named George Holman stated he was in the Melbourne Gaol in January, awaiting trial, and on or about the morning of 17 January he overheard Harding say to Dunstan, 'I want you to stick to me over this and pull me out down here' (meaning St Kilda Court). 'I have told you about Ross, and I will fix you up after the trial.'

Yet the Chief Justice declared he was not satisfied that these witnesses could not have been procured at the trial.

The next affidavit was for Mrs Hannah Lily McKenzie. It took nearly two days' argument before the judges would put her in the witness box. Brennan had difficulty convincing them that the defence could not have called her before, since she had written to Maxwell three weeks before the trial. Maxwell was obliged to explain that Mrs McKenzie's letter was one among hundreds he had received. Since he had no idea who the writer was and because he had not yet been appointed defence counsel, he simply passed the letter to the police, whose response was: 'Oh, we know Mrs McKenzie. There's nothing in this.' Assuming the letter was a hoax, Maxwell dismissed it.

Then, when Mrs McKenzie visited Maxwell after the verdict, he remembered that she had consulted with him previously regarding a will. Now he knew who she was, he notified Brennan and Sonenberg.

Macindoe opposed the admission of McKenzie's evidence, stating that the police had found her claims groundless. Indeed, Macindoe had a copy of the police report before him. Since the defence had made two days' strenuous argument to place her in the witness box, the judges agreed she could be called. However, the Chief Justice warned that there could be no decision at this stage on whether her testimony would be admissible.

Unbeknown to the defence, the elderly Mrs McKenzie was already showing signs of dementia, on occasions failing to recognise even her own son when he passed her in the street and often speaking of her deceased son and daughter as if they were both still living. She sometimes demonstrated more serious psychological disturbances. Some years earlier, at the inquest into the death of her son, Mrs McKenzie had alleged a conspiracy. Now she had written to Maxwell:

> The only man Mr Maxwell that can though [*sic*] light on the murder of Alma Tirtschke is a man called Murdoch [Alma's uncle]. The man the child was with last, he met this child with golden hair, 'Alma', in Russell Street near Kings Theather marshed [*sic*] quickly until he turned into Little Collin Street the direction of the Arcade Friday 3pm ...

On 11 January Mrs McKenzie had written to the Acting Chief Commissioner of Police, with the same allegations, but signing herself L Mack, care of Northcote Post Office. Eventually she was traced and interviewed by Piggott and Brophy. They reported:

> ... [We] asked her how she came to know Mr Murdoch. She stated that she saw him in the shop of TK Bennet and Woolcock, Butchers, Swanston Street, and that he was wearing a long khaki coat, similar to that worn by the Master Butchers in this particular shop. Further, that since she saw him with the deceased on the 30th December, he had grown a small Charlie Chaplin moustache.
>
> ... We then informed Mrs McKenzie that Mr Murdoch was still clean shaved and that he never worked in the shop, and never wore a khaki coat, and that he was always in his own office upstairs.

... Mrs McKenzie then ... appeared to be perfectly satisfied that she had made a mistake. She does not know the murdered girl personally.

... We wish to state that Mrs McKenzie is a woman who claims to have second sight. She has come under the notice of the police on other occasions under similar circumstances and is a woman who cannot be taken seriously.

Macindoe to the witness: 'You signed the letter [to the police] "L Mack", why did you not sign your full name?'

Mrs McKenzie: '... A person wants protection ...'

'From whom? ...'

'My enemies in the dark.'

At the request of Macindoe, five men stood up in the court. 'Can you see Mr Murdoch there?'

One of the five had a small moustache and Mrs McKenzie picked him out. When asked to swear it was Murdoch she refused. Nor did she want to swear he was the man she had seen in the butcher shop until he donned a khaki coat. Once he did so, she said: 'That is the gentleman. I am positive now.'

None of the five were Murdoch, who was interstate on business. The man picked out was Fred Langford, who worked as a checker for Bennet and Woolcock's. He accounted for his movements on 30 December and was corroborated by his boss, Martin Wheeler. Asked how she was able to identify the child she saw as Alma, Mrs McKenzie said she had often seen Alma playing in the street. Alma's grandmother was called as a witness. Mrs Tirtschke said Alma had visited Northcote, where Mrs McKenzie lived, only once, over seven years earlier. During that visit the then five-year-old did not play in the street.

Mrs McKenzie's son, John Alexander McKenzie, also gave evidence as to the poor state of his mother's mind. In the witness box Mrs McKenzie herself admitted that she was a *Herald* reader; her son said that his mother 'was very interested to get news about [the murder of Alma]'. Indeed Mrs McKenzie's story may have derived from a report carried in the *Herald* of 7 January, claiming that the schoolgirl had been seen speaking with a man outside the King's Theatre in Russell Street.

The admission of McKenzie's testimony was a colossal setback for the defence. If Brennan had been granted more preparation time, he could have established that although Mrs McKenzie could present herself as composed and rational, she was seriously deranged. The defence now strove to regain what ground they could with two remaining witnesses, one of whom would be permitted to testify. Brennan also asked the court to consider that Harding may have been planted in the remand yard of the gaol by the police to get a confession from Ross.

Macindoe: 'Why did you not ask the detectives [if they did this]?'

Brennan: 'I knew that I could not get any other answer but "No" from them.'

In an affidavit, Percy Halliwell deposed that on the afternoon of 30 December he was at the wine saloon, drinking in the parlour. When the saloon closed, he, like Rudkin, looked into the beaded room and saw it was unoccupied. He knew Ross and was allowed to remain after closing time, being invited to share a bottle of beer in the cubicle with the Rosses and Bert Evans (a ship's passenger who had since left the country). There was no one else in the cubicle but themselves and when the group left shortly after six, it would have been impossible for anybody else to have been in the saloon without Halliwell seeing them.

The evidence about sharing the beer, Brennan would later suggest, was valuable because it was not mentioned by the Ross brothers. On 5 January, when both were interviewed by the police, neither would have admitted breaching the liquor licensing laws (by serving alcohol after 6pm). Although not disclosed in his affidavit, Halliwell had also evidence regarding Ivy Matthews—that she had helped the police work up their case against Ross.

The Chief Justice: 'Ross could have called this man at the trial.'

Brennan replied that Halliwell had been regarded as a hostile witness. (In fact he knew that Halliwell, although not called to give evidence at the trial, had been intimidated by the police into becoming their witness.)

Brennan: 'The only opportunity we have had to confer with Halliwell has been since the case, and now he knows the mischief he has done and how he has been made a tool of by Piggott and Brophy.'

Both detectives were present, and in response to Halliwell's affidavit, Brophy countered with one of his own stating that Halliwell called at the detective office before the trial and said Stanley and Ronald Ross wanted him to swear he was in the saloon with Colin when they closed up at 6 o'clock on 30 December. Brophy said to Halliwell, 'Were you there?' and Halliwell answered: 'No ... and I am not going to commit perjury.'

The Chief Justice declared he was not satisfied Halliwell might not have been procured at the trial, thus denying Halliwell the opportunity to tell how he in fact had been 'called in'—if he knew what was good for him—by Piggott.

Argument then arose as to the admissibility of the evidence of Joseph Thomas Graham. He was a cab driver, middle-aged, respectable, courteous, intelligent and level-headed. Finally he was heard.

On 6 January Piggott and Brophy had appealed through the newspapers for anyone who may have heard screams in the area of Gun Alley on the Friday afternoon. Graham responded, as did at least two other people: a man and a woman from Ballarat. Graham went to the detective office, but his reception was not sympathetic. Neither Graham nor the Ballarat witnesses were called at the inquest. When Ross was condemned, Graham visited Sonenberg—this was the first the defence knew of him. While reference had been made in the press to the two Ballarat people, nothing was reported about Graham.

Graham's evidence is important for what it reveals about Alma's probable fate and also the detectives' attitude to evidence that did not 'fit' their case against Ross. Were Brophy and Piggott anxious to suppress Graham's information? His evidence conflicted with—to use Piggott's words—the 'chain' being 'forged'. But it was consistent with Mr and Mrs Young's testimony—Alma's last sighting by independent and credible witnesses.

Graham recalled the afternoon of 30 December:

> I was walking slowly up Little Collins Street ... going to Franz's, the grocer's ... It was between a quarter and half past 3. I was opposite the far end of the Little Collins Street frontage of the Adam and Eve Hotel. I heard a piercing scream, followed immediately by others; terrifying screams ... I heard at least 5 screams—more like 6—then the girl seemed to be exhausted. While the screams were echoing and re-echoing, I noticed a man who seemed to be trying to locate the screams. I would say they came from anywhere between Alfred Place and [Pink Alley]. They seemed to be at the back of the Adam and Eve Hotel. They were ... like a little girl terrified at what was occurring or [what was] about to occur. I reported it at the detective office on January 9, after reading the papers.

Macindoe asked whether Graham had described the screaming to Detective Brophy as he had today, and

Graham answered that he had, 'exactly'. Macindoe then read from Brophy's notes of the interview, which indicated Graham had been confused as to the date and place he heard the screaming. Graham denied this.

Macindoe: 'Screaming is a fairly common occurrence in that locality, is it not?'

Graham: 'No, sir; I have been there hundreds of times, night and day ... [and not heard such screams].'

'You say these were the screams of a little girl?'

'I knew it was a young girl by the voice; I should say from 10 years to 15.'

'You are convinced, I suppose, that it was Alma Tirtschke?'

'I cannot think it was anyone else ... It didn't seem to me that a girl was being choked ... It seemed to me as if she was being dragged in somewhere.'

The Chief Justice: 'You realised before the trial was over that your evidence would be extremely valuable in the defence of the prisoner?'

' ... [No,] I didn't ... I told so many people [including the police] and they did not seem to take any notice.'

Brophy, put in the stand, confirmed the evidence of his notes of interview with Graham. He was asked if he inquired where the screams came from. 'Yes ... the Adam and Eve and nobody there heard screams ... [However,] there were frequently screams in that locality; there is a child in the tobacconist's shop, the barber's, who is noted for her screeching.'

'You saw a man from Ballarat?'

'Yes, we took him to the locality, and he said he was inside the gates, and heard only one scream.'

'Did the man from Ballarat fix the time?'

'Yes, he fixed the Friday afternoon and heard only one scream.'

Two newspaper reports drawn from police sources throw more light on this witness. He was actually from

Melbourne, but went to the police while staying in Ballarat. On the Friday afternoon Alma disappeared he had walked along Bourke Street to the Eastern Market. While standing near a door on the southern side of the market, near Gun Alley, he heard 'a piercing scream'. He walked towards the door, but as the scream ceased, he thought perhaps it was a child merely being beaten. He gave the time of the incident as being between 3.05 and 3.25pm, and said one of the stallholders in the market could corroborate him.

The Ballarat detectives forwarded this information to the Melbourne CIB on 9 January. The next day they again questioned the man. He was emphatic he heard a young girl's scream. When asked why he had not come forward earlier, he replied that he had not been in good health and had not wanted publicity. But as nobody else had reported the scream, he decided to tell the police. On the afternoon of 11 January he travelled to Melbourne and was interviewed by Superintendent Potter that evening. Nothing more is known of this witness. However, his evidence correlates in time with Graham's, and the location is very similar. It is conceivable that he heard the girl's final cry.

24. 'Don't let them get you down-hearted'

Mid-afternoon, Monday 20 March: Brennan sought permission to produce fresh evidence volunteered late on Sunday night by a man named Crilley. On Friday the newspapers had reported on the new affidavits read to the court. Certain affidavits—in particular those of Jordon, Halliwell and Graham—hinted at police suppression and manipulation of evidence. These reports struck a chord with George Crilley. He, like Jordon and Graham, had made a report to the police and was interrogated by them on several occasions. Since Crilley had approached the Ross family only the night before, Brennan had not had time to prepare an affidavit. But now the Bench had been sitting for four days, and wanted to end the appeal.

The Chief Justice: 'Before this witness can come before the court it must be shown that the evidence was not available before. In the case of the previous witness there was evidence in affidavit but [not] in this instance ...'

Brennan proposed to put Crilley in the witness box, to say that, between 1.30 and 1.45pm on 30 December, he saw a little girl answering the description of Alma

Tirtschke walking up Little Collins Street. She was in front of him, and a man was walking just behind her. The man appeared to be following the girl so persistently that Crilley was going to speak to him, but he eventually walked on past her. Somewhere about opposite the Eastern Arcade Crilley looked back and saw the man talking to the girl—he was not Ross.

The Chief Justice: 'There is nothing remarkable in somebody being seen talking to the little girl.'

Brennan: 'I submit it *is* important ... the dead girl had been sent on a message and, according to a pile of testimony, she was not the sort of girl who would stop and talk to people in the street. It is extremely important if it is shown that the girl entered into conversation with this man.'

Chief Justice: 'He thought it so important that he did not report it to the police.'

Brennan: 'He *was* interrogated by the police ... and he made a full statement!'

After some argument, the Chief Justice said the court would consider the statement made by Crilley to counsel, but would not accept any further evidence. The judges adjourned to consider their verdict on the appeal.

It was the responsibility of Piggott and Brophy to test the statements of all persons they interviewed, which could mean challenging a witness with contrary statements. However, it appears from the evidence not only of Halliwell but also of Jordon, Allen, Edwards, McLoughlin, Graham and Crilley, that the detectives were dismissing evidence or conveniently adjusting it to suit their case.

Piggott would later admit:

... the public were clamouring for police action and the politicians, of course, were harassing us. They were nervy, thankless days. But we survived the uproar long enough *to plump for the theory*† that Ross ravished and strangled Alma in the saloon ... But we were well aware that our evidence ... was only circumstantial ... [1961]

While I suspected Ross ... [w]e desired to ... build up the chain of evidence that was being forged against him ... [1935]

Thus, when a piece of evidence could not be 'forged' into a link, it seems it was simply discarded.

In his reply to Brennan, Macindoe defended the inconsistencies in the Crown case: they were all before the jury and the jury chose to act on them. On the suggestion that evidence was wrongly rejected, with Jordon for instance, Maxwell had stated during the trial that Detective Piggott had been scrupulously fair. That being so, the evidence could not be admissible.

On the ground that the judge had misdirected the jury Macindoe submitted that Schutt's summing-up was a masterpiece. And on the point of whether the killing of the girl constituted murder or manslaughter, Macindoe said: 'If the prisoner killed the girl in order to cover up the traces of his crime, that must be deemed to have been in furtherance of the crime.' As to whether the public mind had been inflamed, Macindoe said that happened in every trial.

---

†Author's italics

In handing down the Full Court's judgment, the Chief Justice stated that it was no part of the court's function to put aside the verdict of a jury unless a miscarriage of justice could be proved. He then responded to each ground of the application. On the first ground, that the verdict was against the evidence and weight of evidence, he found there was no basis. The second ground, that evidence was wrongly admitted and wrongly rejected, he also denied, and on the fourth ground declared himself satisfied with Schutt's direction.

On the fifth ground, the absence of any express direction as to manslaughter, this 'was an omission, as far as it went, entirely in the prisoner's favour' (because if the jury did not find Ross guilty of murder, they had to acquit him). On the sixth ground: 'There was nothing ... to show this court that the jury who went into that box were in any way influenced by ... public opinion.' With the third ground, the fresh evidence, he found that it might have been discovered before and during the trial, and disallowed it. Thus: '... this application must be refused'.

Ross took the judgment quietly but his mother and sister broke down. Florence Rudkin, who had been seated with the family during the proceedings, sobbed loudly. Outside she bitterly protested Ross's innocence.

As the prison van left the courthouse, Stanley Ross shouted: 'Cheer up, Colin, old man. Don't let them get you down-hearted!' Prior to this day, Ross had replied cheerily to his farewells. This time he did not answer.

A large crowd watched as the van departed.

The *Herald* declared 'Ross's Appeal Fails', and in the same edition that '... an effort will be made to approach the High Court'. So new was the legislation allowing the process of appeal to the High Court that there was no precedent in Victoria for an appeal to it against the death sentence. Ross's counsel were required to bring the matter before the High Court's next sittings: 27 March, in Sydney. The grounds were that the Victorian Full Court judgment was wrong in law. The appeal arguments were to be substantially as before and the affidavits for the presentation of fresh evidence identical, Mrs McKenzie apart. If the High Court decided in Ross's favour, this evidence might be heard at a new trial. Ross remained in Melbourne Gaol. Piggott attended the High Court hearing. Although he would not be called as a witness, he was to serve as a consultant if required.

The application was heard by the High Court's Chief Justice, Sir Adrian Knox, with Justices IA Isaacs, HB Higgins, F Gavan Duffy and HE Starke. At one point Justice Starke said:

> ... It is obvious that the analyst, Mr Price, had not done much of this class of work before. It also seems an extraordinary thing that these little bits of serge should be kicking about the street for nearly a month, and they are not at all alike in texture or colour.

The latter point was also noted by Justice Isaacs.

A second notable moment occurred when Brennan declared that there was a gap regarding the blankets, since it was not shown where they were during the night before they were handed over to the analyst. Justice Starke asked whether this 'sinister suggestion' was put to the officers when they were called at the trial. Brennan replied that it had not. (He had been constrained by Maxwell's leadership.) Macindoe pointed out it was the prisoner himself who had suggested the police put the hairs on the blanket.

Brennan later responded to Justice Starke:

> ... it is not ... a sinister suggestion, but an elementary requirement in proof ... a blow would be struck at the whole administration of justice, if ... the principle were admitted, that evidence, just because it is police evidence, is not to be subjected to the ordinary tests ... a prisoner under the shadow of the gallows, who speaks through his counsel, is entitled to demand the exclusion of every possibility of fraud, even when a man of the standing of Detective Piggott is in charge.

Brennan also anticipated the increasing role science would play in criminal convictions and argued that it should be stringent science. The court adjourned on Friday 31 March.

25. Piggott

Frederick John Charles Piggott was born at Phillip Island, Victoria, in 1874. His father, also Frederick, was a butcher from Beaconsfield, England. His mother was Margaret Dickins, the daughter of John Dickins, farmer, of Bulla, Victoria. Having won a scholarship to attend the Working Men's College in Melbourne, the young Piggott graduated in 1893 and became a joiner and cabinetmaker. He later joined the police because he was 'of an adventurous turn of mind', and his trade was 'not giving him sufficient scope'. The depression of the mid–1890s was probably also a factor. In 1898, Piggott joined the Victorian Mounted Police. He was 176 centimetres tall, had grey eyes, light brown hair, and was of pale complexion and 'respectable' appearance.

In 1899 he married Matilda Holland and by 1904 they had three children, born at various locations as Piggott was posted around Victoria. He was a country constable-in-charge until 1912, when he was posted to the CIB, Melbourne, 'for detective duty at his own request'. Although he was now based at Russell Street, his experience in bushland districts meant he was still assigned to country investigations. One such case—involving sheep stealing—was heard in the Kaniva Court of Petty Sessions in 1915. It was his first taste of cross-examination by Maxwell.

From 1912 to 1922 Piggott assisted in hundreds of investigations, being promoted to senior detective in 1919. In 1920 he and Detective Ashton arrested Dr James Duncan; Josephine Smith, a nurse; and Charles Chapman, chemist, on a charge of conspiracy to produce an abortion.

At their trial, Mr Ridgeway, defence counsel, condemned the tactics of the detectives in laying a trap for the accused by employing an agent, Katherine English, who had, on police instruction, lied. During cross-examination her integrity as a witness was attacked. Allegations were made that she had been gaoled and charged for drunkenness, been fined £10 for indecent language and assault, and arrested for soliciting. English admitted using aliases, lying to the accused under the instruction of the police and that Piggott had paid her for the job. Ridgeway suggested such police tactics, far from preventing crime, were liable to create it. There was also the implication that as Piggott's paid agent, she was still lying in the witness box.

The presiding judge Justice McArthur took exception to Ridgeway's suggestion. While acknowledging there were gaps in English's credibility, he said: 'This was certainly an indelicate and unsavoury sort of trap ... and you cannot expect to find a particularly high-class woman to set [such] a trap.'

Piggott thus received an object lesson in how, despite a vigorous attack on character, a witness might retain credibility. '... [Y]ou cannot wipe out her evidence altogether,' McArthur told the jury.

He added: 'Police "agency" work is as necessary in the detection of crime as espionage is in war ... Criminals work subtly and darkly and cleverly; and they often have their own spies. If crime is to be detected it must be by matching skill against skill. Tactics must be used, and information must be obtained to justify arrest ... It is absurd that the police should have to bear odium because in their unpleasant work they employ agents outside the force ... and in matters of great difficulty the police must act in what appears to them to be the most effective way to protect society ... There are a great many crimes that are difficult to detect and the police have a perfect right to set traps for suspected people when it would be more difficult otherwise to sheet home the crime.'

Piggott pasted all three newspaper reports of McArthur's summing-up into his scrapbook. He and Ashton were commended for their work by Superintendent Bannon. In so doing, he endorsed their methods.

The jury, however, thought differently, declaring the defendants not guilty. Duncan's barrister was Maxwell; the prosecutor, Macindoe.

26. Seeking reprieve

Judgment was divided, the majority being: the Chief Justice Sir Adrian Knox, Justices Higgins, Gavan Duffy and Starke. Justice Higgins, while concurring, wanted also to add 'certain observations'. One judge differed: Isaacs. Although his dissent did not alter the judgment, it is of great importance nevertheless. Isaacs acknowledged that the facts relied on by the Crown might have been 'tainted and discrepant and improbable', and also candidly recognised the possibility of judicial inadequacy.

It was the first capital case appealed to the Australian High Court. In handing down the decision on 5 April, the Chief Justice began by defending the court's political conservatism:

> If throughout Australia it were supposed that the course and execution of justice could suffer serious impediment [or] ... obstruction, by an appeal to this court, then ... a severe blow would have been dealt to the ordered administration of law within the several states ... Accordingly ... we have thought it necessary that the application ... and ... the grounds of the appeal should be examined with extreme care before special leave is given.

Ross's leave to appeal was refused. The High Court agreed with the Victorian Full Court. It also cited the inviolable function of the jury, stating, '... with their decision ... no court or judge has any right or power to interfere'. Even Justice Isaacs agreed here.

So much faith did the High Court judges place in the system of trial by jury (it was, after all, the cornerstone of British justice) that Justice Higgins attached a number of observations which he presumed to draw from the perspective of the jury.

Justice Higgins said that, according to the jury's verdict, Ross must have lied when he denied that he had ever spoken to Alma. The judge further said the two confessions, although they varied in detail, both had the accused admit that he had sexual intercourse with the child and killed her. Higgins deduced that 'if there is any inconsistency, it is an inconsistency in the prisoner's statement, not any inconsistency in the evidence of the witnesses to the alleged confessions'.

Brennan, though, would demonstrate that it was this very matter of 'the points of agreement and disagreement that suggest[ed] so strongly that the two confessions were fabricated'—the points of agreement being only those the police already knew.

Higgins: 'The prisoner has had fair play and due process of law.' He also agreed with the Full Court that 'the absence of any express direction as to manslaughter was an omission ... entirely in the prisoner's favour'.

'I absolutely dissent from that,' said Isaacs:

> A detestable crime has been undoubtedly committed whereby a young girl was deprived of her honour and her life in appalling circumstances ... But, as British law in defending the weak and the innocent against the strong and the guilty demands vindication, and not possible victims, it proceeds by what Lord Shaw aptly

calls 'the ordered march of justice'. The question is whether that has been preserved in the present case, or whether the prisoner was exposed to a peril of conviction for wilful murder which, had the jury been adequately instructed, they might not have arrived at ...

The Crown placed before the jury a mass of evidence, but in that mass there were three principal pieces of testimony [the Matthews, Maddox and Harding confessions]. On certain crucial points they were absolutely inconsistent. But the Crown left to the jury the choice (inter alia) of accepting any one of them as having been made, and as being true. The whole matter now centres around this one vital question—What is the position supposing Ross did make the Harding confession and that every word of it was true? ... [B]eing itself a denial of intention to kill, it at once excludes other evidence relied on to show a contrary state of facts. It is only when the question is lost sight of, and it is conjectured that the jury did an impossible thing— namely accept the Harding confession as the true state of facts, namely that murder was not intended, and at the same time draw from other evidence an inference entirely inconsistent with it, namely that murder was intended—that the verdict can be sustained.

I have accordingly applied that question ... and the answer I find is ... All contrary evidence being excluded, the jury should have been told that the confession did not necessarily amount to murder, but may have been manslaughter.

... I cannot for myself imagine a more serious breach ... than the want of a sufficient instruction to a jury to distinguish between wilful murder and manslaughter where the facts require it.

[Ross] was found guilty of wilful murder, and has been sentenced to death. The Victorian court rejected his appeal. Of the several grounds placed before us, I agree that none are sustainable except ... that the evidence was left to the jury, without sufficiently guarding the accused against the danger of a conviction for wilful murder, upon facts which a jury properly instructed might consider only manslaughter.

... The ground to which I agree to a rejection of all the other grounds brought forward by Mr Brennan is that, however powerful the considerations he advanced, however tainted and discrepant and improbable any of the facts relied on by the Crown might be, that was all matter for the jury alone ...

[D]uring the argument before this court, the learned Crown Prosecutor ... admitted that the words deposed to in the Harding confession did not necessarily mean that Ross intended to kill. That admission, in my opinion, practically concludes the matter.

... In my opinion, and without hesitation, I hold there should be a new trial ...

When the judgment of the High Court was handed down, the blow to the Ross family was severe. It was arranged that a Baptist clergyman, the Reverend JH Goble, whom the family had known for over 20 years, should break the news to the condemned man. On being told, Ross became agitated and declared: 'I am innocent, and if they hang me they will hang an innocent man.'

The *Herald* to Sonenberg: 'Can you appeal to the Privy Council?'

'I do not know yet,' said Sonenberg.

Founded in 1833, the Judicial Committee of the Privy Council—its full title—was, and still is, the ultimate British court of appeal. Strict limitations, however, apply to the cases in which leave to appeal will be granted. For an appeal in a criminal case to be successful it would have to be shown that a substantial and grave injustice had occurred.

Good Friday was only a week off. The Easter break might give Ross's family and sympathisers time to marshal the resources for the appeal to London. The case had already cost the Victorian government a considerable amount in legal and other costs, even without the £1000 reward. Premier Lawson summoned his ministers for a special Cabinet meeting on 10 April. If they decided the sentence of death should be carried out, a draft Order in Council would be forwarded to the State Executive Council, which would then be submitted for the Governor's approval. If the Governor approved the order, the date of execution would be fixed: usually the second Monday following the ratification of the sentence. Lawson wasted no time: a meeting of the Executive Council would directly follow the special Cabinet meeting.

Hanging Ross would support the police, and by implication, the Government too. The *Midnight Sun*:

> If the death sentence were being reviewed by a Labor government, Ross would probably be reprieved ... One prominent Laborite remarked this week: 'Of course we wouldn't hang Ross: we don't believe in hanging.' On the whole the sentiment of modern times is inclining to the Labor view. At any rate, it has got as far as this—that the extreme penalty should be reserved for murders of a really calculated and cold-blooded kind.
>
> [But Ross's] fate is to be decided by a Conservative administration, which ... is very liable to be influenced by public opinion ... The hue and cry has not yet died

down ... the trial was conducted in a super-heated atmosphere ...

Has the Lawson Government the moral courage ... to reprieve Ross? Or will it act on Monday as it thinks the people with the loudest voices (and longest purses) would like it to act?

That Monday morning of Holy Week, 1922, Victorian Attorney-General Arthur Robinson received a small deputation, with a letter from Sonenberg announcing his intent to appeal to the Privy Council. A fortnight's stay of proceedings was requested.

The deputation was led by EC Warde, MLA, and included Dr Charles Strong of the Australian Church, and Mr HB Heathy, an opponent of capital punishment. Dr Strong stated there was a doubt as to the prisoner's guilt and that the Attorney-General ought give the prisoner the benefit of any doubt.

Mr Byrne, representing the Ross family, said he could produce an affidavit from Halliwell indicating that the detectives were prepared to fabricate evidence in order to get Ross convicted. He added that, like Justice Starke, he did not think the government analyst knew enough to speak about the hair found on the blankets.

Robinson replied that seven judges had already upheld the verdict, and that appealing to the Privy Council would upset the principle that sentences should be expeditious: '... it would be wrong of me to hold out any hope to you'.

That the Governor would approve the sentence was a formality. It was now merely a question of following the established protocols, and the execution was set for 24 April.

At 5.40pm that Holy Monday, Mr Barclay, the governor of the gaol, came to Ross's cell and gave him the news. Ross did not speak. His head drooped. Subsequently he became greatly distressed, sobbing for a long time as he lay on his bed, before finally sinking into a profound and exhausted sleep.

A flurry of letters was sent to the Governor, imploring mercy. There were anonymous letters professing to be from the real killer. By far the most convincing of these letters Brennan would publish in his book.

Mrs Ross attracted the sympathy of many women. A subscription list was circulated by the women's committee of the Victorian ALP, with the object of 'giving Colin Campbell Ross a proper opportunity of proving his innocence'. On 13 April, Holy Thursday, Mrs Ross visited the Attorney-General seeking a reprieve. She told him she had sold her house and now had the means to go to the Privy Council. She produced a bundle of sympathetic letters. Robinson did not bother to read them, and replied in similar terms as he had to the deputation.

'My boy is as innocent as me,' declared Mrs Ross.

Robinson: 'An appeal to the Privy Council would not depend on his innocence. It would be based on ... a plea that the offence committed on the unfortunate child was not murder but might be regarded as manslaughter ...'

'Excuse me,' Mrs Ross persisted, 'but my son is innocent.'

Robinson: '... I am perfectly satisfied that you are wasting your time and money ...'

'He wants to prove his innocence,' said Mrs Ross. 'He is not guilty, and it is a disgrace to humanity to hang an innocent man.'

She also wrote to Anglican Archbishop Lees, who had publicly commented on the evils of wine saloons, but he declined to get involved. On Good Friday, 14 April, she travelled to Castlemaine where the Premier, Mr Lawson, was spending Easter. Mrs Ross was permitted a short interview, pleading for clemency. While the Premier admitted there were some weaknesses in the Crown case, he would not stay the execution. In speaking of this interview Mrs Ross recalled:

> [The Premier] commented on the character of Harding and on his evidence, but added that my son had been very cheeky in his attitude. I told him that that was not surprising after the indignities he had been subjected to, and I asked Mr Lawson if a man had to hang because he was cheeky.

Finally Lawson sent her away, saying that the law must take its course. Sonenberg also petitioned, writing to Attorney-General Robinson, pleading for a stay of execution until the Privy Council could be approached:

> ... I would ask you, Sir, before hurrying this man to his doom, to consider for yourself the nature of the evidence on which he has been condemned ... never since the times ... [of Titus Oates, in 1678] has a man been convicted of murder either in Great Britain or Australia on two discordant confessions which he is alleged to have made, but which he on his oath has denied having made, and in support of which not one particle of direct or circumstantial evidence has been adduced ... We have now a mass of evidence available which will throw a totally different light on this case. [It] will show almost beyond doubt ... that that little girl was not in the wine saloon ... I therefore earnestly appeal to you not to shut out this unfortunate man's last hope of life and last chance of clearing his name.

On Easter Tuesday (18 April) William Henry Dooley, a school inspector, happened to be walking past the

Melbourne Gaol. He found an envelope on the footpath, addressed to Ross, with a message in pencil from Ross. He took it to the *Herald*, the 'Gun Alley Journal'. Postmarks showed the envelope had been posted and received on the previous day. Governor Barclay had initialled and dated it, as was the custom. On the verso was written:

> Dear Friends, outside, a few words from Colin Ross who is going to hang an innocent man. I appeal to the people of Australia to see that I get justice. My life as [*sic*] been sworned [*sic*] away by Police and wicked people. I ask you this because if they will do it to me they will do the same to you take this to some paper office for me please, I am an innocent man.

Herald reporter Thomas Kelynack took the envelope to the gaol next morning. Barclay winced; the envelope had undoubtedly been inside the gaol and in the possession of the prisoner. He told Kelynack that Ross was under the very closest surveillance and searched every day. Ross was not permitted a pencil, because it might easily be converted into a stabbing weapon. He could not have written the note without alerting the warder. And he would have had to throw it over a gaol wall 6 metres in height.

When Kelynack had gone, Barclay sent for Senior Warder Gloster, who said he had never seen the prisoner with a pencil. He had observed Ross reading his Bible and noticed the pages were pencil-marked.

Ross was searched in the exercise yard, and a small lead pencil was found and presented to the governor. Ross confirmed he used it 'for marking special texts in his Bible ...' Barclay questioned Ross, who admitted writing the letter and throwing it over the wall. Warder Kelly was on duty Tuesday morning, but he denied that Ross had any opportunity to throw the note over the wall. Nonetheless Ross had got the message out.

The *Herald* reported its discovery, only to be scooped by *Smith's Weekly*: 'IVY MATTHEWS TELLS IT ALL'. Among other things, Matthews declared that she had received two letters from Ross while he was imprisoned. Reporter HC Maddison postulated that since Ross, pre-sentencing, was able to associate with other men awaiting trial, he must have arranged to have the messages smuggled out by prisoners who were due to be discharged.

Allegedly the first letter arrived two days before the inquest. Pencil-written 'on a dirty piece of paper of the kind that is used for wrapping round butter', it was brought to the house in Rathdowne Street by 'a man who handed it to Matthews without any remark'. She did not explain how the man got past the police guard. It read:

> A man is settled in here. Surely you will not turn on him now. For my mother's sake, stick to me, and I will make it all right for you when I get out. (Signed) Colin.

The alleged second letter arrived on the day after the inquest, brought by a young boy who handed the maid a piece of light blue paper rolled into a ball. He said that a man had asked him to deliver it. It too was written in pencil and addressed to Matthews.

> You dirty bitch. Just wait till I get out of this and I'll fix you. My word will be taken in the criminal court before yours, and you will be in here instead of me. If I do go in for a stretch — will fix you. (Signed) Colin.

Subsequently Mrs Ross called, so Matthews tore up the letters. Thus the story was conveniently impossible to confirm. Mrs Ross had already stated at the trial, under oath, that she had only visited Matthews once—at the time of the shooting affair.

Meanwhile, Harding had returned to prison on 10 April following his conviction for receiving. Having turned shelf, he was a marked man and subject to threats. He managed to get onto the gaol's sick list and, drawing upon his background in medicine, secured a privileged position as an assistant in the dispensary. Yet even there, Harding was not immune: he could be reached, he was assured, and accidents could happen.

While in prison, Harding read Matthews's claims. He was permitted to write to HC Maddison, and asked the reporter to visit him. Maddison then reported that Harding had received a note from Ross and had impulsively destroyed all but a fragment of it. Harding did not tell the prison governor until the 20th—the day after the note found in Russell Street was reported in the *Herald*. Barclay now had to relay a second report of misconduct at his prison to the Inspector-General:

> Harding informs me that the note led off with 'Mr Harding, thank you very much for sending me to my death. I hope you get as much enjoyment out of it as I do [in dying].' Then [the message] went on to say 'You have a mother of your own and I want you to think of my poor mother. You could easily have said that I did not intend to murder. Surely you can do something. If you don't you will be guilty of the murder of my mother.'

The surviving fragment of the note was attached to Barclay's report. It is certainly in Ross's handwriting.

> Mr Harding I thank you very much for sending me to my death, I hope you get as much (jory) [*sic*] out of it, as I do in dring [*sic*].

The fragment has certainly been torn, but there is no indication the tearing was impulsive. Considerable care has been taken to preserve exactly the note's first sentence. What followed afterwards was very likely damning, but to Harding rather than Ross. Brennan would later comment:

> ... there is in Melbourne one man at least whose lightest word would carry more weight than Harding's most solemn oath, who knows that Ross did write a letter to Harding, knows its contents, and knows that, so far from it containing an implied admission of guilt, it contained exactly the opposite.

Was the mystery figure, perhaps, Governor Barclay? In the Public Record Office, the Inspector-General's report on the Ross letters can be found. It contains Harding's fragment and also Ross's pencil: a stub of only 5.6 centimetres.

With Ross to hang in less than three days, a further deputation which included the Reverend Dr Strong, representatives from the Footscray community and Colin's brother Stanley visited the Attorney-General late on Friday 21 April. If Sonenberg's letter had failed to sway Robinson, its publication in the press had prompted many to think again. The deputation presented a petition signed by 2000 people, plus statutory declarations from the new witnesses, including Halliwell. His declaration contained damning revelations as to the preparation of the police case against Ross.

It stated that on 9 January, three days before Ross's arrest, Ivy Matthews called at Halliwell's Fitzroy home and said: 'I told the detectives you made the key for Colin Ross for the gate of the arcade.' Halliwell denied it. At this time the problem of how Ross, if he were the murderer, got back to the arcade was bothering the police. Matthews knew Halliwell was a locksmith. Now she wanted him to confirm her evidence that he made the key, and also to tell the police about a conversation he had with Ross—which had never occurred. Halliwell:

> Ivy Matthews further said to me, 'I've got a friend down at the corner in a motor. He is very much interested in this case and I want you to tell him what I have said to you.' I then accompanied Ivy Matthews to Westgarth Street, Fitzroy, where I saw a motor car, and when I got up to the car I saw Detective Piggott sitting on the back seat. Piggott said to me, 'Sit in the front seat with the driver.' I then sat in the car as directed, and Ivy Matthews sat next to Piggott. Piggott said to me, 'Now what about those keys?' I said, 'I know nothing at all about them.' Piggott said, 'I want you to come up to the detective office with me.' Ivy Matthews said, 'I want to see him during the afternoon.' Piggott and Ivy Matthews then had a conversation.
>
> Subsequently Ivy Matthews said to me, 'I want you to meet me ... this afternoon' ... I then got out of the car. On the same afternoon I saw Ivy Matthews at the time and place appointed. She said, 'Come up here; I want to have a word with you.' I accompanied her to a house in Rathdowne Street, Carlton.

Matthews supplied Halliwell with drink. She said: 'Remember, I don't want you to slip [up] in anything I told you this morning. What did you tell Piggott you never made the keys for?'

Halliwell replied, 'I was telling the truth when I said it.' His deposition continues:

> Ivy Matthews said, 'Go round to the detective office and tell them what I have told you to say.'

I ... proceeded to the detective office in Russell Street ... Piggott said, 'Step inside; you are the man we want. When were you in Colin Ross's saloon?' I said, 'On Friday.' Piggott said, 'No, it was on Thursday, and you were there on the Saturday afternoon, and Colin Ross spoke to you and said to you he was blamed for the murder, and you said to him, "What do they want to blame you for?" and Ross said, "I've never been a shelf."' After further questioning Piggott said, 'I want you to sign this,' and I signed a piece of paper with writing on it.

That Piggott was framing information to fit the case against Ross and that Ivy Matthews was cooperating with him are grave charges. If false, Halliwell should have been prosecuted for perjury and libel, yet there was no response when his controversial claims were published in the press a fortnight later, and subsequently in Brennan's book.

27. The mysterious woman

Ivy Matthews decided to give an extensive biographical account of herself to HC Maddison, published on 8 March. 'I want the readers of *Smith's Weekly* to know the real facts of my life and to let them know who and what this "mysterious Matthews woman" is.

'I am an Australian. I was born at Burnie, Tasmania, on 2 September, 27 years ago [1894]. My real name is Ivy Florence Matthews. My father died when I was 3 [and] ... two years later, my mother married Patrick Dolan and I took his name.'

It should be straightforward to confirm these facts—a birth, a death and a marriage—at the Tasmanian Registrar General's Office, but a comprehensive search failed to locate any certificate. Throughout the island from 1880–1901 no birth was recorded for a child named Ivy Florence Matthews. Nor was there any marriage registered involving any Dolan and a Matthews.

'I was 9 years old when I was sent ... to live with an aunt, Mrs Julia Atkinson, in Caroline Street, South Yarra. I remained with this aunt until I was about 15 years old.

[Then] I left school and took a position as a junior saleswoman in Reid's stores in Prahran, working in the haberdashery. I remained there for nearly 4 years, and worked afterwards at Love and Lewis's in the same city.

'Soon after, I returned to Tasmania to my parents. There I met for the first time my future husband. His name is William Henry Sutton ... His present address is a private hospital in Ipswich, Queensland, where he is dying of cancer.

'Our marriage was ... none of my seeking. At that time I had it in my mind to become a nurse. He was a wealthy mining manager—a member of the Melbourne Stock Exchange ... He was 20 years older than I was—old enough to be my father, but my stepfather was bent upon the marriage ...'

The *Midnight Sun* responded:

Mr Sutton is not, and never was, a member of the 'Change. Inaccuracy number one. [8 April 1922]

Of Sutton, Matthews said: 'I had no real affection for him at the time, but we were thrown into one another's company for 12 months, and eventually I agreed to marry him. We were married on March 18, 1914 ... The wedding took place at the Methodist church, at Burnie ...

'We lived together for just 2 weeks. I had found that I had made a mistake ... One day I decided to take a boat to Melbourne and left a note on the dressing table informing him I was not coming back ... I went back to work. I got employment as manageress of the Union Manufacturing Co. in Elizabeth Street, Melbourne, where I stayed for 2 years.'

The *Midnight Sun*:

Inquiries ... reveal the fact that Miss Matthews was only employed at this firm for a period of seven months—

from July 1916 to February 1917, and not in the capacity of manageress at all, but that of a saleswoman. Inaccuracy number two.

The *Midnight Sun* concluded: '[T]he question of to what extent [Matthews] can be relied on, either in speaking of herself or of others, is a very open one, indeed.' It was something of which Piggott was aware, since he had pasted into his Gun Alley scrapbook both the Maddison article and the *Midnight Sun*'s refutations.

The possibility of Matthews's unreliability is supported by a Tasmanian certificate of marriage for a William Henry Sutton and an Irene Florence Dolan. The bride's handwriting is identical with that of Matthews. The certificate stated that Sutton was a 'mining engineer'. He was 50 years old, a childless widower, and the marriage was solemnised 'according to the usages of the Methodist Church' in March 1914 at Burnie.

Most of the information supplied by the bride contradicts *Smith's Weekly*. She gave her age as 24, implying she was born in 1890—*not* 1894—and thus was 32 in 1922—*not* 27. Moreover, on the certificate, Matthews gave her birthplace as 'Prahran, Victoria', and her present and usual residence as 'Brunswick, Victoria'. She gave her father's name and occupation as 'Alfred Arthur Dolan—bricklayer', and her mother's name as 'Margret [*sic*] Atkin'.

In his 1965 book, *Crime Chemist*, Alan Dower disclosed some aspects of Matthews's life after the Ross case. She accrued a substantial number of charges in Victorian police records under various aliases. Dower:

> She was an abortionist. Her dossier number—531/33—records charges of abortion, receiving, unlawful possession and insulting words since 1933. Always she appeared in court under assumed names—Irene Cholet,

Irene F Sholet, Nurse Mack, Florence Mackie, Irene Smith and Patricia Cholet—that never revealed her true identity.

... Late in 1963 ... [Sergeant] Jack Ford [of the homicide squad] led a raid on a house at Kew ... They surprised a woman allegedly in the act of conducting grave illegal operations and charged her to appear before the Criminal Court. The hearing was delayed several times as the woman suffered repeated heart attacks. Finally it was listed for a Wednesday in September, 1964. Four days before this date the woman suffered another heart attack. She died the morning she was to have appeared in that court, prepared to admit her guilt in the name of Irene Cholet and go to gaol so that the case would be dealt with swiftly and her name, life and times as Ivy Matthews might never be revealed.

The informant for the death certificate was Francis Daniel Cholet, husband of the deceased, of Kew. The couple had married in 1933 in a Methodist ceremony at Albert Park, Melbourne. The groom described himself as a bachelor, aged 36, and a coppersmith. The bride declared herself to have been widowed '23/12/30'. This time her story was that she was born in 'Burnie, Tasmania'; aged 33 (ie born in 1900); that she was a nurse residing in Albert Park; that her father's name was John Murphy, 'mine manager', and that her mother's name was Florence Mack. The Cholets were childless.

One final point: when Brennan asked Matthews in February 1922, 'Is your name Ivy Florence Matthews?' and Matthews replied on oath, 'To the best of my belief it is', she committed perjury. Matthews's two marriage certificates show that from 21 March 1914 (the actual date of her first marriage) to 9 March 1933 (the date of her second marriage), her name was Irene (Patricia) Florence Sutton (née Dolan).

28. The myth of instant death

Theoretically, in the ideal hanging the condemned man drops, stopping with a jerk of sufficient force to snap the neck instantly. Thus the prisoner is rendered unconscious, and simultaneously the noose forcibly closes to a diameter of three inches (7.5 centimetres), compressing the neck. Stoppage of arterial blood to the head deprives the brain of oxygen, with total brain death in six to eight minutes. Compression of the windpipe means air cannot get into the lungs. The remainder of the body becomes starved of oxygen and its systems begin to shut down. Reflex muscular spasms occur, with erection of the penis and evacuation of the bowels and bladder. The heart continues beating until its own supply of oxygen is depleted. Finally there is fibrillation and eventual stoppage.

Such was the ideal, but in practice instantaneous death was not inevitable. The condemned might die only after a lengthy agony of shock and asphyxiation. Between 1894 and 1924 there were 19 hangings in the Melbourne Gaol. Of these, at least eight (42 per cent) were botched.

In 1892, the British Home Office began developing some

fundamental guidelines for hanging. The lighter the weight of the condemned, the further they had to fall in order to reach the neck-snapping force necessary for instantaneous death. Conversely, the heavier the condemned, the shorter the distance they had to fall. The force necessary for snapping the human vertebrae was, on average, 840 foot-pounds. The principle translated to a table of drops calculated by dividing 840 by the weight in pounds of the condemned person in their clothes.

The Home Office Table of Drops cautions that: 'no drop should exceed 8 feet'. Otherwise the condemned's head might be torn off. Instantaneous death would result, but with tremendous bloody mess.

Neither hangmen nor the government medical officers necessarily had expertise. The executioners might be ignorant or inept. Their job was unpopular, and those willing to do it were otherwise undesirables. Robert Gibbon, Victoria's hangman from 1897 to 1907, was a mentally deficient child-sex offender.

The duty of the medical officer at a hanging in the Melbourne Gaol was to stand below the gallows trap, awaiting the fall of the condemned. The hangman, his assistant, the governor of the gaol, the sheriff and the chaplain all stood above, on the gallows platform. Journalists were permitted to see the body of the condemned fall, a split-second after which a green curtain was released, immediately screening the hanging body from view. The death throes were then observed by the medical witnesses only.

Because government medical officers knew much could go wrong, it was required that the hanged person should remain suspended on the rope for one hour after dropping. Even in well-managed hangings the heart could take some time to cease beating, and it was essential that no chance whatever exist for the revival of the hanged man or woman.

From 1916 to 1918, the government medical officer required to attend executions at the Melbourne Gaol was Dr O'Brien. He documented the four executions prior to Ross, all of them bungled. His notes demonstrate: the incompetence of the hangman; official indifference towards humanitarian concerns; and the bureaucratic intransigence preventing reform. O'Brien knew the Home Office regulations and tried to introduce them, but was repeatedly thwarted. Not until 1939 and the execution of Thomas Johnson were some of the regulations applied, and even then the hanging was botched, Johnson dying of asphyxiation. Officially hanging was proffered as a humane form of execution, but O'Brien shows it was not. Three of the hangings witnessed by O'Brien involved near-decapitations; in the fourth the rope stretched.

Ross would be the 174th person executed by hanging in Victoria. The public was informed a new hangman had been appointed, but what was kept secret was the experiment planned, involving a kind of rope that had never before been tried, and for which there was certainly no recommendation in the instructions of the Home Office. The experiment would fail—appallingly for Ross.

29. A dandy 'D'

Interviewed shortly before his death at age 93, ex-superintendent HR (Bill) Donelly, a founding member and eventual chief of Melbourne's homicide squad, recalled that Detective Piggott's successful involvement with the 'heavier inquiries'—elaborate swindles, illegal abortions or especially mysterious murders—meant his name was frequently in the press. He was highly rated not only in the public eye but also by the police. Ex-inspector George A Newton, who entered the force as a constable in 1923, remembered that Piggott was considered generally to be 'the leading detective of that period'.

Even Melbourne's underworld agreed. After Ross's failed appeal to the Victorian Full Court, gangster Joseph Leslie 'Squizzy' Taylor sent off the following to the *Herald*, which he prefaced with: 'For the old saying goes—'

> Ashes to ashes, dust to dust;
> if Brophy don't get you,
> well, Piggott must.

The jingle almost certainly dates from the Gun Alley case, for Piggott and Brophy did not generally work together. Neither man had been teamed on a case of any particular stature since 1913.

Jim Rosengren joined the Victoria Police in 1932, becoming Assistant Commissioner (Crime) in 1964. He recalled that in his six years with the CIB he often heard the jingle when reference was made to Brophy or Piggott. But Rosengren was emphatic that Squizzy was misquoted: 'Piggott's name came first. Piggott was always given precedence ...'

The precedence of Piggott, both professionally and in the CIB's version of the rhyme, was borne out in interviews with both George Newton and ex-brevet sub-inspector Fred Hobley. Newton recalled that Piggott '... had a sophisticated personality ... He spoke very well ... He never used any sort of language that was ever crude or anything like that. [He was a] well-groomed, well-dressed—superbly dressed—man ... [Indeed,] on some occasions ... he overdid it ... [He was] like one of these stock exchange men that you'd see walking with a walking stick—in that period anyway—and gloves on and all the rest of it, in Collins Street ...'

An anonymous newspaper satirist gave the same impression:

A dandy 'D' is Piggott
When he's out upon a case
He makes the tales of Sherlock Holmes
Seem tame and commonplace.

He runs the thief and forger down,
He corrals up the crook;
And many a daring criminal
Has Piggott brought to book.

Piggott was instrumental in establishing the Victorian Police Association in 1917 and was voted vice-president in its first election. Even after retirement he kept up the connection. In a 1961 claim for a pay rise, Piggott, then 87, spoke on the association's behalf at a hearing of the Police Classification Board. He was quoted on the use to which he put the detectives' allowance of 5/6 a day. This sum, allocated to detectives to 'buy information', had remained unchanged for more than 40 years. Piggott stated: 'I spent the lot.' The remark gives not only an indication of the extent to which his success as a senior detective in the 1920s relied on bribes, but it also demonstrates his acceptance of this practice as normal and ethical. The most disturbing feature about his testimony is the suggestion that if the price was right, a criminal might be purchased.

Piggott also stated that in the 1920s the allowance was fair, but in the present day it would represent only a fraction of a detective's pay cheque. 'My pay then was about 12 shillings a day. So the extra allowance—about half my pay—went far to getting the information that brings criminals in.'

In the decades since, times had changed, and the function of the allowance was no longer admitted to be for quite the purposes Piggott was suggesting. In fact, here Piggott did little to aid the cause of the association that he himself had—in an earlier, harsher and more desperate policing era—helped to establish. The pay claim was refused.

Fred Hobley: '... of the two, I think Piggott was a few steps ahead of Brophy ... in getting information. Of course, you understand, they had their contacts ...'

> Ashes to ashes, dust to dust;
> if Piggott doesn't get you,
> then Brophy must.

30. Farewell

The family and friends of a condemned person were freely permitted to visit the prisoner until the morning of the day prior to execution, and the number of Ross's visitors was a record for the Melbourne Gaol. Since the execution was set for Monday morning, Anzac Day eve, visits would not be permitted after Sunday morning. Ross last saw a small group of his family, including his mother and sister. It was later said that Ross was the most composed; the consoler rather than the consoled.

Two warders watched outside the cell door. One visitor at a time was permitted to approach the door, to a distance not less than 3 feet, and from there speak with Ross. Everything took place within the sight and hearing of his guards and it was strictly forbidden to pass any article to the prisoner. The permitted length of the visit was generally half an hour.

When it came time for Mrs Ross to farewell her son, she stood before the bars of his cell. She could not at first speak.

Colin: 'Mother, all I want you to do is not to watch the clock tomorrow. I thank God you and Ronald know me innocent. Hold your head up wherever you go. And tell the boys not to do anything rash. I want you to live, Mum. Until my innocence is proved. And then—'

'What, Colin?'

'And then—' continued Ross, stretching his arms through the bars, 'I want to take my mother home.'

Mrs Ross: 'Colin, you know, I will fight for you while I have breath.'

Time was creeping on and the interview would have to end. Mrs Ross asked: 'Can I embrace my boy once before his journey?'

The warder shook his head. He was sorry, but it could not be done. Nor was a parting kiss through the bars permitted; and so Mrs Ross took leave of her son. It was said that, subsequent to this visit, a supreme calm fell upon Ross. Having said farewell to his family, Ross was returned to the exercise yard. At 6pm he was taken into the condemned cell, where the Reverend Goble visited him.

It seems the purpose of the visit was to write a letter to Ross's mother. Presumably as a special favour Goble interceded to permit Ross the use of a pen. The letter would be delivered after the execution. During the writing, Ross occasionally appealed to Goble regarding spelling, but otherwise the chaplain sat quietly by. Ross wrote:

> Goodbye my darling mother and brothers. On this, the last night of my life, I want to tell you that I love you all more than ever. Do not fear for tomorrow, for I know God will be with me. Try to forgive my enemies—let God deal with them. I want you, dear mother, and Ronald, to thank all the friends who have been so kind to you and me during our trouble. I have received nothing but kindness since I have been in gaol. Say goodbye to Gladdie for me, and I wish for her a happy life. Dear ones, do not fret too much for me. The day is coming when my innocence will be proved. Goodbye, all my dear ones. Some day you will meet again your loving son and brother.
> Colin X X X X X X X X

31. Execution

The day before Anzac Day: dark skies; rain drizzled down the slates and windows of the city, of the gaol. At 9.15am Acting Chief Warder Matthew Ryan and three other warders stood outside Ross's cell.† The prisoner was informed that he was to be taken to the death cell on the gallery above. Ross declared his readiness to go with the warders.

There was absolute silence in the corridor. All the other prisoners had been brought in from the exercise yards and were in their cells. Ross walked without hesitation to the death cell. He was led inside and the door closed. At 9.20am the Reverend WL Fenton, the official Presbyterian chaplain to the prison, and the Reverend Goble entered the cell. To Goble Ross said: 'I am ready now to face the highest court of appeal, where there is no law—but justice.'

A crowd of more than 1000 gathered outside the gaol. The opinion was freely expressed that the condemned man would confess his guilt at the last minute. Motor cars, jinkers and tradesmen's carts also pulled up. Out on the road traffic was practically blocked.

---

†It is not recorded why Chief Warder John Gloster could not, or would not, accompany Ross to the scaffold on this day.

The witnesses to the execution, some 30 people comprising policemen, officials and journalists, entered the gaol at about 9.30am and waited in the anteroom near the main entrance. At 9.55am they were led through the courtyard and up a short corridor where, passing through a barred door, they went into a space between two iron staircases running up to the gallery. Looking up, they could see the gallows: a heavy beam let into the walls above the lintels of two cells, in one of which was the condemned man with his chaplains, in the other the hangman and his assistant. The floor space between the cells was mostly occupied by the trapdoor.

Just before 10am a procession headed by the governor of the gaol arrived. It included Dr Godfrey, the government medical officer, who took up his position under the scaffold.

Governor Barclay led the way up the stairs and faced Sheriff Miller.

'I demand from you the body of Colin Campbell Ross,' said the sheriff.

'Where is your warrant?' asked Barclay.

The sheriff gave the document to the governor, who knocked on the door of the death cell. Simultaneously, the masked executioner emerged with his assistant. The warders opened Ross's cell. Preceded by the governor, the executioners entered the cell and pinioned Ross's arms behind his back.

A few minutes earlier Ross had farewelled Goble with a friendly pressure of the arm that was, the chaplain would later say, 'more eloquent than words'. Fenton would accompany Ross to the scaffold. He had earlier conferred with Ross over the biblical verses to be read at this point.

Ross's executioners led him to the centre of the trapdoor, only a few paces from the doorway of the cell. Fenton read: *This is a faithful saying and worthy of all acceptation that Christ Jesus came into the world to save sinners of whom*

I am chief. [1 Timothy 1: 15] Ross stood on the drop while his ankles were strapped together. *He is able to save them to the uttermost that come unto God by Him, seeing He even liveth to make intercession for them.* [Hebrews 7: 25]

The executioner adjusted the noose round Ross's neck, placed a white cap over his head, its peak lifted, and stood aside.

Wherefore gird up the loins of your mind. Be sober and hope to the end for the grace that is to be brought unto you at the revelation of Jesus Christ. [1 Peter 1: 15]

Miller: 'Colin Campbell Ross, have you anything to say before sentence of death is carried out?'

Ross was silent. He then spoke clearly and slowly—

I am now face to face with my Maker, and I swear by Almighty God that I am an innocent man. I never saw the child. I never committed the crime, and I don't know who did. I never confessed to anyone. I ask God to forgive those who have sworn my life away, and I pray God to have mercy on my poor darling mother, and my family.

Some would suggest Ross lied in this statement. He had freely admitted he had seen Alma. However, he could simply have meant that he had not seen the girl except as he had already admitted.†

When Ross ceased speaking, the sheriff waited a few moments. He motioned to the executioner, who placed the flap of the cap over Ross's face. The lever was pulled, and Ross fell through the gallows trap. The green cloth

---

†It was later revealed that Ross intended to say more than this. His chaplains knew he had proposed denouncing some of the Crown witnesses. They urged him to make peace with the world. He accepted the cut, but may have excised more than intended, like a qualifier to: 'I never saw the girl.'

attached to the side of the gallery was released, hiding Ross as he fell from the view of those below. Less than two minutes had elapsed since the executioner entered Ross's cell. Fenton, who had been quietly reading aloud prayers from the burial service, continued until the lever was pulled.

Warders quickly escorted the guests back the way they had come. A cup of tea was available for those wanting it.

Behind the green curtain, Ross rebounded on the rope, his throat and neck taking the impact, his body revolving slowly. But the noose had closed to only 4 inches. The knot did not run freely. Ross had sustained a fracture to the second cervical vertebra with pressure on the spinal cord within. But the cord was not severed, the medullary centre not paralysed. His diaphragm contracted as he inhaled, with a wet guttural sucking. His windpipe was torn, and obstructed by the fragments of his larynx.

Blood vessels haemorrhaged into the structures of his throat, and Ross convulsed on the rope. He struggled against the bonds, flexing his arms at the elbow, his knees bending. Three times he assumed this posture, before finally becoming limp. Although the length of time it took for Ross to die is not officially recorded, the physiological indications suggest a timeframe of between eight and 20 minutes.

Ross's body hung from the beam until 11 o'clock, when it was removed to the gaol morgue to await inquest.

Outside the gaol a great silence had descended on the crowd. In Russell Street a police inspector told them it was all over. By 11 o'clock most had gone. They had neither seen nor heard anything of the execution. No flag was raised. No bell was tolled. Their curiosity had remained unsatisfied.

It is hard to imagine more going wrong with a hanging than that of Colin Campbell Ross. Much of the problem can be attributed to the experiment with a type of rope (four-stranded, rather than three-stranded European hemp) not previously used in executions in Victoria. It was not prescribed for use by the Home Office.

In the Melbourne Gaol's *The Particulars of Executions*, red ink was used for the first time, so that it might never be forgotten. EA Hughes, senior hospital warder, wrote:

NOTE: A four-stranded rope was used for the first time. Never use it again. Important.

The red ink has smudged across the page, like blood. In his confidential report, Dr Godfrey summarised the problems. The rope could be blamed in part, but so could the hangman:

The rope was less pliable than usual ... the knot was unnecessarily large. The knot did not run freely ...

Again the drop was vastly in excess of that prescribed by the Home Office. Ross's weight on the day before his execution was 153½ pounds, requiring, according to the Home Office calculations, a drop of 5 feet and 5 inches. He instead was dropped 8 feet 5 inches. Godfrey claimed, 'the rope itself stretched approximately 9½ inches', thus contradicting his earlier statement that 'The rope was less pliable than usual ...' So remarkable a stretching of the rope suggests the problem was more due to the hangman's inexperience.

The gaol's authorities, the community and its judicial system, all relied on Godfrey to certify that Ross's death was instantaneous. To do otherwise would incur some responsibility for error. As the presiding medical officer, he should ensure the execution was conducted humanely.

Godfrey would tender his post-mortem report to the coroner at an inquest at the gaol that afternoon. On this occasion the coroner, Dr Cole, could not be present, instead sending his deputy, Alexander Phillips, a man with no practical experience of judicial executions. Worse, newsmen would be attending. What if word got out about the botched execution?

Godfrey:

> I have made a post-mortem examination of the body of Colin Campbell Ross with regard to the structures of the neck. I found the second cervical vertebra was fractured with pressure on the spinal cord. The cause of death was fracture of the spine. I was present at the execution of deceased. The arrangements were conducted with strict regard to humanity and death was instantaneous.

This report, which Godfrey placed on the public record, is very different from his notes made that same day in *The Particulars of Executions*.

Dropping such a distance, Ross would almost certainly have been decapitated—if the knot had fully tightened. The noose did not close to the requisite 7.5 centimetres around his throat, but only 10 centimetres, which ensured air could still enter his trachea. Ross suffered a prolonged and agonising asphyxiation, and Godfrey noted the classic physiological responses of death by throttling.

Shortly after 6 o'clock that night, Ross's body was buried in the unconsecrated ground of the gaol's cemetery. Quicklime was scattered over his remains to hasten decomposition. Persons executed had no claim to memory and by an Act of Parliament their remains were forfeited to the state. Mrs Ross made concerted efforts to have her son's body returned for interment in the family's burial ground in the Footscray Cemetery, but she was continuously rejected.

Before he left the death cell, Ross gave Fenton a Bible inscribed: 'This Bible is the kind gift to me from my chaplain, Rev W Fenton. Thanking him for all his help and kindness to me.' Ross intended the Bible to be passed on 'To my Darling Mother'. It survives in the care of the Ross family.

Colin marked off and annotated certain verses, underlining particular words and phrases. He thus reshaped the text into a commentary on his recent life. Some idea of the annotations is shown in the following extracts. Where a marked passage bears some commentary by Ross or he has replaced an existing word with one of his own, the annotation is shown in italics.

> 'False witnesses rose up against me; they laid to my charge things that I knew not. *time will tell*' (Psalms 35: 11, 12)
>
> '... for I have seen violence and strife in the city. *Melbourne.* Day and night they go about it upon the walls thereof: mischief also and sorrow are in the midst of it. *The Police.* Wickedness is in the midst thereof: deceit and guile depart not from her streets. *Melbourne.*' (Psalms 55: 9–11)
>
> 'Gather not my soul ... with bloody men: In whose hands is mischief, <u>and their right hand is full of bribes</u>.† *This is our Police force which our people think so much of.*' (Psalms 26: 9, 10)
>
> '*Piggott.* ... posterity approves his sayings ... death shall feed on him ... and his beauty shall consume in the grave from his dwelling ... Though while he lived he blessed his soul ... he shall go to the generation of his fathers; they shall never see light. Man that is in honour, and understandeth not, is like the beasts that perish.' (Psalms 49: 12–14, 18–20)

---

†Ross's underlining

Among the verses Colin marked were several clearly intended as a farewell to his mother.

> 'Let not your heart be troubled ... I go and prepare a place for you ... I will not leave you comfortless ...' (John 14: 1, 18)
>
> 'If God be for us, who can be against us?' (Romans 8: 31)
>
> 'Who shall separate us ...? ... For I am persuaded that neither death, nor life, nor angels, nor principalities, nor powers, nor things present, nor things to come, nor height, nor depth, nor any other creature, shall be able to separate us ...' (Romans 8: 35, 38, 39)

32. Brophy

John O'Connell Brophy had come from a police family: his father was a mounted constable. In March 1900 the then 21-year-old joined Victoria Police. His first beat was in the city division, as would be all his service. 'Well conducted, intelligent & efficient', wrote one of his supervisors in 1910. Brophy was accepted into the CIB in 1912. He had already passed his examinations for sergeant (1905) and even officer rank (1907) but would not be promoted to senior level until he had served a further eight and a half years. After achieving many significant arrests, Brophy was promoted to senior detective on 11 February 1921.

Journalist Tom Gurr described Brophy as '... jovial, well-rounded. He wore a black Homburg hat and a heavy gold watch-chain across his egg-shaped middle.' 'A cheerful personality,' remembered Fred Hobley, '... easy to get on with ... Brophy was the easier man to approach. Piggott was rather conservative ... [not] as talkative discussing things as Brophy.'

Brophy's role in the arrest and conviction of Ross, was, Superintendent Potter wrote, '... deserving of special promotion'. He received five subsequent promotions in the following 14 years, culminating in April 1936 in the role of chief of the CIB. Brophy was now close to the chief commissioner's office—a position occupied since 1925 by former military man Brigadier-General Sir Thomas Blamey. Within a month, however, Blamey would be disgraced.

Both men's careers, in fact, would end after a Friday night at the Melbourne Zoological Gardens. At 10.45pm, 22 May 1936, a small dark car drove along the dirt road that formed the perimeter of the zoo. At distances along the road vehicles had parked in the quiet dimness of the tree-lined track. This car pulled off the road behind a Daimler owned by Mrs Madeleine Orr, a hotelier and friend of Brophy's.

From the dark car two men, possibly three, emerged.

There are several accounts of what happened next. The most official is the report of a royal commission headed by the then Judge Macindoe, who later admitted that he had held Blamey in good regard and had tried 'to steer him to the truth'. But in the end Macindoe could only report euphemistically that Blamey 'gave replies which were not in accordance with the truth'—to conceal that 'women were in the company of Superintendent Brophy'.

The account that follows has not previously been published, but its source is impeccable: ex-superintendent HR (Bill) Donelly, a former chief of Melbourne's homicide squad. Donelly knew Brophy and was working as a detective under his authority during the 1930s.

In October 1995, Donelly offered to be interviewed for this book. He agreed to discuss his recollections of Brophy and Piggott and understood that the information was intended for publication. He died in 1996, aged 93. His disclosures about that May night in 1936 are controversial. He would say only that his information came from 'a senior source in whom I have the utmost confidence'.

Donelly explained that the road around the zoo was notorious as a lover's lane, but by the mid–1930s was also attracting a reputation for thuggery. On the night in question, said Donelly, Blamey had compelled Brophy to drive him to the zoo. Blamey and a prostitute were in the back of the Daimler. Brophy and Mrs Orr were in the front. Blamey was drunk and had 'stripped off' the prostitute in the back seat. He was engaged in a sex act with the prostitute and had his head 'down' when three men appeared around the car. One man threatened Brophy through the open window on the driver's side. According to Donelly, Brophy pushed him away and the man fell to the ground. Brophy wound up the window. The man on the ground 'growled like a dog', Donelly said, and pulled out a gun, wounding Brophy with three shots.

Donelly was on duty the night of the Brophy shooting. At Russell Street a telephone call was received from Mrs Orr, asking to speak 'to someone senior'. Donelly claimed Brophy was made to wear the blame for the dishonourable conduct of his superior officer, Blamey. Both men left the force under a cloud—Blamey in 1936, Brophy in 1937.

Brophy died in October 1946 of lung cancer and heart disease, aged 68.

33. Ghurka's fortune

By mid-June the Ross reward had been paid to its various beneficiaries.† Ivy Matthews received a total (comprising the government and *Herald* allocations) of £437/10/-. Madame Ghurka received £31/5/-, for services never officially disclosed, though she later claimed it was for housing Matthews prior to the trial.

That month the friendship between Ghurka and Matthews ended. Madame Ghurka submitted to Matthews an account for boarding: £104/1/-. At first Matthews declined to pay and Madame asked her to leave. Madame referred the account to her solicitor and Matthews then paid it.

Fewer and fewer businesses would occupy rooms at the now notorious Eastern Arcade. In 1923 the City Tyre and Tube Repair Company occupied the former wine saloon rooms. But in 1924 the rooms were again vacant, as were many others on the ground floor. In the huge gallery only

---

†See table on page 349 showing reward and sustenance payments.

six tenants remained. No one else would ever rent Ross's rooms.

In 1926 the Eastern Arcade's new occupiers, Clauscen and Co, undertook a complete refurbishment of the interior. The building was converted into a furniture emporium. Madame Ghurka hung on to her rooms at the arcade until the very end. She then moved to Drummond Street, Carlton, to continue her practice as a character reader aka fortune-teller, and as Julia Gibson, dressmaker. Her income, though, derived largely from the former. She would be convicted twice in 1929 and once in 1933 for 'using a subtle craft and certain devices by palmistry to defraud or impose'. She would also intervene as a psychic in several murder cases.

Another source of income was from lawsuits. One example: in May 1951 the then 80-year-old Ghurka was awarded £1000 in a libel suit against the *Herald*. The latter had reported the recent sale of the Rathdowne Street house, and referred to the building as 'Carlton's ghost house ... where the notorious fortune-teller Madame Ghurka used to live'. It is now the Quit Campaign headquarters of the Victorian Anti-Cancer Council.

One final note: in July 1922 Ghurka gave evidence in a divorce suit involving one of her boarders, a Mrs Kerr, who had been having an affair with Alexander Olsen, Madame's son. Justice McArthur heard Ghurka's evidence, and described her as a 'bitter and vindictive woman', and 'the sort ... who would say anything, whether it was true or false'.

An analysis of the evidence

34. Brennan's book

In October 1922, Alma's uncle, John Murdoch, wrote to the Attorney-General asking him to prevent the imminent publication of *The Gun Alley Tragedy* by TC Brennan:

> I ... with the other relatives of the family feel somewhat distressed to think that a book is to be published which may be once again bringing forward all the harrowing details ... [I]t is to be a criticism of the verdict and ... this is not a desirable procedure ... without taking into consideration the feeling of the relatives.

Robinson regretted he had no power to prevent the book being published, though he told Murdoch he regarded the publication as 'a reprehensible and even dangerous precedent'.

Brennan noted in his introduction:

> ... for a generation to come the name of a Ross will never be mentioned without recalling that particular bearer of it who died an ignominious death for a revolting murder. If all the truth has not come out, the community owes it to those of his blood left behind him that it shall be brought

out. It is largely at the solicitation of those bearers of the name that this review is being written.

In the book Brennan demonstrated that the Harding and Matthews confessions agreed on almost all the points that were already known to the police. These were: that Alma Tirtschke was in the vicinity of the Eastern Arcade at about 3 o'clock; that Ross had been speaking to Gladys Wain both outside and, for an hour after 4 o'clock, inside the saloon; that he went home to Footscray for tea; he met with Gladys again in the saloon for over an hour after 9.15pm; and that he went home late by train and tram. All this information came from Colin's and Stanley's statements of 5 January, and Gladys Wain's statement of 12 January. They also knew that the body was not in the alley at 1 o'clock, that Ellis had said that he had seen a man going in and out of the arcade near that time, and that Ross suffered from a venereal disease.

But on the five aspects about which nothing was known to the police, the two confessions are absolutely at variance: 1. How did the girl actually get into the saloon? 2. How did Gladys Wain fail to see anything of the girl when she was there in the afternoon? 3. What was the exact manner of the girl's death? 4. How was Gladys Wain prevented from seeing the body when she came in at 9 o'clock? 5. How did Ross get back from Footscray late at night to dispose of the body? These five points had to be somehow answered if Ross were to be made responsible for the crime.

Brennan concluded that Matthews and Harding were provided with certain facts about Ross by the police, but were compelled to fill in the gaps themselves. They could not have been drawing from the one alleged source (Ross) when they differed so absolutely as to the essential circumstances of the crime. Indeed, by the time of publication, Brennan knew the source of Harding's information: Detective Walshe. Brennan observed that had the defence known of this at the time of the trial, it would 'have given the jury something to consider ...'

Regarding the philosophy behind the police methods used to convict Ross, Brennan quoted two passages from *Taylor on Evidence*. The first concerns the caution necessary in considering all police evidence:

> With respect to policemen, constables and others employed in the detection of crime, their testimony against a prisoner should usually be watched with care not because they intentionally pervert the truth but because their professional zeal, fed as it is by an habitual intercourse with the vicious, and by the frequent contemplation of human nature in its most revolting form, almost necessarily leads them to ascribe actions to the worst motives, and to give a colouring of guilt to facts and conversations which are, perhaps, in themselves, consistent with perfect rectitude. 'That all men are guilty till they are proved to be innocent' is naturally the creed of the police, but it is a creed which finds no sanction in a court of law.

The other passage deals with the dangers of circumstantial evidence:

> It must be remembered that, in a case of circumstantial evidence, the facts are collected by degrees. Something occurs to raise a suspicion against a particular party. Constables and police officers are immediately on the alert, and, with professional zeal, ransack every place and paper, and examine into every circumstance which can tend to establish, not his innocence, but his guilt. Presuming him guilty from the first, they ... determine, if possible, to bag their game. Innocent actions may thus be misinterpreted, innocent words misunderstood, and as men readily believe what they anxiously desire, facts

the most harmless may be construed into strong confirmation of preconceived opinions. It is not here asserted that this is commonly the case, nor is it intended to disparage the police. The feelings by which they are actuated are common to all persons who first assume a fact or system is true, and then seek for argument to support and prove its truth.

Nobody took Brennan to court over his book. To do so might not only have confirmed his allegations, but also exposed the tainted methods of the police. In fact Brennan anticipated the damning observations of Sir Frederick Mann, Chief Justice of the Victorian Supreme Court. In 1936, Mann denounced the criminal investigation work of Victorian detectives as 'the crude and unbridled doings of untrained investigators, who depended too much on informers and ... coercion ...'

Mann had tried a libel case in November 1925 in which Madame Ghurka appeared. *Truth* had published an article in which it claimed Ghurka had said she had seen Alma Tirtschke enter Ross's wine saloon. *Truth* suggested Ghurka could have saved the child's life, but had not acted. Subsequently Ghurka denied ever making any statement about seeing Alma Tirtschke and took *Truth* to court. The case meant that some of Ghurka's claims, made in her own booklet *The Murder of Alma Tirtschke: A Challenge to T.C. Brennan*, could be tested in court. For instance, she admitted to various conversations with Matthews on the Saturday and Sunday after the murder:

> Matthews came to live at my place shortly after she left the employ of Ross. I pitied the unfortunate woman and befriended her ... On Saturday [31 December] ... she came down to [my office in the arcade] ... I was not busy at the time and I asked her to come inside and sit down. The conversation turned on the murder.

Ghurka said Matthews became pale and uneasy as they talked:

> Suddenly she rose, and without making any remark left my office. I followed her to the door and watched her. She went to the door of Ross's saloon, slowly passed it, and then came back again and looked towards the interior. It seemed to me as if she were trying to attract the attention of someone on the inside. Ross came out in his shirt sleeves, and spoke to her. Presently ... the two walked together out into Little Collins Street.
>
> That night, at my home, Matthews and I had a conversation ... I purposely brought the conversation round to the tragedy.

According to Ghurka, Matthews shuddered and would not meet Ghurka's gaze. When Ghurka pressed the point with the words 'I think Ross knows something about it', Matthews became agitated. Ghurka wanted her to go to the police but Matthews left.

In Ghurka's book she claimed that on the Saturday night, she had 'learnt something in the interval between Matthews and Ross's meeting that afternoon', which justified her suspicion of Ross. During the 1925 case, Ghurka admitted under oath she had no grounds whatever to suggest that she suspected Ross on that Saturday night.

Mr Dixon (for *Truth*): 'Did you not get the news late on Saturday and ring the police straight away?'

Madame Ghurka: 'No, that was on Monday or Tuesday.'

'Well, you say in your book late on Saturday; how did that get there?'

'The man must have made an error ...' answered Ghurka, referring to Welch, her ghostwriter.

Dixon: '... On page 45, the book says, "Late on the same Saturday I heard that a man named Hines had told two people ... that Olive Maddox ... had seen the child in the saloon on the afternoon of the murder." Isn't that what you mean when you say you learnt something in the meanwhile?'

Ghurka: 'No, that must be a mistake of the corrector.'

Dixon: 'In black type at the top of the page you have the words "WHY I SUSPECTED ROSS". Do you mean to tell the jury what you have just said is true?'

Ghurka: 'It is right, I can't speak English too well; that is the reason I make mistakes.'

It is clear Ghurka was eager to implicate Ross from the start:

> [I] ... immediately ... called up the CIB office. I asked that one of the detectives on the Gun Alley murder be sent out to my place at once, as I had something to communicate of the very greatest importance ...
>
> Early the next morning detectives Piggott and Brophy arrived at my house. I took them into the presence of Ivy Matthews, saying, 'I think this woman (Ivy Matthews) has something to tell you.'

But Matthews declined to speak, perhaps because she had not yet worked out what the stakes were, and what she would have to say.

Ghurka won her suit and was awarded £100 in damages, despite having sued for £1000.

35. Piggott recalls

After a distinguished career Superintendent Piggott retired on his 60th birthday in 1934. Within months the *Herald* ran a series of interviews with him: 'Secrets of Melbourne's Most Sensational Crimes—Leaves from the Private Diary of ex-Superintendent Frederick J Piggott'. Piggott's 'private diary' was actually his four scrapbooks, containing his snapshots, some taken by government photographer Walcott, handwritten notes and many pages of news cuttings.

Hugh Buggy was the journalist assigned to do the interviews, which appeared in the *Herald* from 26 January to 6 February 1935. Two articles were devoted to Gun Alley—but they were riddled with inaccuracies. Similar mistakes occurred in a 1950 *People* magazine interview by journalists Tom Gurr and HH Cox. The next journalist to take an interest in Piggott was the *Herald*'s 1950s police roundsman, Alan Dower. In 1959 he was writing rehashes of old cases. 'Auburn Hairs Hanged Him' was the story for 5 September. The article again contained inaccuracies, including that Piggott was dead. Still very much alive, Piggott responded, which resulted in his final interview, recorded in Dower's 1965 *Crime Chemist*.

Piggott: 'There was a lot of bitterness about the case ... But because there was no doubt in my mind that Ross was the guilty man, I will release some facts not known ... when Ross was tried.'

It was not the first time Piggott had offered 'new evidence hitherto undisclosed': such a claim had been made to Buggy 26 years earlier. Both interviews made clear the circumstantial nature of the evidence and Piggott's implied admission that there was no solid evidence at all. He declared to Buggy, 'I *felt*† morally certain' of Ross's guilt, and to Dower—

> [W]e were well aware that our evidence to back our reasoning was only circumstantial ... [But w]e were sure we had our man ... We still had to hope that, by hard slogging, we would get even more positive evidence that would stick hard in court ...

These admissions confirmed what Brennan had intimated in his book about the detectives' methods. Moreover, Piggott conceded to Dower that Matthews *may have lied*.

> ... several persons claimed [Ivy Matthews] lied. But even if she did, I still believe the guilt of Colin Ross was indisputable.

In both the Buggy and Dower interviews Piggott put forward evidence that was discredited at the trial or subsequently refuted, such as Francis Upton's testimony. Even Macindoe had abandoned this evidence in his closing address—the *Herald* reports of which Piggott had pasted into his scrapbook. In the Buggy interview Piggott declared candidly that he was willing to mislead the press to suit the Gun Alley investigation.

Some of the statements made by Piggott in these articles suggest that both Buggy and Dower asked some of the

---

†Author's italics

unanswered questions about the Gun Alley investigation, such as whether Matthews lied. Similarly, when Buggy raised the matter of the cleanness of the serge found along the Footscray Road, Piggott responded defensively. While declaring 'it would be conspiracy on my part if I had obtained a piece of clean cloth and induced witnesses to swear to it', Piggott also said, 'It was quite reasonable for the police to shake the dust out of the cloth ...' Why? '... so that its texture and stitching would become visible'. Piggott eventually admitted: 'The fact was that when the cloth was picked up I did brush the dust and grass seeds from it.' In fact, Piggott was not present 'when the cloth was picked up' by Mrs Sullivan.

In the Buggy interview Piggott added that had a new trial been ordered for Ross, 'We could have strengthened the Crown case with new evidence ... After the fragment [*sic*] of blue serge had been found ... Detectives Saker and Lee combed a large area there. In some bushes they picked up a billiard table brush ... Adhering to the bristles of the brush was a strand of blue thread ... similar to the thread in the girl's blue frock.' By the time Piggott related the story of the brush to Dower, however, it had evolved. This time Piggott said, 'On this brush we found a piece of the same material [as Alma's tunic] about five-eighths of an inch square.' These exaggerations can be attributed to lapses of memory over time. However, in the Buggy and Dower interviews Piggott stretches his imagination to link the brush to Ross. In both Piggott begins by saying that the brush had been used for grooming a horse. He deduced this from what he believed were the marks of the teeth of a currycomb on the wooden back of the brush. Ross owned a trotter, kept at the back of the family property in Footscray. But many people kept horses and stables were frequently attached to hotels.

Further, Piggott said 'it was evident' the brush had been used as a scrubbing brush. The apparent link here is to

Harding's claim that Ross said he scrubbed out the cubicle and part of his saloon. Piggott adds: 'Ross was known to possess such a billiard table brush when he conducted a hotel at Donnybrook.' That this was in fact 'known' is questionable. There were no billiard tables in Ross's saloon.

Piggott also claimed he had asked Matthews if Ross owned the brush. 'She told me Ross had such a brush and used it when grooming his pony at his house.' How could Matthews know this? Her relationship with the Rosses was no more than business. It is improbable that Matthews visited the Ross home.

Piggott to Dower:

> I didn't doubt, either, that this brush had been used to clean up the cul-de-sac when Alma's body was dumped there, because there were brush marks and other signs that the killer had tried to force the body down the drain, but had been disturbed.

But nothing to this effect was tendered at either the inquest or the trial. The police evidence at both hearings was that the locality was thoroughly searched, and showed nothing significant. Concluding his comments on the billiard table brush, Piggott claimed, 'The reason this was not submitted as evidence at the trial was that it was found after the inquest.'

But then, so was the serge.

Piggott to Buggy:

> A woman had seen the girl drop her parcel in Little Collins Street. This woman gave the girl sixpence, saw her turn back into the arcade, and saw Ross speak to

the girl at the doorway of the wine saloon. She saw the girl actually enter the wine shop.

Neither Gurr and Cox nor Dower mention this woman in their articles, which is surprising given that her evidence supported the Crown's case. Piggott claimed she came forward only after the trial. However, Mrs May Young had deposed at the inquest she had seen Alma drop her parcel—on the corner of Alfred Place and Little Collins Street. Mrs Young did not speak to Alma, nor give her money. The reference to the sixpence is probably Piggott getting his wires crossed. His interview with Buggy was 13 years after the murder of Alma Tirtschke and more than ten years after the somewhat similar murder of another little girl.

The body of 11-year-old Irene Tuckerman was found in a chaff bag in a Caulfield gutter in August 1924. She had been sexually assaulted, and strangled with a length of clothesline. Piggott was assigned to head the police inquiry. During his investigations, the following item appeared in the press:

NEW CLUE
Irene's purchase of sweets
Where did she get the money?

A *Herald* reporter ascertained that Irene Tuckerman purchased 6d of sweets on Saturday morning ... This was not known to members of her family, who do not know where she obtained the money for the purchase.

This item appears in Piggott's scrapbook, suggesting that he confused the two cases.

One major problem with the Crown's case against Ross had been the contradictory evidence as to Alma's character—between the quiet and shy child recalled by her family, and the 'cheeky' and 'forward' girl of the confessions. Piggott to Buggy:

> It was ... too readily presumed by the public that Colin Ross was an entire stranger to the girl. Had there been a second trial we would have sought to show that ... it was probable that Ross had chatted with the girl at times before December 30, 1921.
>
> A gardener in East Melbourne came forward after the trial and told us that on several evenings he had identified Ross as a man he had seen loitering near the Jolimont tennis courts.
>
> There, Ross was in the habit of watching a number of schoolgirls playing tennis.

Piggott accepted the gardener's claim. However, there are problems with it: primarily that there was no place that can be readily identified as a tennis court in Jolimont circa 1922.

Nonetheless Piggott postulated:

> If the girl had chatted with Ross earlier, possibly near the tennis courts, her willingness to enter the wine saloon would have been understandable.

How else could Piggott explain away the evidence that Alma could not—and would not—sit willingly for three hours drinking in a wine saloon when she had been given an errand by her Grandma? 'It was totally opposed to the picture of the girl's temperament, which we had secured from sources that were absolutely trustworthy,' Piggott himself admits.

... we felt convinced that Ross had met and spoken to the girl *during these visits*† to the tennis courts. Had he been a complete stranger to the girl on December 30 he could not have so won her confidence as to induce her to go and sit down in the wine saloon.

In an interview in 1996 Alma's sister Viola responded to questions regarding Piggott's story. The first question concerned whether Viola thought it possible that Ross could have met Alma at any time prior to the day of her murder. Viola: 'No. Definitely not.'

The second question put—prior to any disclosure of Piggott's allegation—was whether she knew any reason why Alma might be persuaded to drink in Ross's wine saloon. Viola:

There was no need for her to go in there at all ... we had to be home at the right time. If we were late home from school my grandmother would be halfway on the way to school, if not right there; so she was very, very strict ...

Thirdly, on the question of whether Alma played tennis, Viola stated that in later years she herself would take up an interest in both tennis and basketball. Of Alma's interest in the sport, Viola could only suggest:

I was the tennis player, not Alma ... She certainly didn't play when I lived with her in Connell Street.

School documents, supported by interviews with Alma's contemporaries, show that the two sports for girls at the Hawthorn West Central School were basketball and rounders. In 1921 few schools had courts and racquets, and balls were expensive. Viola recalls:

---

†Author's italics

> Tennis wasn't [widely] known. I myself, I taught myself tennis. I didn't even learn it at the high school ...

When told about Piggott's allegations of her sister meeting Ross at 'the Jolimont tennis courts', Viola responded—'Jolimont? There was a tennis court at Jolimont?' Pressed further, Viola paused before replying: 'I don't believe it ... [then again, softly, but with much conviction:] I don't believe it.'

After a few moments Viola returned to the subject of Piggott's allegation:

> [People tell so many] stories about things. To me, they made them up. People say a heck of a lot of things you know, and they're not, they're most untruths [sic].

The inescapable conclusion is that Piggott's 'new evidence' was spurious, a mixture of speculation, merged cases, blurred truths and factual errors. For an ex-superintendent of Piggott's reputation, these errors indicate an unconscionable carelessness in not checking detail—especially since his scrapbooks, which he had before him during the interviews, could have provided corrections. Allowing these errors to pass unchecked suggests a disregard for the truth.

Why would Piggott allow himself to be the source of so many fallacies about this case? Put simply, he had returned from service in a bitter war where 'results' counted more than the means by which they were obtained. The overriding impression of the interviews is of a man trying to vindicate the prosecution of Ross. He told Buggy:

> During the trial ... it was suggested in defence that I or some of my colleagues on the investigation might have placed hairs on the blankets to help to secure a conviction. It was hinted that we were out to catch someone, anyone, to appease an incensed public ...

As a police officer directly concerned in the investigation I had no right or opportunity then to challenge such implications. But now I ... feel that it is only just that I should tell the public ... emphatically that my work on the Ross case and the work of all those associated with me was done in a straightforward and conscientious manner.

... For anyone to hint or suggest by innuendo that detectives would stoop to such a despicable act to secure a conviction was not only unjust, but placed a stigma on them and members of their families. A charge of this kind injures the reputation of a detective and paves the way for counsel to fling sinister hints at him in any important succeeding case ...

Now I want to say this to the public. If such a charge or suggestion that I placed hairs from the girl's head on the blankets taken from the home of Ross was true, the only place for me would be behind the bars ... It was absolutely false ... The hairs we cut from the dead girl's head never at any time came into contact with those blankets ...

There is no evidence that Piggott placed Alma's hair on the blankets. In that at least he is innocent.

36. The evidence of the hair

Officially the case was closed. The public, the press, the police and the government all had their man, and he had gone to the gallows. Henceforth, officialdom would present a wall of silence on the Ross case. It was history.

Piggott was adamant that Price and Taylor 'put the rope around Ross's neck'. Yet in 1995 leading consultant forensic pathologist Vernon D Plueckhahn examined a copy of Taylor's admissions to Dower regarding the handling of the hair samples in the Gun Alley case (including Taylor's description of his and Price's antics with redheads in the city's streets). Plueckhahn's response: '... that sort of evidence wouldn't have got to first base these days. It would be laughed out of court.'

Jane Taupin, the hair analysis expert at the Victoria Police Forensic Science Centre, supports Plueckhahn, stating that: 'Today it is unlikely that a prosecution would succeed if the only evidence in the case was the physical matching of hair. In Australia today [such] evidence is considered to be similar to fibre evidence, where no statistical probabilities may be given.'

In the early 1920s the justice system was not equipped to deal with scientific evidence. It had few safeguards to prevent so-called experts from presenting shonky science, such as that of Price and Taylor.

The three crucial hair specimens in the case of *R v Ross* still exist; they were found by the author in 1995 at the Public Record Office, Melbourne. Each of the three specimens is mounted on a white card, and they comprise a specimen of hair from the deceased, from the 'brown–grey' blanket and from Gladys Wain. Of particular importance are samples A and B, 'Hair from Head of Deceased' and 'Hair from Brown–Grey Blanket'. After more than 80 years, Alma's hair still shows vibrant hue, unequivocally auburn. Sample B is gingery brown. Sample C, from Wain, fits Price's description: 'golden blonde hair of very fine texture'. The difference in appearance between samples A and B is obvious to the unaided eye. Was it part of Price's persuasive strategy that he first acknowledged the obvious variations—such as colour and diameter—before delivering his explanation as to why the samples were similar rather than different in convoluted (and contradictory) language?

Following consultation with the Public Record Office of Victoria and the Victorian Office of Public Prosecutions, which are the agencies responsible for the file containing the hair exhibits, it was agreed that the exhibits be made available for a thorough microscopic examination and mitochondrial DNA (mtDNA) testing. The microscopic examination was undertaken by Dr James Robertson, Director of Forensic Services with the Australian Federal Police, Canberra, a world expert in forensic hair comparisons. The mtDNA tests were undertaken on samples A and B by the Molecular Biology Department of the Victorian Institute of Forensic Medicine. Due to insufficient DNA in the samples used for testing, the first test in November 1998 yielded a result so weak no conclusion could be drawn. A second test in March 2004 showed the DNA of the blanket hair was contaminated by extraneous DNA—presumably from persons who had handled the exhibit during the past 82 years—and again no conclusion could be drawn. Until such time as techniques for removing contaminants are improved and mtDNA testing becomes more sensitive, the remainder of the hair in the exhibits will be preserved.

The microscopic examination by Dr Robertson, however, was more conclusive:

> The hairs from all three sources, Tirtschke, Wain and the blanket, were all easily differentiated at the stereo microscopic level based on colouring. This was confirmed at a more detailed microscopic level where there were very clear differences in colour, pigmentation and other features. In my opinion, the hairs recovered from the brown–grey blanket could not have come from the deceased Tirtschke, or from Wain.†

---

†Dr Robertson's full report appears as Appendix 2 on page 350.

Who killed Alma Tirtschke?

37. Following the trail

Bennet and Woolcock's butcher shop was located at 154 Swanston Street, between Bourke and Little Collins streets. From here, Alma's most direct route to Masonic Chambers was up Little Collins Street and then to Collins Street via either Alfred Place or Exhibition Street. The Eastern Arcade was not a short cut for Alma. That she diverged from her route to walk slowly around to its Bourke Street entrance is significant.

Bill Tate, the porter at the Victoria Coffee Palace, saw her walking 'very, very slowly' along the southern side of Little Collins Street at 2pm. Having presumably walked down Russell Street, she was next seen in Bourke Street, entering the Eastern Arcade a little after 2.30pm. She was back in Little Collins Street, at the corner of Alfred Place, by around 3 o'clock. She was then an easy ten-minute walk from Bennet and Woolcock's, but it had taken her over an hour. From the time Alma left the butcher's at 1.30pm to the time she stood at the corner of Alfred Place and Little Collins Street at 3 o'clock, all those who saw her—including Ross—describe the girl as being in a state of apprehension or distress. 'She was walking along looking up at the buildings very slowly,' said Tate. 'I wondered what was wrong—whether she had lost herself or was looking for somebody ...' He last saw her 'walking towards Russell Street'.

Alma continued up Bourke Street where she encountered Mrs Edmonds and her daughter, Muriel. Alma entered the Eastern Arcade ahead of them. Mrs Edmonds: 'She turned round twice as if afraid or nervous.' Identifying Alma from her school photograph, Mrs Edmonds recalled: '... she is smiling here ... She was not smiling when I saw her. She looked scared, she looked very nervous.'

Ross was the next to see Alma. At 3 o'clock the Youngs saw the 12-year-old leave the arcade, walk across Little Collins Street and stand at the corner of Alfred Place, where she dropped and picked up her parcel. Mrs Young: 'She looked to me like she was frightened. She looked back twice as she was standing there ... She seemed to me as if she were waiting for somebody and she was looking into the arcade.' Mr Young confirmed this.

Whoever or whatever was causing Alma's distress, one thing is certain: it had begun, as Tate's testimony indicates, prior to her reaching Russell Street, let alone passing Ross's saloon and reaching the arcade.

The dearth of clues not only made the killer difficult to identify, but suggests something important about him. This person was not stupid or careless, may indeed have been educated, and appears to have known about techniques of crime detection, as they were then applied, and the state of forensic medicine in 1922. The killer disposed of the child's clothing, partly washed her body, and conveyed her to the lane in a wrapping that left no fibre on her body. Might the killer have been a medical man or a detective himself, someone with a good knowledge of the state of forensic science in 1922?

What more can be deduced about Alma's killer? It appears that he was someone possessed of a clear mind, capable of thinking ahead, and aware of the sorts of clues that might disclose his identity. Ross, in contrast, was an impulsive, bungling criminal, acting without forethought, as exemplified by him proposing at gunpoint to Lily Brown, and the planned robbery that went awry when Walsh shot Bayliss. He could be stupid, to put it frankly. This fact makes it impossible to accept that Ross could have planned and cleanly executed the numerous sequential steps—as alleged by the police and their witnesses—necessary in disposing of Alma's body.

The night before Ross was hanged, Sonenberg received a letter. The original text is lost, but it is quoted in Brennan's *The Gun Alley Tragedy*.

Colin C. Ross,
Melbourne Gaol.

You have been condemned for a crime which you have never committed, and are to suffer for another's fault. Since your conviction you have, no doubt, wondered what manner of man the real murderer is who could not only encompass the girl's death, but allow you to suffer in his stead.

My dear Ross, if it is any satisfaction for you to know it, believe me that you die but once, but he will continue to die for the rest of his life. Honoured and fawned upon by those who know him, the smile upon his lips but hides the canker eating into his soul. Day and night his life is a hell without the hope of reprieve. Gladly would he take your place on Monday next if he had himself alone to consider. His reason, then, briefly stated, is this: A devoted and loving mother is ill—a shock would be fatal. Three loving married sisters, whose whole life would be wrecked, to say nothing of brothers who have been accustomed to take him as a pattern. He cannot sacrifice these. Himself he will sacrifice when his mother passes away. He will do it by his own hand. He will board the ferry across the Styx with a lie on his lips, with the only hope that religion is a myth and death annihilation.

It is too painful for him to go into the details of the crime. It is simply a Jekyll and Hyde existence. By a freak of nature, he was not made as other men ... This girl was not the first ... With a procuress all things are possible ... In this case there was no intention of murder—the victim unexpectedly collapsed. The hands of the woman, in her frenzy, did the rest.

May it be some satisfaction to yourself, your devoted mother, and the members of your family to know that at least one of the legion of the damned, who is the cause of your death, is suffering the pangs of hell. He may not ask your forgiveness or sympathy, but he asks your understanding.

It is not possible to prove whether or not this letter was a fake. The author was certainly literate and educated. Brennan stated that the letter 'bore on its face some suggestion of genuineness'. He noted: 'The envelope bore the postmark of a small country town, but there was nothing otherwise to indicate whence or from whom it came.' Brennan edited it 'with the elision of a sentence or two, rather Zola-esque for publication'. As a result, a frustrating ambiguity is given to the fragment '... This girl was not the first ...' Not the first *to be killed*? Or not the first to be sexually assaulted?

Either way, this statement is consistent with what we know today of the recidivism of paedophiles. When and where might this criminal have offended previously? Did he subsequently offend after 1922? It has been mooted in some quarters, most notably by writer John Gribbin, that the killing of Chrissie Venn a year earlier may have been related to Alma Tirtschke's case. Venn was murdered in Tasmania and, like Alma, she was intercepted by her assailant during an errand. The similarity ends there. Where Alma's killer systematically eliminated clues, Venn's murderer left the ground littered with debris from the crime. Her body was found crammed into a hollow tree stump. No attempt had been made to wash evidence from the body, nor dispose of the clothes. She had been garrotted with a length of hay band wire. Notwithstanding all the evidence, the police were never able to secure a conviction. Finally, Venn was 14, '... weighed over 8 stone, and had the development of a woman'. She was not a child, like Alma.

Likewise, any relationship with the rape and killing of Irene Tuckerman, murdered in Caulfield in 1924, can be ruled out. Tuckerman was aged 11½ and her body was found in the gutter. She had been strangled with a length of clothesline rope, with no effort made to dispose of evidence. She was found fully clothed and bent double in a sack.

It is unlikely Alma was an early victim of Arnold Karl Sodeman, hanged at Melbourne's Pentridge Prison in 1936 for raping and killing four girls aged between six and 16 years from 1930 to 1935. Sodeman did not wash the bodies or eradicate evidence and bound his victims in a trademark fashion. He confessed to all of his murders, forcing the police to drop charges against three men wrongly suspected of the killings. If Sodeman had had any involvement in the killing of Alma Tirtschke he is likely to have boasted about it.

It has also been suggested the killer may have been a prominent figure of the Melbourne underworld. Hugh Anderson implied in his 1971 book *Larrikin Crook, The Rise and Fall of Squizzy Taylor* that 'Squizzy' Taylor may have known something about the Gun Alley crime. When some of the contents of Taylor's scrapbook, found in his

Elwood flat, were published, it appeared that: 'His fancy, according to the pictures he had culled from newspapers, [ran] along sensational lines, the pride of place [being] given to a large picture of Colin Campbell Ross.' However, there is no evidence that Squizzy Taylor was responsible for Alma's death.

38. At the edges of identity

In a series of interviews over a two-year period, Viola spoke on various occasions about her dreams since her sister's death. For the purposes of presenting a complete and cohesive narration, the following extracts from interviews have been compressed and edited, with dates given to indicate the shifts in time.

'I've had a lot of nightmares ... lots and lots of terrible nightmares. But when I was with Grandma, later on, in apartments and flats and everything, if I had a nightmare I'd get up and go into her bed, you know; she always let me go into her bed ... [But] I never went to Grandma's room in Hawthorn; [it was] only afterwards.' [7 December 1995]

While living with Alma at Hawthorn, Viola cannot recall Alma having had bad dreams, nor Alma ever going to Grandma's room.

'... [But] some of the nightmares—I know when we were in [East Melbourne], Grandma was in—I was on the veranda—and Grandma was in the bedroom and I got up because a face came through the window.' [5 December 1997]

'—a man put his head through the window ... he came in and looked at me and said "I came home at one o'clock"!' [8 February 1996] 'And I got such a heck of a fright I got up and got into my grandmother's bed ...' [5 December 1997]

Viola had a recurrent dream of being chased through dark places. 'I'd even jump our front fence and go into a neighbour's place and hide ...' [5 December 1997] The dreams began: '... because of being chased by him [at the age of 16], and the persistence in which he—' [5 December 1997]

This dream persisted even after Viola had married and settled with her husband in the suburbs. She attributed it to the husband of an older cousin, whom she is certain wanted to assault her sexually, theorising that he was frustrated in his own marriage. 'I think he wanted children and she didn't have any children.' [27 February 1996] Viola says he pursued her vigorously throughout her youth. In 1928 Viola was 16 and lived with her grandmother in an apartment at Masonic Chambers.

'... When I went to [live in] the city at the age of 16, he asked me to marry him, to go away and marry him and ... I said no straight out. Then there was another time. We were all playing cards up in our room, and Auntie Maie sent me downstairs [to fetch] something [from] her place. I went out and he followed me—and they still didn't do anything about it—any rate he followed me and, believe it or not, he chased me in and out of 19 and 31—where the hall was—where our rooms were in 19, he chased, and I had to go round the other part, past the hall into Auntie Maie's part. He chased me round and around and around right out into Collins Street. I finally got back inside quick enough up the stairs and into the room, sat down and played cards. He came in and sat down and played cards. And nothing was ever spoken ... No good telling them anything, they wouldn't believe me.' [5 December 1997]

At first it was a name given out by inference only.'He got married again later on and they had children I think. I never ever saw him after that really; after he got married the second time I never ever saw him. And Jessie died. Jessie died.' [27 February 1996]

A figure moving at the edges of identity ... 'When we went into town to see the parades, the Anzac marches, I used to ask another cousin to keep close to me so that he wouldn't come anywhere near me.' [27 February 1996]

'... I didn't want George Murphy at the back of me ... And every Anzac Day that's exactly what happened. But I kept out of his way. It's marvellous how I knew, that instinct was in me—which it doesn't always happen but it did happen to me ... as early as the age of five.' [5 December 1997]

Viola had feelings from an early age that Jessie's husband was not safe to be around. 'But he never did anything to me—he only started ...' [27 February 1996]

'... I was about five and this happened in Hawthorn. This is when that George Murphy came out with the aunts and things like that, and my sister—(breaks off)' [5 December 1997]

'... [T]hat was only the first time. I don't know about Alma, whether he did or he didn't. We ... didn't talk about things like that. It was somehow or other he just put his hand up my legs. And that's as far as he got ... and I knew from that instinct that I must keep away from him ... We didn't talk about things like that. I just got on with life. I was told to come out into the family and the family spoke to me and I told them what he did ... they didn't believe me and that was the end of that. I forgot after that. We didn't talk about things like that. [27 February 1996]

'... I was given at the age, at the early age of five, I was given ... something inside, to know what to do. I guess that's been with me all of my life ... But today we do know there's a lot of child abuse and apparently I was given something, and I don't know why but I know my sister got up and went to the toilet and then the next thing I heard these footsteps coming up the passage and I knew who it was and I just got out of bed and got into the wardrobe ... Any rate, he went back and said "Vi's not in her bed." It's a wonder he did that, he was a bit stupid really: he shouldn't have said anything. Any rate, I was called out in ... front of my aunties and that, and asked about it but they took no notice of me and practically said I was telling lies: so I got nowhere. But from that day on ... (trails away)' [27 February 1996]

She would return to this incident in a later interview.

'[With me] he had tried, he never ever did, but he did try and ah, when my sister got up to go to the bathroom, I got out of bed and went into the cupboard ... I was questioned about it and I told them exactly why I got into the wardrobe. But they didn't believe me and they didn't take any notice of it at all.' [5 December 1997]

The line between what was dreamt and what was real could become tenuous.

'There was a strange thing that happened ... with Alma, when I was in bed with Alma, I, we, still don't know. We were both sent to—we always had a handkerchief when we were sent to bed. And I slept nearest the window. And one night I felt somebody there and I put my—incredible—I put my hand out and I pinched their nose. They stole my handkerchief and believe it or not that handkerchief was never found. But nothing else was—we could never ever understand what happened. I've never been able to solve that. But I [can vividly] remember feeling that nose. They said something, you know, and I put my hand out and felt the nose ... I don't know [what they said]. I wouldn't remember ... And that handkerchief was never found ... I told Grandma. We looked for it everywhere ... it's been a mystery all my life. Now whether it was a nightmare ... or not—but the strange thing was: the handkerchief was gone. I cannot—we cannot—solve that.' [7 December 1995]

The son of a bootmaker, George Francis Murphy was born in Collingwood in 1895. At the age of 16 he was granted, on the strength of his school results, a four-year training bond with the Department of Lands and Survey. The bond was to expire in March 1916, but World War I intervened. In December 1915, two days past his 20th birthday, Murphy enlisted. He embarked overseas in 1916 and did not return to Melbourne until 1918, spending a month in the military hospital in Caulfield. Murphy was discharged DAH—a Defective Action of the Heart—and categorised as 'permanently unfit' for further military service.

Murphy's contact with Alma and Viola coincided with his courtship of Jessie, which occurred after his discharge in 1918. Thus his attempted molestation of Viola most probably occurred in her sixth or seventh years, ages consistent with the timing given in her recollection of the intruder in her bedroom.

Murphy would be married to Jessie for eleven years before separating from her. Jessie died in the mid–1950s. Murphy remarried, but was childless in both unions. He had been infected with gonorrhoea in 1916—an era in which the disease was without medical cure. Murphy probably infected his wife.

Murphy also suffered a severe nervous disintegration. Assessing him in November 1917, Captain Jamison, Medical Officer, reported: 'Up till six months ago he could carry on alright, when after the Bullecourt attack he became very ill and could not carry on ... he gets very short of breath and dizzy; gasps for breath. Sleeps badly. He can feel his heart thumping.' Another report made during Murphy's shipboard return to Australia records that he '[has difficulty breathing], giddy, gnashes his teeth and sleeps badly'. On arrival at Caulfield, his condition was assessed as 'DAH Arrhythmia—No lesion detected—Tachycardia—Neurosis'.

On discharge, Murphy was expected to be proud of his military service and to keep his chin up. Tears and moping—which today would be recognised as symptoms of depression—did not figure in those assumptions. Today, psychologists acknowledge that if suppressed, traumas can fester like any physical wound. Did this festering take the form of molesting one, or even two young girls with a German-sounding surname?

No file relating to Murphy nor any reference to him exists at Victoria Police Information Bureau Records (IBR). However, it should be noted that, as part of a culling program, all police files for persons born pre–1900 have been destroyed. Did the police even know that a close relative of Alma had tendencies towards paedophilia? At an interview in 1997, Viola was asked whether she was questioned about Alma's death by her grandmother. She replied that she wasn't questioned—neither by Grandma nor the police. 'I was kept right out of it. Right out of it altogether.'

39. Who killed Alma Tirtschke?

Following his military discharge, Murphy returned to work at the Department of Lands and Survey. Due to ill-health he was unable to complete the surveying part of his training. Consequently, he qualified as a draughtsman only. In 1921 Murphy was working for the Office of the Registrar-General and Registrar of Titles, in Queen Street, Melbourne. His position title was 'draughtsman', with duties described as: 'examines plans of survey'. It was here that Murphy was working in December 1921, when Alma made her fatal trip to the city.

Was Murphy focusing his sexual attentions on Alma? With her departure for Maffra now imminent, was he afraid Alma would speak to her father about him? Had Murphy been threatening her? Of the two Tirtschke children, Viola (who had been taken to Maffra the previous August) was always the more assertive and strong-willed. She resisted Murphy and had attempted to speak up about him. Alma, on the other hand, was more submissive, trusting and obedient; she was also the more diffident. If she felt threatened she might only have been able to speak about it indirectly, through alluding to a clairvoyant.

Which brings us to Friday 30 December 1921, not a holiday for public servants other than teachers. Since leave and other personnel records for the Registrar-General's Office no longer exist, it is not possible to determine for certain whether Murphy attended his workplace that day. He may have been on leave due to ill-health. He may have worked part of the day and finished at lunchtime. In any case Alma's troubles that day began in the latter lunch hour of the working day, between 1 and 2pm. If that afternoon is reconstructed on the assumption that someone (Murphy?) had been harassing Alma, a picture emerges that is infinitely more coherent and more consistent with witness testimonies than the Crown's case against Ross.

To begin with, in just a few days Alma was to be returned to her father. It can be inferred that she knew this move would free her from Murphy's advances and threats. He was perhaps afraid that the move might give her the nerve to denounce him. When Alma arrived at the butcher's at 1.15pm, nothing in her manner betrayed distress. At 1.30pm she left the shop and set out on the most direct route to Masonic Chambers: Little Collins Street. It was at this point that her difficulties started.

At around 1.30pm George Crilley saw a child answering the description of Alma Tirtschke walking up Little Collins Street. A man was just behind her, apparently following persistently. Crilley was going to speak to him but he eventually walked on past the little girl. Somewhere about opposite the Eastern Arcade Crilley looked back and saw the man (who was not Ross) talking to the girl. Brennan saw the significance of Crilley's evidence—that if Alma was speaking to the man, he was known to her.

The meeting altered Alma's course. She diverged from the route to Masonic Chambers, only 10–12 minutes away, because it was no longer a sanctuary. Her Auntie Maie had instructed her to leave the parcel there saying: '... then go straight away back to [Grandma's] flat in Jolimont—do not wait for me'. Alma was due back at Jolimont for lunch, but she knew her Auntie Maie was not at Masonic Chambers this afternoon and that it would be some time before she returned.

Alma dallied anxiously in the street. In 30 minutes she progressed no more than 400 metres down Little Collins Street from the corner of Swanston Street. At 2 o'clock she was still on the southern side of the street, at the back of George and George's, where she was seen by Tate, the coffee palace porter. Did she fear Murphy would be waiting for her at Masonic Chambers, or some other point along her route? Disobedience was not in her nature but already she was much later than she ought to be for this errand. If she could not speak of the problem to Grandma, how could she tell a stranger, such as a policeman? Viola tried to explain and was not believed by her own family.

It appears to have taken about 30 minutes, but Alma finally decided to change course. She crossed Little Collins Street and wandered down Russell Street. She walked slowly, feigning interest in the buildings and window displays. She dawdled, stalling for time. She may have imagined she would be safe if she stayed in reasonably populated public places. But what if he came to get her?

At 2.30pm Alma was seen in Bourke Street by Blanche and Muriel Edmonds, who followed her into the Eastern Arcade. Everything about Alma's body language—as it was observed by the Edmondses, the Youngs, and even Ross—was consistent with, or suggestive of, an imminent anticipation of being followed and accosted.

Mrs Edmonds: 'She turned round twice as if afraid or nervous ... She looked scared, she looked very nervous.'

Ross's glimpses of the schoolgirl suggested an equivocation over where she ought to next go. As was proven by Mr and Mrs Young when they saw Alma outside the arcade a few minutes later, Alma did not enter Ross's wine saloon.

Above and to the right of Alma, Blanche and Muriel Edmonds proceeded along the gallery to shop 54, where Mrs Edmonds visited her masseur. The overhang of the arcade's western balcony obscured Alma from the sight of both women. It was 2.45pm when Muriel and her mother ascended the staircase and lost sight of her. Only minutes afterwards, Ross saw Alma walking towards the arcade's Little Collins Street entrance.

Outside, the Youngs passed the Eastern Market, approaching the arcade entrance as they moved west along the northern side of Little Collins Street. Alma emerged from the arcade ahead of them, and they saw her walk across the road to the corner of Alfred Place and Little Collins Street, where the Adam and Eve Hotel stood. It was now nearly 3 o'clock.

'She appeared to be frightened when we first saw her come from the arcade,' recalled Stanley Young. 'She kept looking around behind her. She was looking back towards the arcade when standing on the corner.'

Did Alma know that Murphy was looking for her? Did he now catch up with her? Stanley Young again: 'It would take us two or three minutes to go to Russell Street ... But when we looked around again from Russell Street she was gone ...'

Some minutes later, Joseph Graham walked up Little Collins Street from Russell Street, on the same side as the Youngs. He passed Alfred Place. When he was about midway between Alfred Place and Pink Alley, 'opposite the far end of the Little Collins Street frontage of the Adam and Eve Hotel', he heard cries. He stopped in his tracks, transfixed. He stood 30 metres from the market gate, where the Ballarat man caught the most piercing cry ...

Graham:

> ... It was between a quarter and half past 3. I heard a piercing scream, followed immediately by others ... I heard at least 5 screams—more like 6—then the girl seemed to be exhausted ... They seemed to be at the back of the Adam and Eve Hotel. They were terrified screams, like a little girl terrified at what was occurring or [what was] about to occur ... It seemed to me as if she was being dragged in somewhere.

The fact that Graham favoured that part of the block nearest Alfred Place—the part occupied by the old Adam and Eve Hotel—as the most likely origin of the screams is significant for its correspondence in time and place with Alma's last sighting by the Youngs. Was it here that Murphy lay in wait for Alma to come down Alfred Place? Did he now drag her in somewhere—into a disused stable, an easement, a fenced-off or gated recess behind the delicensed Adam and Eve?

Had it only been thought to interview Alma's ten-year-old sister, Viola, and had the credibility of children as witnesses been more widely respected in 1922, a quite different perspective on Alma's fate might have emerged.

Postscript

Subsequent Histories

ALBERTS, David At the time of the trial, Alberts had a number of previous convictions in Brisbane and New South Wales. By 1925 he was serving time in Pentridge under the name of Frederick D Stirling. He was convicted of robbery on 4 May that year in the court of general sessions.

BRENNAN, Thomas After the Ross case, he was largely responsible for reforming the High Court's practices for the hearing of criminal appeals. In so doing Brennan inscribed into the judicial system a silent and ongoing memorial to Colin Ross. He became a KC in 1928 and stood for parliament unsuccessfully. In 1931, as the result of a vacancy, he was appointed to the Senate. He served as minister without portfolio for several years and served as acting attorney-general and acting minister for industry in 1935–36. He was defeated in the 1937 election. He died in 1944, and received a state funeral.

DUNSTAN, Joseph Sentenced to a prison term with Harding for his part in a housebreaking offence, he received a pardon and was told to leave Victoria. No further prison terms are recorded for him in the Victorian prisoners' register.

GUN ALLEY In 1923 Lane's Motors, which abutted Gun Alley, applied successfully to erect a new building over a portion of the alley. By the end of the year, the lane was little more than an access-way to Lane's new building. In 1937, Lane's extended further and in that year Gun Alley ceased to exist. In its place stood Lane's gleaming new showrooms. Today the octagonal skyscraper Nauru House stands on the site.

HARDING, Sydney John In April 1922 Harding petitioned for an early release from his sentence, which was approved. Harding and Dunstan each entered into a £50 good behaviour bond for five years, and in July 1922 were released. That September, Harding was arrested on a charge of indecent language. He was bailed out by Superintendent Potter himself. The next morning the case was struck out and Harding sent to New South Wales. There, he encountered two notorious Pentridge escapees, Loughrey and Higgins, in Newcastle. Harding informed the police who captured the escapees. He went further north to Queensland, but was now in failing health. Having squandered most of his funds—none of which had gone to the Children's Hospital—he was near destitution. He found work as an itinerant slaughterman and stationhand, and died in the Queensland town Hughenden in 1924.

MACINDOE, Hugh Campbell Gemmell Judge Macindoe retired from office in 1946, and died the following year.

MADDOX, Olive Maddox spent the rest of her days in and out of gaol on charges of prostitution and drunkenness. In 1925 she was in the dock yet again, where she wept and begged not to be sent back to Pentridge. 'They have put two or three hundred injections into me, but they cannot cure me. Let me free so that I can get proper treatment.' Despite her pleas and protestations, she was returned to prison.

PIGGOTT, Frederick John In December 1922 Piggott's wife Matilda died after a long illness, and his only son Fred was killed in a motorcycle accident several weeks later. Piggott retired with the rank of superintendent in 1934. He died in August 1962, aged 88.

POMMEROY, Robert Two weeks before Ross's execution, Pommeroy appeared in Melbourne's criminal court. He was found guilty on a charge of larceny and sent back to prison—yet another addition to a record rivalling that of Harding.

ROSS, Mrs Elizabeth Campbell Colin's mother continued to live with the rest of her family in Footscray. Although frail, she continued to campaign for her son, forming the Ross Vindication Committee. In an interview in 1925, Mrs Ross said: 'All I want is to live to see my boy vindicated. I don't want anybody else punished. I haven't any hard feelings against any of them. I have had a lot of people come to me with information ... but nothing has ever come of any of it.' She died at the Victorian Benevolent Home in Royal Park in 1932, aged 63 years. Of her surviving children, Ronald died at Footscray, in 1948; Stanley, in Coogee, NSW, in 1973; and Thomas died in Sydney in 1963. Alexandrina lived longest, until 1979.

SCHUTT, William John His colleagues believed his early resignation was associated with his having passed sentence of death on Ross. In retirement he travelled, and died from a shipboard fall in 1933.

TIRTSCHKE, Elizabeth (Grandma): Grandma Tirtschke was admitted to Wesleyan hostel care shortly after Viola came of her majority and moved out of her grandmother's charge. Mrs Tirtschke died in 1939, aged 92.

TIRTSCHKE, Viola Married at the age of 21, she has a daughter and a son who today live in Melbourne. Viola is the grandmother of six children, and the great-grandmother of five children.

UPTON, Frank Lane (Darkie) He left Victoria for interstate, fearing the vengeance of the condemned man's friends. He vanished without a trace.

Appendix 1

Totals of Reward and Sustenance Payments

Beneficiary	Government reward	*Herald* reward	Total sustenance payment (if applicable)	TOTAL
Ivy Matthews	£350	£87/10/–	£37	£474/10/–
Sydney J Harding	£200	£50	£27	£277
Olive M Maddox	£170	£42/10/–	£74	£286/10/–
George A Ellis	£50	£12/10/–	–	£62/10/–
Joseph Dunstan	£50	£12/10/–	–	£62/10/–
David Alberts	£30	£7/10/–	–	£37/10/–
Madame Ghurka	£25	£6/5/–	–	£31/5/–
Maisie Russell	£25	£6/5/–	–	£31/5/–
Blanche Edmonds	£20	£5	–	£25
Muriel Edmonds	£20	£5	–	£25
Francisco Anselmi	£20	£5	–	£25
Violet Sullivan	£20	£5	–	£25
Michelucci Nicoli	£20	£5	–	£25
Frank L Upton	–	–	£30/12/6	£30/12/6
Robert Pommeroy	–	–	£6/4/9	£6/4/9
TOTALS	£1000	£250	£174/17/3	£1424/17/3

Appendix 2

Dr James Robertson: Report of Examination of Hair Samples in the Case of *R v Ross* (1922)

Background

The central technique used in the forensic analysis of hairs is examination using microscopes. This will usually start with examination at quite low magnification (up to ×30 or ×40) and usually with overhead light or epi-illumination. At this magnification and with reflected light the overall shape of the hair, its colour, condition and the appearance of the root and tip ends can be assessed.

Hairs consist of three anatomical parts: the outer scales and cuticle; the body of the hair called the cortex; and a central canal called the medulla. The latter is not always present in human scalp hair. The medulla can be seen at low magnification if hairs are placed in a suitable mounting medium (a liquid chosen for its optical properties) on glass microscope slides.

The visual colour of hair results from a visual perception but at a microscopic level the presence of pigment in the cortex is the main determination of colour. The detail of the pigment particles or granules and their arrangement into groups can only be seen using transmitted light at higher magnification of up to ×400 total magnification. At this level other detailed features can also be seen in the cortex. The presence or absence of these features is used along with the previously mentioned features, to differentiate hairs from different people.

This is the basis of the forensic examination of hairs and it relies on the variation in these microscopic features being less in the hairs from one person than hairs from different people.

In fact, the examination process relies on the scientist looking for differences. Only when no significant differences exist can an inclusionary opinion be considered.

The final step in the examination process involves direct comparison of two hairs using a comparison microscope. This consists of two transmitted light microscopes linked with an optical bridge, which allows the examiner to compare the two hairs side by side.

The basics of the above process have changed little this century and much of what is known about the microscopic features of hairs was known in the early decades of the 1900s.

Today it is possible to conduct DNA testing on some hairs. Where this is not possible or not successful the fundamental examination process is the same today as 100 years ago.

Finally, as the differentiation of hairs from say two persons is based on there being greater recognisable differences (variations) between the hairs of individuals than within the hairs of each individual, an essential prerequisite for a meaningful examination is to have enough hairs from each individual to reveal the range of variation within and between individuals. It is generally considered for a meaningful examination, a sample from an identified (known) source should consist of from 40 to 100 complete hairs. These would usually be pulled or combed to ensure the roots were present.

The Ross case

The sample relating to the 1922 Ross case consists of three pieces of cardboard onto which are attached three separate samples of hair. From information supplied to me along with the samples I understand that Colin Campbell Ross was convicted of the 1921 murder of a 12-year-old girl, Alma Tirtschke, and that evidence was presented at trial in 1922 that a number of hairs, recovered from a brown–grey coloured blanket from the lodgings or house of Ross, were said to have come from the deceased. The precise nature of the latter evidence is not the subject of this report. I further understand that a Mrs Wain, a female friend of Ross, was excluded as the source of the hairs on the blanket. Ross was convicted of the murder and hanged.

Re-examination of hair samples

I received three items as follows:

1. A piece of brown card which was labelled 'Hair from head of deceased Alma Tirtschke'. On this card was a group of visually reddish-brown hair in the rough shape of a figure eight. The hairs were held by a glass slide and tape. I removed ten hairs from this sample and placed them on individual glass microscope slides in a semi-permanent mounting medium (Hystomount) for further examination.

The hairs ranged in length from about 4 to 17 centimetres. None had a root present and most had been cut at both ends and hence were segments of hair shafts. All had a distinctive reddish/orange brown colour. The central medulla was visible in some of the hairs. I also recorded the detailed microscopic features of five hairs.

2. A brown piece of card which was labelled 'Hair Mrs Wain'. On this card was a circular group of hairs held on the card by a broken glass slide. I removed ten hairs from this sample and prepared them as for the hairs from Tirtschke. The hairs ranged from about 7 to 13 centimetres.

Three had roots present. The remainder had cut or broken ends. All had a light yellow–brown hue. Detailed microscopic examination revealed the hairs to be relatively featureless.

3. A brown piece of card which was labelled 'Hair from Brown-Grey Blanket'. On this card was a lightly configured group of hairs in the shape of a figure eight. The hairs were held on the card by a piece of (browning) clear adhesive tape. I removed eight hairs from this group due to the smaller number present and the desire to maintain the integrity of the appearance of the group. These hairs ranged in length from 7 to 20 centimetres and only two had roots present, the remainder having cut ends. One hair had a so-called club root, which is normally associated with hairs which have been naturally lost. The second had what appeared to be a so-called ribbon-shaped root which would normally require some force for removal, such as combing. I examined all hairs in detail and recorded their microscopic features. These hairs had more visible features than hairs from the two known samples 1 and 2. Furthermore, the microscopic features would support a conclusion that the hairs in this sample were from a single source.

Conclusion

The hairs from all three sources, Tirtschke, Wain and the blanket, were all easily differentiated at the stereo microscopic level based on colouring. This was confirmed at a more detailed microscopic level where there were very clear differences in colour, pigmentation and other features.

In my opinion, the hairs recovered from the brown–grey blanket could not have come from the deceased, Tirtschke or from Wain.

This conclusion must be tempered by the following:

(a) As the hair sample from Tirtschke was cut it was not possible to examine the microscopic features at the root end of the hairs.

(b) As all of the hair samples are over 70 years old there may have been changes in colour.

Despite the above potential limitations the extent of the differences and the very distinct colour of the Tirtschke hair are such that I consider it very unlikely the hairs on the blanket could have come from Tirtschke.

No hairs were received from Ross and hence no conclusion can be reached as to whether or not the hairs could have been his own. In the absence of hairs from Ross any inclusionary conclusion would have been unsafe, regardless of any findings or conclusion resulting from examination of other hair samples.

> James Robertson, Director, Forensic Services
> Australian Federal Police
> 30 November 1999

Appendix 3

Letters Written to Colin Ross During his imprisonment

The following two letters were sent by Colin's aunt, Lillian Blake (née Eadie), Mrs Elizabeth Ross's first cousin. In the first, undated, letter, Lillie writes to Colin in gaol during the course of his trial, probably soon after 21 February 1922.

Letter 1

My dear Colin,

The last sheet in the tablet so must make the most of it. Was out at your home last night (it's open house there now). A regular mothers' (and fathers') meeting held most nights in the week I think. Talk about 'talk', the Yarra bankers are not in it with us. But the worst of it is that everyone wants to say his (or her) say at once, and the consequence is that the gems of logic with which yours truly is brimming over, is lost in the clatter. We hold discussions on the subject of the Law of Today, etc. We also vie with each other in the picking to pieces of Brains and Reasoning Powers, as well as the supposed doings of a certain person whose surname begins with R. Well, to quit foolery, lad, I may tell you that the public is beginning to use its brains now instead of its spectacles in regard to your case. Its gospel up to now has been that newspaper, which I think I once mentioned to you as being a very good paper (to use to wipe one's razor on) but take it from me the majority are using their thinking boxes now. I know from what I hear 4 out of 5 saying. I believe one man who rarely takes strong drink, took more than was good for him yesterday in the lunch hour, because out of a crowd of people airing their views in the precincts of the Courts, for and against you, he found only 3 of the latter. So the spirit of conviviality was so strong upon him that he had to ask one or two to have 'wan'. Well that's the way of it, lad, I'm pleased to tell you.

I was telling them last night that I'm going to stand for the hire of a piano at your home when we have that celebration, but I'm thinking the house will only hold a handful of the number that will want to be shaking you by the hand (you'll have to do as the Prince did, Colin, give your left to rest the right), so was thinking it wouldn't be a bad plan to ask the Governor of the Castle, to let you hold your levee there. That butler who ushers in your visitors now†, would come in handy. Well, I don't know of any more to say, lad, this time, except that you are losing me a lot of sleep the last couple of months (excitement and suspense) so the sooner I'm able to order that piano the better for us all. I think your folk are wonders, there's no downing them (I don't think anyone's tried an ... [word illegible] on them yet, but they've had enough hard knocks goodness knows to flatten them out).

Carrie* and your mother heard you call 'Tata' on Wednesday. With love—From Auntie.

---

†'That butler' is probably Melbourne Gaol senior warder John Gloster.
*Carrie, ie Carol Ross (née Ballantyne), Thomas Ross's wife.

Letter 2

In this further undated letter, Lillie writes to Colin on the eve of his execution. The date is therefore around 22 April 1922.

My dear brave lad

I am trying to screw up my courage to write you a few last lines as you wished, as I am not brave enough to accompany your aunt tomorrow. Besides, I feel I should be with your poor mother, tho' there is not much I can do or say to comfort her. Everyone is most kind but she seems to rely on me—even though we just sit silent, for we can't talk of tomorrow—not now—

We are all keyed up, but hoping and praying that even at this the 11th hour, God will touch the heart of one of those perjurers and liars, bad as they are. But as Mr Maxwell told the jury, there is not a scrap of conscience among the lot, all are underworld, crooks and prostitutes.

Still—we hope.

We, none of us, went to bed last night—just lay down now and then—or outside walking up and down.

I am sorely tempted to ask is there an Almighty? Who permits this awful sacrifice of an innocent person, but I must not; for God must have answered my prayers, to help me bear up and enable me to be a little help and comfort to your dear mother through these last awful days.

We are all very proud of the brave way you are bearing this shocking cruel thing and I can't tell you how thankful we are that you have Mr Goble to help you. He speaks so well of you Colin and said he would as soon believe his own son to be guilty of that vile crime as you.

Your mother has received piles of letters from every state, all showing that the writers see this thing as a frame up. I shall not forget the promise I made you lad to be as a sister to your dear mother and be with her as much as possible—I do so dread tonight for her, tho' up to now she has been as brave as you.

Oh Colin I just can't believe this awful injustice will be carried out to the bitter end. Something surely will happen to prevent it.

'Some day we'll understand.'

Goodnight dear Colin. Be your own brave self. May God sustain and comfort you is the wish of your Unhappy Aunt Lillie.

Your aunts Teenie† and Annie*, also Lexie will stay tonight. I'm glad that Lex was able to see you today—she was so heartbroken we thought she would not be able to, as it would only break down your control if she broke down.

'Lead kindly light, amid the encircling gloom.'

---

†Teenie, Christina Bourke (née Ross), an aunt of Colin's
*Annie, Teenie's daughter, and therefore Colin's cousin

Appendix 4

Letter to the People of Australia from Mrs Elizabeth Campbell Ross

The following letter appeared in *Smith's Weekly* shortly after Ross's execution.

To the Public of Australia

As my dear son Colin has suffered all that the law can do to him—and has gone to the highest court of all where, without passion, prejudice or revenge he will receive (what he did not get here) justice, I now make a mother's appeal to the public of Australia, to help me clear my son's name from the terrible stigma that has been placed upon it. I view with horror the awful crime for which my son was wrongly executed. I can quite understand the indignation and wrath that must sway the judgment of the public at the committal of the shocking deed. But as his mother, I protest with all my soul that my boy should be made the innocent victim of that indignation and wrath. I know that Colin is not guilty. I know that he could not have committed the crime at the time alleged. I know when he came home—when he left home—and when he returned on that fateful day and night. But because I was his mother I was not believed. I have gone from place to place, from one to another, pleading for my boy's life, pleading for justice and mercy—only to be turned away without hope. The cruellest slanders have been heaped upon my character. I have been wickedly misunderstood just because I was Colin's mother—and mother-like I have spent everything—and done everything a mother could to clear her son's name—and save his life. Nearly everybody's hand has been turned against my boy. His words have been twisted, distorted and exaggerated and made to imply what I know he never meant, even when his last words upon the gallows were taken from their connection and made out to be a lie. There was no mercy for my dear lad. Now I ask those who have judged so harshly to read Colin's last letter to his mother. I gave him my last earthly goodbye outside the prison bars of the condemned cell on Sunday morning, 23rd April (I shall never forget it)—and the last Sunday night of his life—in the condemned cell—with his minister by his side—he wrote me a farewell note:†

It speaks for itself. It shows the true heart of my boy as I knew it. I cannot yet forgive his enemies as he has done. Perhaps some day his spirit may be mine. But I am convinced he is the victim of a foul conspiracy, prompted by motives of revenge, jealousy and cupidity. Colin died believing his name would one day be cleared. It is that hope that is keeping me alive. I have received hundreds of letters from all over Australia. These have comforted me more than words can express. I ask those who think Colin is guilty to suspend judgment—until the day comes as it surely will—when false witnesses shall be confuted and my dear son's memory cleared of the stain of the abominable crime for which he has innocently suffered. Till that day I remain

His broken-hearted mother,
EC Ross

---

†Colin's farewell note to his mother is reproduced on page 293.

Select Bibliography

Spatial constraints do not permit a complete listing of sources; however, the following were of particular importance.

Public Record Office, Victoria

VPRS 30/P (Criminal Trial Briefs)

Unit 1953 File 1922/92 for *R v Ross 1922* includes: transcript of the inquest into the death of Alma Tirtschke, giving the depositions of witnesses and Piggott's account of his exchanges with Ross. Also includes: statements of trial witnesses; notices to the defence to call new witnesses; an application from Sonenberg for an independent test of the hair and the Crown Solicitor's negative reply; letters from Mrs McKenzie to Maxwell and from Ronald Ross to Ivy Matthews (reflecting on the terms of her employment); the police report on Mrs McKenzie; and the reports of doctors Godfrey and Rennie on Ross's condition.

Unit 1943 File 587/1921: the Eastern Arcade shooting incident.

VPRS 1100/P1 (Capital Sentences)

Unit 1 contains the 'Police Report as to Antecedents of Prisoner (Colin Campbell Ross)' dated 27/2/1922.

VPRS 515 (Central Register of Male Prisoners)

Volumes 58 and 61, of which folios 128 and 133 respectively are for prisoner 32060: Sydney John Harding (aka John Corlette, aka Sydney J Hennesy). Volume 69, folio 88, is for 35134, Joseph L Dunstan. Volume 71, folio 299, is for 36188, Frank Rhodes Walsh. Volume 71, folio 378, is for prisoner 36267, Colin Campbell Ross.

VPRS 266P (Law Department Inward Registered
    Correspondence)
Units 829 and 830 provide files 22/1134 and 22/1684, showing
    the extent of payments to Crown witnesses as 'sustenance'.
Unit 837 File 22/5914 contains the attorney-general's reflection
    on Brennan's book.
VPRS 264/P Unit 30 (Capital Case Files)
VPRS 3992/P (Chief Secretary's Inward Registered
    Correspondence)
Unit 2227 File H5223 for the official reward papers.
Unit 2227 File G5106 for William Henry Dooley's statutory
    declaration and the inquiry papers on Ross's stub of
    pencil.
Unit 2590 File L9916 for official papers on the third degree.
VPRS 1187 (Chief Secretary's Outward Letter books)
Unit 208, Letter 3098 is a negative reply to one of Mrs Ross's
    requests for return of her son's body for interment in the
    Footscray Cemetery.
VPRS 3994/P (Chief Secretary's Inward Registered
    Correspondence)
'M'- Register (for 1924), folio 310, shows a letter was received
    by the Chief Secretary's Department from Mrs EC Ross on
    this matter dated 8/7/1924—the file number given is
    M7939, but the file is missing and, despite exhaustive
    searching, remains elusive.
VPRS 7575 (Inward Registered Correspondence)
Unit 15 File 22/302 for letters received by the governor in
    relation to the Ross case.
VPRS 24 (Inquests)
Unit 1018, File 168 provides the inquest papers for Charles
    Henry Tirtschke.

Probate Office, Melbourne
Probate papers for Emily Kate Tirtschke.

Victorian Supreme Court
Case no. 1925/691 for Julia Gibson's 1925 *Truth* libel case.

National Archives
Series A10074/1, Item 22/14: Full Court Case Records.
Australian Archives (ACT)
WWI Records Series B2455: Personnel Dossiers for 1st
    Australian Imperial Forces Ex-service Members; ex-
    service members numbers 14163/65464 Sydney John
    Harding; 7236 George Francis Murphy; 181 Ronald
    Campbell Ross; W30770 Hugh Campbell Gemmell
    Macindoe.
Australian Archives (Victoria)
WWI Personnel Records Series MT1486, items V51729 and
    V63948 for Henry David Errington.

Victorian Education Department
Pupils' Register for the State Elementary School at Hawthorn
    West No 293; enrolment number 817: Alma Tirtschke, for
    the date of Alma's qualification.
Hawthorn West Central School Inspector's Report Book, page
    58—reports of inspections 14 June 1920 and 13–15 July
    1921 for the number of grade six students obtaining their
    qualifying certificate in 1920.
The Hawthorn West Central School Register of Marks 1919–25:
    F Form (Girls) 1921, for school report for Tirtschke, Alma.

Brighton Cemetery Trust
Forms of Instruction for Graves, order numbers: 16418 for
    Alma's burial on 3/1/1922; 18932 for Alma's disinterment
    and re-burial on 7/8/1923; 15842 for the burial of HCA
    Tirtschke on 5/8/1921; 16544 for Charles Henry Tirtschke;
    22034 for the interment of Alma's uncle in 1925.

Victoria Police History Unit
Police Records of Conduct and Service: James Thomas
    Arrowsmith (4803); Ernest Graham Ashton (4628); Leslie
    Alexander Baker (6031); James Joseph Bates (6523);
    Clement Bell (5172); William Thomas Brooks (5697);
    John Brophy (2642); John O'Connell Brophy (4844);
    William Thomas Brough (5043); Frederick William

Chanter (6193); James William Chanter (5849); Robert Corrie (4469); Ellen Frances Davidson (7709); Hugh Rupert Donelly (7740); Robert John Dower (5123); Edmond Ethel (5064); William Herbert Harper (5864); Frederick Hobley (7265); Edward Holden (4802); Henry William Kroger (4170); Andrew Clifford Lee (6162); Cedric Leslie (6304); George Herbert Mason (5407, 6402); Martin Thomas McGinty (5561); Walter Moyle (6303); Elijah Napthine (4243); George Alexander Newton (6938); Madge Irene Connor (7711); Patrick O'Mara (4114); Leo Ambrose O'Sullivan (6290); Albert William Henry Peach (5534); Frederick John Piggott (4713) George Portingale (5571); Lionel Frank Potter (4428); Harry Rand (6249); Harold Garfield Saker (6348); John Patrick Salts (4662); John Edward Sheehan (5253); Lily Eva Ruby Smith (8504).

NSW Police Service
Personnel record for John Henry Michael Eugene Walshe (9308).

Other Records
Marine Register for Deaths (July 1922), entry for Emily Kate Tirtschke; register held in the General Register Office of the Office of Population Censuses and Surveys, Smedley Hydro, Southport, London.

Extract of Master's log (SS *Runic*) recorded on the Return of Death at Sea for Mrs Ellen Tirtschke (registered February 1915)—National Maritime Museum, Greenwich, London.

'Enclosure 2 in Confidential Circular dated 24th March 1905—Executions—Table of Drops (April 1892)' which has been transcribed into the front of *The Particulars of Executions 1894–1967*, a record of the Sheriff's Office of Victoria.

Melbourne Diocesan Historical Commission, Records of Newman Society.

Private Papers
Ross, Tirtschke, Brennan and Piggott family papers.

Interviews
Reg Allen, 17 July 1995, 20 July 1995, 30 April 1996.
Eric Beissel, 31 May 1995.
Columb Brennan, 24 April 1995.
Niall Brennan, 29 April 1995.
HR (Bill) Donelly, 20 September 1995.
Fred Hobley, 26 September 1995.
Ida Murdoch, 12 March 1996.
George A Newton, 13 September 1995.
Vernon D Plueckhahn, 20 October 1995.
Aggie Reid, 24 July 1995, 24 August 1995, 27 May 1996.
Ed Reilly, 24 August 1995.
Charlie Rixon, 26 October 1995.
Jim Rosengren, 9 September 1995.
Viola Tirtschke, 24 November 1995, 7 December 1995,
    8 February 1996, 27 February 1996, 26 November 1996,
    5 December 1997.
For Walcott's photographic duties at the Melbourne Gaol and
    elsewhere:
Charlie Rixon (former employee of the Government Printing
    Office, Melbourne) interview 26 October 1995; and Fred
    Hobley, 26 September 1995.

Newspapers/Periodicals
Age, *Argus*, *Herald*, *Midnight Sun*, *Truth* (Melbourne), *Smith's Weekly* (Sydney), January–April 1922.
Christ Church Chronicle, January–February 1922 (Christ Church parish archives, Hawthorn).
Tribune 27 April 1922, *Mercury* (Hobart), 23 March 1921, *People*, 15 March 1950.

Books and Articles
Bowden, Keith Macrae, *Mollison's Forensic Medicine Lectures: Revised, Enlarged and Illustrated* (W Ramsay, Melbourne, 1949)
Brennan, TC, *The Gun Alley Tragedy: Record of the Trial of Colin Campbell Ross, Including a Critical Examination of the Crown Case with a Summary of the New Evidence* (Gordon & Gotch, Melbourne, 1922)

Dower, Alan, *Crime Chemist: The Life Story of Charles Anthony Taylor, Scientist for the Crown* (John Long, London, 1965)

Ghurka, Madame, *The Murder of Alma Tirtschke: A Challenge to T.C. Brennan: With a Reply to his Book 'The Gun Alley Tragedy'* (Fraser & Jenkinson, Melbourne, 1922)

Gurr, Tom, and Cox, HH, *Famous Australasian Crimes* (Shakespeare Head Press, London, 1957)

Haldane, Robert, *The People's Force: A History of the Victoria Police* (Melbourne University Press, Melbourne, 1986)

Meates, Ian, 'History of the Victoria Police Vehicle Fleet', in *Journal of Police History*, Vol 2 No 2, October 1994.

Mollison, CH, *Lectures on Forensic Medicine* (W Ramsay, Melbourne, 1921)

Ritchie, John (Ed), *Australian Dictionary of Biography*, Vols 11, 13 (Melbourne University Press, Melbourne, 1990)

Taylor, John Pitt, *A Treatise on the Law of Evidence as Administered in England and Ireland with Illustrations from Scotch, Indian, American and Other Legal Systems* 10th Edition (Sweet & Marshall, London, 1906)

Victorian Law Reports 1922, pp 329–39; *Australian Law Times*, Volume XLIII, pp 187–90. *Commonwealth Law Reports*, Volume 30, pp 256–70; *Victorian Law Reports 1922*, pp 345–359.

Note: The author has retained all his original footnotes. Anyone wishing to enquire about a specific quotation or source is welcome to contact the author via the publisher.

Index

A

Alberts, David (aka David Stirling, Frederick D. Stirling), 82, 181, 190, 345

Alger
  Ellen Emily Eliza. *See* Tirtschke, Ellen Emily Eliza (née Alger) 'Nell'
  Emily Louisa Alma (née Holder), 210-1
  Henry Charles, 210, 212

Allen, Albert, 48, 171, 182, 250, 260

Anderson, Hugh, 332

Annand, George, 237

Anselmi, Frank, 83-4, 138, 245

Ashton, Senior Detective Ernest Graham, 30, 39, 51-3, 98, 165, 266-7

Atkin, Margret (sic), 284

Atkins, Mr, 227

Atkinson, Julia, 282

B

Baker, George McPherson, 100, 105

Ballantyne
  Alice, 183, 192, 194-5, 203-4, 235
  Mrs, 202

Bannon, Superintendent, 108, 267

Barclay, Henry, 273, 276, 278-9, 295

Bayliss, John James, 115-6, 118-9, 124, 330

Beamish's Livery Stables, 27

Beissel, Eric, 237

Bell, Detective Clement, 231

Bennet, and Woolcock (butchers), 4, 69, 72, 252-3, 328

Billings, Mr, 144-5

Blamey, Brigadier-General Sir Thomas, 303-4

Bolan, Joe, 50

Bradley, George Frederick, 192, 202

Bremner, Mrs, 81

Brennan, Thomas Cornelius, 124, 133-6, 140-6, 154-9, 164, 181, 192, 195, 203-5, 239-42, 245-51, 254-5, 259-61, 263-4, 269, 271, 281, 285, 308-11, 315, 330-1, 341, 345

Brophy, Senior Detective John O'Connell, 10-12, 23, 25, 30, 34, 38-40, 44, 49-52, 55-7, 63-4, 68, 80, 83, 108-9, 126, 128-30, 174, 178, 186-7, 194, 200, 204-5, 208, 250, 252, 255-7, 260, 289-91, 302-4, 313

Brown, Lily May, 111-2, 330

Brown, Mary, 218

Brown, SJ *See* Harding, Sydney John (aka SJ Brown)

Buchanan, AJ, 249

Buggy, Hugh, 32, 36, 48, 314-9, 321

Byres, Sub-Inspector, 67

Byrne, Mr, 273

C

Castles, Cyril, 4

Cavour Club. *See* Circolo Italiano Cavour

Chaplin, Charlie, 252
Chapman, Charles, 266
Cholet
    Francis Daniel, 258
    Irene Florence. *See* Sutton, Irene (Patricia) Florence
Circolo Italiano Cavour, 32, 83–4, 138
Clarke, William Henry, 46, 139, 192
Clauscen and Co, 306
Cole, Dr Robert Hodgson, 66, 69, 89–90, 96, 109, 299
Connor, Madge Irene, 126
Cooper, Ellen ('Auntie Nell'), 212
Corlette, John. *See* Harding, Sydney John (aka John Corlette)
Cox, HH, 49, 315. 318
Crilley, George, 259–60, 341
Cullity, Jack, 104
Cussen, Mr Justice, 242

D

Darkie. *See* Upton, Frank Lane
Dawsey, Oscar 172, 184, 190, 202
Diamond, Mr, 145
Dickins
    John, 265
    Margaret. *See* Piggott, Mrs Margaret (née Dickins)
Dixon, Owen, 312–3
Dobson, Florrie, 74
Dolan
    Alfred Arthur, 284
    Irene Florence, 284
    Patrick, 282
Donelly, Hugh Rupert ('Bill'), 289, 303–4
Dooley, William Henry, 275
Dower
    Alan, 36, 62–3, 165, 284, 314–8, 323
    Sub-Inspector Robert John, 36
Doyle, Sir Arthur Conan, 11
Duncan, Dr James, 266–7
Dunstan, Joseph L, 100, 105–6, 128, 162–3, 198, 201, 204–5, 251, 345–6
Dyson, Jean, 73

E

Edmonds
    Mrs Blanche, 70–1, 138, 198, 329, 342–3
    Muriel, 70–1, 138, 329, 342–3
Edwards, Herbert William Victor, 250, 260
Elliget, Patrick, 231
Ellis, George Arthur, 32, 35, 38, 82–3, 138, 245, 309
English, Katherine, 266
Ermakov, Zakaree. See Gibson, Henry (aka Zakaree Ermakov)
Errington
    Eva, 1–2
    Henry David, 1–2, 10, 11, 30, 68–9, 137
Evans, Bert, 254

F

Fenton, Rev WL, 294–7, 300
Fleming, Alexander, 125
Ford, Jack, 285

G

Gavan Duffy, Mr Justice F, 263, 268
Ghurka, Madame. *See* Gibson, Julia (née Glushkova)
Gibbon, Robert, 287, 296
Gibson
    Henry (aka Zakaree Ermakov), 124
    Julia (née Glushkova, aka 'Madame Ghurka'), 20, 75, 100, 116–8, 120–1, 123–4, 126, 154, 159, 182, 305–6, 311–3
Gloster, John, 276, 294
Glushkova, Peter, 123
Goble, Reverend JH, 271, 293–5
Godfrey, Dr Clarence George Sheffield, 125, 238, 295, 289–9
Graham, Joseph Thomas, 255–60, 343–4
Gray, Helen Phyllis, 115, 117–21
Gribbin, John, 331
Gurr, Tom, 49, 302, 314, 318

H

Halliwell, Percy, 254–5, 259–60, 273, 279–81
Harding
  Ruby, 100, 162
  Sydney John, (aka John Corlette, Sydney J Hennesey, SJ Brown), 85, 99–107, 125, 128, 136, 139, 160–4, 175, 179–80, 186, 188, 198–9, 201, 204–5, 236, 238, 242–5, 247–8, 250, 254, 270–1, 275, 278–9, 309, 317, 345
Harper, Detective William Herbert, 12, 25, 39
Heathy, Mr HB, 273
Hennesey, Sydney J. See Harding, Sydney John (aka Sydney J Hennesey)
Hepburn, May, 218–9, 221
Higgins, Justice HB, 263, 268–9
Hobley, Brevet Sub-Inspector Frederick, 9, 290–1, 302
Holden, Senior Detective Edward, 39, 116–7, 119
Hollow, Rev Stanley, 15
Holman, George 251
Holmes, Sherlock, 290
Hoppner, Mrs E, 112–4
Hughes, EA, 298
Hyde, Mr, 331

I

Irvine, Chief Justice Sir William, 240–2, 247–8, 250–1, 257, 259–60, 262, 268
Isaacs, Mr Justice IA, 263, 268–71

J

Jamison, Captain, 338
Jekyll, Dr 331
Johnson, Thomas, 288
Jordon, Harold Leslie, 250, 259–61
Juror X, 234, 237
Juror Y, 234–7

K

Kane, Sub-Inspector, 59
Kearney, James, 221
Kee, Mary, 172, 184, 189–90, 202
Kelly gang, 26
Kelly (warder), 276
Kelynack, Thomas, 276
Kennedy, Agnes, 55, 188–9, 193
Kerr, Mrs, 306
Kinleyside, Sergeant, 59
Kinsella, Mr, 182, 185
Knox, Sir Adrian, 263, 268
Kroger, Sergeant Henry William, 164

L

Lane's Motor Garage, 2, 27, 31, 346
Langford, Fred, 253
Lawson, Premier Sir Harry, 26, 42, 272–3, 274–5 236, 238–9
Le Maitre, Elizabeth. See Tirtschke, Elizabeth (née Le Maitre), 'Grandma'
Lee, Detective Andrew Clifford, 25, 51–2, 126–7, 142, 316
Lees, Archbishop, 274
Lewers, Mr, 121
Lewis, Mr, 171
Linderman
  Agnes, 184, 192, 193
  Gladys. See Wain, Gladys Cecilia (née Linderman)

M

Macindoe, Hugh Campbell Gemmell, 134–7, 139, 145, 148–53, 167, 175–81, 183–6, 188–96, 200–4, 240, 251, 253–4, 256–7, 261, 263, 267, 303, 315, 346
Mack, Florence, 285
Mack, L. See McKenzie, Mrs Hannah Lily (aka L Mack)
Maddison, Hugh C, 223, 277–8, 282
Maddox, Olive May, 72–81, 86, 94–5, 126, 147–8, 155, 174–6, 182, 195–6, 198. 201–5, 208, 239, 246, 270, 313, 346–7
Mahomet, Faiz and Tagh, 210184
Manchester, Mr, 112

Mann, Justice Frederick, 120, 240–1, 311
Mason, Constable George Herbert, 10
Matthews, Ivy Florence. See Sutton, Irene (Patricia) Florence
Maxwell, George Arnot, 120. 133–7, 139, 148, 150, 160, 163, 167–9, 170–5, 181, 183, 195–201, 208–9, 240, 247–8, 251–2, 261, 263, 266–7
McAdam, Alice, 3–4
McArthur, Justice, 266–7, 306
McCole, James, 230
McGinty, Constable Martin Thomas, 53–4, 98, 128
McKay, Mrs, 70
McKenzie
  (Mrs) Hannah Lily (aka L Mack), 251–4, 263
  John Alexander, 253
McKenzie, Mr RW ('Jack'), 39, 45, 47–8, 50, 90
McLoughlin, Victor, 250, 260
McNamara, Albert, 238
McPherson, WM, 21
Menzies, Sir Robert, 134
Miller, Sheriff James Taylor, 295–6
Mollison, Dr Crawford Henry, 6–8, 13–4, 41, 69, 136–7
Moore, Notley, 112
Morrison, Mary, 123
Murdoch
  John Bedford ('Uncle John'), 3–5, 16, 68–9, 137, 219, 228, 252–3, 308
  John Gordon, 3, 228–31
  Maie Henrietta ('Auntie Maie'), 3, 69, 137–8, 212, 235, 335, 341–2
Murdoch, Sir Keith, 133
Murphy, George Francis, 214, 336–44
Murphy, John, 285

N

Newton, George A, 289–90
Nicoli, Michelucci, 83–4, 138, 245

O

Oates, Titus, 275
O'Brien, Dr J, 69, 288
O'Halloran, Constable William, 112, 121
Olsen
  Alexander, 82, 123, 126, 138, 306
  Christian, 123–4
Orr, Madeleine, 303–4

P

Park
  Ivy ('Auntie Ivy'), 14, 212
  William (Uncle Bill), 14
Patterson, James, 162–3, 185–6, 191
Phillips, Alexander, (JP), 69, 299
Piggott
  Fred, 347
  Frederick, 267
  Senior Detective Frederick John Charles, 11–12, 23, 25, 30–41 44–5, 48–53, ,55–9, 61–4, 68, 107–8, 126, 128, 131, 135, 138, 173, 175, 178, 182, 195, 199, 208, 237, 250, 252, 255–6, 260–1, 263–7, 280–1, 289–91, 300, 302–3, 313–23, 347
  Margaret (née Dickins), 265
  Matilda (née Holland), 265, 347
Plueckhahn, Vernon D, 323
Plum, Mrs, 222–3
Pommeroy
  John, 129–31
  Robert (aka Albert Ernest White), 108–9, 128–32, 174, 178, 186, 200, 205, 347
Pooley
  Melvina (Melly), 15
  Mrs, 220–1
Porter, Lou, 50
Portingale, Detective George, 12, 14–5, 25, 39, 98, 165–6
Potter, Superintendent Lionel Frank, 11, 38, 108, 126, 208, 252, 302

Price, Charles Albert Edward, 62–5, 86, 99, 165–9, 195, 248, 263, 323–4

R
Ramsay, Constable, 5
Rand, Constable Harold, 25
Reid, Aggie, 218–9, 221, 224, 227
Reilly, Ed, 17
Rennell, Mrs Emily Kate, 232
Rennie, Dr Hilda, 125
Ridgeway, Mr, 266
Robertson, Dr James, 324–5
Robinson, Arthur, 209, 273–5, 279, 308
Rollandi, Baptisti, 84, 138–9
Rosengren, Jim, 210
Ross
    Alexandrina ('Lexie'), 111, 262, 292, 347
    Caroline (Mrs Tom Ross, née Ballantyne, 'Carrie'), 51, 182, 192–4, 202–3, 235
    Colin Campbell Eadie, 39, 44–61, 67–8, 71–9, 81–3, 85–96, 98–9, 101–6, 108–22, 125, 129–31, 133–6, 139–40, 143, 149, 151, 154–60, 162, 164–5, 170–201, 203–9, 234–42, 245–51, 255–6, 260–3, 269–74, 276–81, 288, 292–301, 305, 308–9, 311–2, 314–7, 319–24, 328–30, 333, 341–3
    Donald, (JP), 53
    Elizabeth Campbell (née Eadie), 39, 52–3, 57, 60, 68, 109–111, 120, 129, 131–2, 173, 182–4, 190, 202, 237, 262, 274–5, 277, 292–3, 299–301, 347
    Ronald Campbell, 52–3, 56, 60, 68, 94, 110–3, 121, 129–31, 173, 182–6, 190–1, 203, 255, 292–3, 347
    Stanley Gordon, 44–7, 48–51, 55, 86–7, 93–4, 111–3, 121, 127, 149, 152, 155, 170, 181–2, 184, 203, 243–4, 248, 255, 262, 279, 309, 347

    Thomas (Mr Tom Ross), 53, 110–1
    Thomas McKinley, 47, 110, 171, 183–5, 190, 194, 347
Rudkin, Florence, 239–40, 250, 254, 262
Ryan, Matthew 294

S
Saker, Detective Harold Garfield, 25, 51–2, 126, 316
Salts, Senior Constable John Patrick, 10, 12–3, 24
Schutt, Justice William John, 135, 139, 144–5, 149–52, 154, 157–8, 189, 191, 195, 204–8, 240, 242, 246–7, 250, 261–2, 347
Scott, Alice May ('Auntie Alice'), 5, 212, 232
Scott, Robert, 116
Scott Murphy, RL, 69, 81, 86, 89–90, 101, 104, 108–9
Sharp
    Doris, 15, 220
    Mrs, 220–1, 223
Sherrard, William Henry (Bill), 66, 137
Sinclair (prisoner), 100, 105
Smith, Josephine, 266
Sodeman, Arnold Karl, 332
Sonenberg, Naphtali Henry, 57–8, 67, 69–70, 75–8, 83, 89–99, 104–9, 118, 134–5, 155, 169, 174, 191, 239–40, 249, 251, 255, 271, 273, 279, 330
Stanley's barbershop, 2, 11, 27
Starke, Mr Justice HE, 263, 238, 273
Stirling, David (aka Frederick D Stirling). See Alberts, David
Strong, Rev Dr Charles, 273, 279
Stuart
    Elizabeth ('Auntie Lizzie'), 212–4
    James ('Uncle Jim'), 213
    Jessie, 213–4, 336, 338
Studd, Herbert, 172, 190–1, 202
Sullivan (Detective), 116
Sullivan, Violet May, 163–4, 316

Sutton
　Irene (Patricia) Florence (aka Ivy Florence Matthews, Irene Patricia Cholet, Irene Sholet, Florence Mack, Florence Mackie, Irene Smith), 39, 48, 51, 78–9, 81, 85–97, 99, 100, 113–22, 126, 139, 148–60, 170–9, 181–3, 186, 192, 198–201, 204–5, 208, 236, 240, 242–8, 250, 255–6, 270, 277–85, 305, 309, 311–3, 315–7
　William Henry, 283–4

T
Tate, William (Bill), 69–70, 328–9, 342
Taupin, Jane, 323
Taylor, Charles Anthony, 62–3, 165–6, 323–1
Taylor, Joseph Leslie ('Squizzy'), 289–90, 332–3
Tirtschke
　Charles Henry (Harry), 16, 210–2, 216–7, 228–31
　Elizabeth (née Le Maitre), 'Grandma', 3, 5, 18, 41, 210, 212–3, 215–7, 219–20, 222–6, 231–2, 253, 319, 334–5, 337, 339, 342, 348
　Ellen Emily Eliza (née Alger), 'Nell', 210–2
　Emily Kate (née Rennell), 216, 230–3
　Heinrich Charles August ('Grandpa'), 210, 212, 216–7, 223
　Nell Alma, 3–8, 13–7, 26, 31–5, 41–2, 44, 59, 64–79, 85–8, 98, 109, 115–6, 124, 127, 129–30, 135, 138, 147–50, 152, 165–9, 171, 175, 178, 181–2, 194–5, 198, 204, 210–24, 226–8, 233, 236, 239, 248, 253, 256–61, 269, 296, 309, 311, 318–22, 324–5, 328–34, 336–44
　Viola, 152, 211–7, 219, 222–5, 228–33, 320–1, 334–40, 342, 344, 348
Tuckerman, Irene, 318, 332

U
Upton, Frank Lane ('Darkie'), 50, 127–8, 139–46, 174, 182, 198, 202, 204, 235, 315, 348

V
Veal's quarries, 111
Venn, Chrissie, 331–2

W
Wade, Mr TB, 59–60
Wain, Gladys Cecilia (née Linderman), 46–8, 50, 54–6, 152–3, 155, 172, 176, 178, 181, 184, 186–9, 193, 195, 201, 203–4, 243–4, 246, 293, 324–5
Walcott, Arthur E, 61, 66, 314
Walsh, Frank Rhodes, 115, 117–21, 124, 330
Walshe, Detective John Henry Michael Eugene, 39, 51, 107, 131, 309
Warde, EC, (MLA), 273
Watkins (butchers), 2
Waugh, Arthur, 230
Welch, Mr, 108, 274
Wheeler, Martin, 253
White, Albert Ernest, See Pommeroy, Robert (aka Albert Ernest White)
White, Harry, 228
Williams, Mr, 39, 50
Woodhouse, Clem 230–1

Y
Young
　May, 71, 138, 256, 318, 329, 342–4
　Stanley, 71–2, 138, 195, 198, 200, 256, 329, 342–4
Young and Jackson's Hotel, 131